MILITARY ADVISORS IN KOREA: KMAG IN PEACE AND WAR

by

Major Robert K. Sawyer

Edited by

Walter G. Hermes

OFFICE OF THE CHIEF OF MILITARY HISTORY

DEPARTMENT OF THE ARMY

WASHINGTON, D.C., 1962

Library of Congress Catalog Card Number 62–60015

Reprinted 1970

For sale by the Superintendent of Documents, U.S. Government Printing Office
Washington, D.C. 20402 - Price $4.25

ARMY HISTORICAL SERIES

Stetson Conn, General Editor

Advisory Committee
(As of 25 October 1961)

Office of the Chief of Military History

Brig. Gen. William H. Harris, Chief of Military History

Foreword

The mid-twentieth century has added new dimensions to the roles and missions long performed by the United States Army. In many lands whose peoples speak alien tongues and observe strange customs, the American soldier is now living and working as ally, friend, and counselor. As a representative of the American way of life, as a persuasive advocate of his country's modern equipment and tactical doctrine, as partner in a global system of achieving security for the entire free world, he is called upon to demonstrate a variety of talents—patience, tact, linguistic ability, and superior professional knowledge, among others. In all that he does, he must make a supreme effort to understand people and traditions often vastly different from his own.

One of the pioneers in this new type of Army endeavor was the Military Advisory Group to the Republic of Korea, commonly known as KMAG. The men and officers who served in KMAG during the early days came to know all the frustrations and triumphs, the problems and partial solutions, the failures and successes that characterize new ventures.

Major Sawyer and Mr. Hermes have vividly recaptured the spirit and actions of the men of both nations whose joint efforts established a remarkable record of achievement. Though this volume describes the Army's experience in Korea only, the lessons it contains have great value to an officer assigned to advisory group duty in any nation. The book will also introduce the general public to the manner in which the United States soldier can and does meet the ever-changing tasks demanded of him by his countrymen.

A professional soldier and a professional military historian pooled their talents to prepare this work. Major Sawyer, presently attending the Command and General Staff College at Fort Leavenworth, Kansas, wrote his manuscript while on duty with the Office of the Chief of Military History from 1951 to 1955. A combat veteran of both World War II and the Korean War, he received a battlefield commission in France in 1945 and fought in Korea in 1950 with the 25th Infantry Division. He holds the Silver Star, the Bronze Star Medal, and the Purple Heart.

Mr. Hermes, also a World War II veteran, is a graduate of Boston University, where he received an M.A. degree in 1942, and is currently completing requirements for a Ph.D. degree in history at Georgetown University. A staff member of the Office of the Chief of Military History since 1949, he is the author of *Truce Tent and Fighting Front*, a forthcoming volume in the series UNITED STATES ARMY IN THE KOREAN WAR.

WILLIAM H. HARRIS

Washington, D.C.   Brigadier General, U.S.A.
15 December 1961   Chief of Military History

Preface

In an era when United States military assistance groups are scattered all over the world and probably will be for some time to come, the story of one of the earliest of these groups is of more than passing interest. The U.S. Military Advisory Group to the Republic of Korea, or KMAG as it was frequently called, was not only one of the first advisory groups to be formed but also one of the few that had to operate both in peace and war.

The problems that KMAG had to face in Korea in organizing and developing native forces differ only in degree from those that confront many American military advisors working in the more recently founded nations of Africa and Asia today. In substance they are essentially the same: the problem of communication between a highly skilled and competent group of technicians on the one hand, and an eager and willing yet often uneducated and untrained people on the other; the need to establish a military language comprehensible to both teacher and pupil; and the task of forging a military instrument out of the raw materials at hand under conditions that may be quite primitive by American standards.

From the KMAG experience in coping with the questions that arose and the solutions that were devised or sometimes improvised, much can be learned. Some of the pitfalls that marked the path of the KMAG military advisors are bound to be encountered again under similar or varied guises. If this study can illuminate a few of the problems involved and help to lessen or eliminate difficulties that are liable to come up, its purpose will have been accomplished.

Although officially KMAG's history does not begin until 1 July 1949 when the group was formally established, the genesis of its mission can be found in the immediate post-World War II period. During the 1945–48 period, the seeds were planted and the area of development was laid out. Thus, the story of the formation of Republic of Korea's armed forces must properly start at the close of World War II when the nucleus for the future ROK Army came into being and American military advisors first were assigned to the task of organizing and training security forces.

During his assignment to the Office of the Chief of Military History in 1951–55, Captain Sawyer completed a draft manuscript covering the period of origins and carrying the KMAG story through the first year of the war. This was the era of greatest stresses and strains on the advisory group and the ROK Army, since they had first to undergo the pangs of birth and of growing up and then to be tested in the crucible of war before they were properly prepared. With the initiation of the truce negotiations and the slowdown in the action at the front in mid-1951, KMAG entered a more leisurely period and was able to rebuild on a more solid foundation. The groundwork that was laid in the 1951–52 period put KMAG and the ROK forces on a firm footing that continued to the conclusion of the truce and beyond. Therefore, this work projects itself into the second year of the war insofar as it is necessary to establish the pattern for the future.

Since Captain Sawyer was no longer available for the task of revising his manuscript, I undertook to provide a slightly broader framework for the narrative and to furnish the projections into 1952 that were needed to bring the story to a more logical stopping place. In the process, I reorganized and rewrote some of the material to conform with the changes introduced into the text. Otherwise, the account is Sawyer's, and my efforts were confined to the details of polishing up the draft manuscript for publication.

One of the great problems in the preparation of a history of KMAG is the dearth and inadequacy of official records. Since it was impossible to fashion a continuous and complete narrative from the extant files, Captain Sawyer had to depend heavily upon the memories of the men who participated in the KMAG experience. He collected their personal accounts through interviews and letters, and, frequently, by viewing their personal papers. On behalf of the author I would like to acknowledge his deep debt to each member of the KMAG team who aided him in this respect. The responsibility for the use of this material and for any errors that may have been made in this book is, of course, the author's alone.

For guidance in the writing of this study, the author has expressed his particular gratitude to Dr. Stetson Conn, now Chief Historian of the Office of the Chief of Military History, as well as to Dr. Kent Roberts Greenfield, the former Chief Historian. Dr. Louis Morton and Lt. Col. Roy E. Appleman, both of OCMH, made many helpful suggestions. Mrs. Marion P. Grimes was copy editor for the manuscript. Mrs. Eileen Blandford, Miss Barbara A. Smith, and others helped cheerfully in repeated typings. Miss Mary Ann Bacon provided many sage comments in the literary editing of the volume; Miss Ruth A. Phillips selected the photographs that brighten its pages.

Washington, D.C.   WALTER G. HERMES
15 December 1961

viii

Contents

Charts

Tables

Maps

Illustrations

All pictures in this volume are from Department of Defense files.

MILITARY ADVISORS IN KOREA:

KMAG IN PEACE AND WAR

CHAPTER I

The Background

Introduction

On 8 September 1945 the vanguard of the U.S. 7th Infantry Division arrived at the Korean port of Inch'on and began to disembark. The following day elements of the division moved on to the capital city of Seoul, where the Japanese officially surrendered their authority in Korea. With conclusion of World War II, the U.S. occupation forces turned to the dual task of disarming and repatriating Japanese nationals and preserving law and order until such time as the Koreans themselves could once again take over the responsibilities of government.

To the great majority of the occupation troops, Korea was little more than a place on the map—a temporary stopover before they returned home. The dramatic collapse of Japan after the atom bombs were dropped and the USSR entered the war had allowed little time for the occupation troops to be prepared properly for the problems that lay before them. With the Russians moving south into Korea from Manchuria and the U.S. forces hundreds of miles distant from the peninsula, a quick and supposedly temporary arrangement on the occupation areas had to be worked out with the USSR. Under the agreement, the Russian troops would accept the surrender of Japanese forces north of the 38th Parallel and the U.S. units would perform the same function to the south of the Parallel. To ensure against any long delay in the arrival of the U.S. forces, General of the Army Douglas MacArthur, Commander, United States Army Forces, Pacific, had been forced to select the units to be assigned for occupation duties on the basis of availability of troops and transport. Thus the first arrivals had little knowledge of the land and the people they were destined to control.

Although Korea had undergone troublesome times in the twentieth century, it was one of the earliest of the modern national states to emerge with essentially the same language, boundaries, and ethnic composition that it has at the present.[1] During the seventh century the kingdom of Silla had emerged triumphant from the petty wars that plagued the peninsula. With Chinese help, Silla was able to consolidate its gains and to introduce a golden period in Korean art and literature. Chinese influences in government, law, and ethics soon became prevalent, and the Koreans adopted the Confucian system of social relationships. Under this system the Korean rulers assumed the role of sons or younger brothers to the Chinese emperors. Despite later barbarian attacks from the north and a devastating Japanese invasion in the late sixteenth century, Korea remained faithful to its tenuous relationship with China.[2]

In the nineteenth century Korea became an unwilling pawn in the power struggle between China, Japan, and Russia for the dominant position in the Far East. By applying pressure upon the declining Chinese empire, Japan secured a commercial treaty with Korea in 1876 that fostered Japanese economic penetration. To counter Japanese ambitions, China proceeded to encourage other nations to seek similar privileges.

In 1882 the United States concluded a treaty of peace, amity, commerce, and navigation with Korea. When the treaty was ratified the following year, the Korean king asked the United States to send military advisors to train his army. Five years later—in 1888—the United States finally dispatched three officers as its first military advisory group to Korea. The long delay and the smallness of the mission did little to sustain Korean confidence in the value of U.S. friendship.[3]

The Japanese began to move more aggressively toward control of Korea in the closing years of the century. In the Sino-Japanese War of 1894–95 they effectively eliminated China as a rival, but then proceeded to underestimate the Korean people. Japanese involvement in the murder of the Korean queen in 1896 led to a wave of popular indignation, and the king was able to bring the Russians in as a counterweight. The respite was only tem-

---

[1] Edwin O. Reischauer and John F. Fairbank, *East Asia: The Great Tradition* (Boston: Houghton Mifflin Co., 1960), p. 411.

[2] For an excellent account of the earlier period of Korean history and the Confucian system, see M. Frederick Nelson, *Korea and the Old Orders in Eastern Asia* (Baton Rouge: Louisiana State University Press, 1946).

[3] Tyler Dennett, *Americans in East Asia* (New York: Barnes and Noble, Inc., 1941), p. 481.

porary, however, for the jealousy between Japan and Russia came to a head in 1904–05. The Russo-Japanese War resulted in a decisive victory for the Japanese, and this time they were determined not to forfeit the spoils. During the next five years they strengthened their hold on Korea and won recognition from Great Britain and the United States of their special interests in that area. In 1910 Japan formally annexed Korea to the Japanese empire.[4]

The forty years of Japanese occupation witnessed the transformation of Korea into a Japanese colony. Administrators, officials, and police descended en masse upon the peninsula and assumed complete control of all the important phases of Korean activity. Japanese became the official language of the government and courts, and the Shinto religion was given a favored place. Through the use of spies, police, and the army, the Japanese governors were able to exercise a tight rein over the political scene and to curb quickly and ruthlessly any signs of nationalistic unrest.

To provide for the needs of Japan, the Korean economy was reshaped. Korea became the rice bowl of Japan and essentially a one-crop country insofar as exports were concerned. Natural resources necessary to complement but not to compete with Japanese production were developed, usually under Japanese ownership and management. Industry and communications facilities were built up to promote the Japanese exploitation of Korea and to support the Japanese war machine.

Until the end of World War II, the Japanese kept an iron grip upon the positions of political, economic, and military importance on the peninsula, and few Koreans were given an opportunity to gain high-level experience in responsible jobs. In the few cases where Koreans rose to important positions in government, industry, and the army, they were usually regarded as collaborators by the people. Thus, trained native administrators,

---

[4] For detailed accounts of Korea under the Japanese, see: (1) George M. McCune, *Korea Today* (Cambridge: Harvard University Press, 1950); (2) Andrew J. Grajdanzev, *Modern Korea* (New York: The John Day Co., 1944); (3) Robert T. Oliver, *Korea—Forgotten Nation* (Washington: Public Affairs Press, 1944); (4) E. Grant Meade, *American Military Government in Korea* (New York: King's Crown Press, Columbia University, 1951).

technicians, and military leaders, untainted by association with the Japanese, were extremely difficult to find in postwar Korea.

Despite forty years of repression, the Korean people had not lost their national self-consciousness. After a revolution in 1919, an independent Korean Provisional Government had been established in Shanghai with Dr. Syngman Rhee, as president, and although it had undergone a number of vicissitudes it was still in existence in 1945. Numerous splinter groups also existed, both within and outside the country, whose aim purportedly was independence. Extreme factionalism, however, appeared to be an inherent Korean trait, and the Japanese had carefully nurtured this destructive tendency of Korean political parties to fragment themselves into warring groups at the slightest provocation.

The disposition toward internecine strife came to the fore when Japan surrendered in 1945. A plethora of political organizations, approximately seventy in number, sprang up overnight, each claiming popular support as the party that would lead Korea out of the political wilderness. Since the Allied leaders had promised at the wartime conferences at Cairo in 1943 and Potsdam in 1945 that Korea would in due course become free and independent, the Koreans assumed that independence would come almost immediately.[5] The misconception was abetted by the fact that the Korean language had no expression that conveyed the meaning of the words "in due course."

Thus, when the first U.S. forces landed in Korea, the situation was hardly encouraging. The Korean people expected quick liberation and independence, although they were not adequately prepared for self-government and lacked trained administrators. The Korean economy was in a state of deterioration, for the dislocation of the close economic ties with Japan could not fail to have tremendous effect upon the entire nation until new markets were established and industry was rehabilitated and reoriented toward Korean rather than Japanese requirements. In addition, the Japanese had resorted to the use of the print-

---

[5] For a summary of events relating to Korean independence questions, see Department of State, *Korea's Independence* (Washington, 1947).

ing press during the closing days of the war and paved the way for a tide of inflation.

With an unbalanced economic structure on the one hand and a nation divided physically by the Russo-American occupation agreement and politically by the internal factional groups on the other, the U.S. troops began their mission in Korea. The task of establishing a viable and stable economy and enforcing internal order until Korea attained full independence promised to be a challenge demanding the highest degree of effort, skill, and tact.

The First Steps

General MacArthur selected Lt. Gen. John R. Hodge as the Commanding General, U.S. Army Forces in Korea (USAFIK), and assigned the U.S. XXIV Corps, composed of the 6th, 7th, and 40th Infantry Divisions, as the occupation force. To handle civil affairs, Hodge appointed Maj. Gen. Archibald V. Arnold, commanding general of the 7th Division, as the head of the United States Army Military Government in Korea (USAMGIK).[6]

After the surrender of the Japanese, General Arnold and his assistants began the task of setting up a Korean government for the U.S. area of occupation. Dozens of political parties clamored for recognition, but none seemed to have the support and confidence of a large segment of the population or to offer candidates of proven ability and experience. Thus the U.S. officials decided to retain the Japanese incumbents during the period of transition until the Koreans attained more political maturity and were able to take over the administrative machinery.

The unwisdom of this decision was immediately apparent as a bitter wave of resentment swept South Korea. After forty years of Japanese rule, the Koreans wanted to erase all enemy control at once. In their opinion, retention of the Japanese officials, even on a temporary basis, was unthinkable. In any event, the Korean reaction was so intense that the U.S. authorities

---

[6] Hq, U.S. Army Military Government in Korea, Statistical Research Division, History of the United States Army Military Government in Korea, September 1945–30 June 1946, MS in OCMH files, pp. 23ff. Hereafter cited as Hist of USAMGIK.

216–985 O–66–2

DR. RHEE AND GENERAL HODGE WITH (CENTER) DR. KIM KOO,
*President of the Provisional Government of Korea in exile, during a
meeting in 1945.*

abandoned the idea and began to replace the Japanese as
quickly as possible, at first with U.S. personnel and later with
Koreans as they became qualified.[7]

In the process of eliminating Japanese influence, one of the
first steps taken by the U.S. officials was to seize control of the
Bureau of Police.[8]   Since the Japanese police were hated and
feared by the Korean people because of their harsh repressive
measures, the U.S. military government leaders felt it necessary to remove them at once and set up a Korean police agency.
Brig. Gen. Lawrence E. Schick, Provost Marshal General, XXIV

[7] *Ibid.*, pp. 73–135.
[8] Interv, Col Reamer W. Argo, 21 Nov 51. Colonel Argo arrived in Korea on
6 September 1945, two days before the general landing by U.S. XXIV Corps troops,
as a military government representative in the Advance Party of Americans. On
the following day he was ordered by Brig. Gen. Charles S. Harris to oust the Japanese Commissioner of Police.   See McCune, *Korea Today,* pp. 25, 26. Unless otherwise indicated, all interviews were conducted by the author in Washington, D.C.

Corps, took over this task.[9] He abolished all functions normally considered to be outside the scope of police activity such as the Economic, Welfare, and Thought Control Sections. In the matter of personnel he had to proceed more slowly since only 30 percent of the police force at the time of the surrender were Koreans and they were almost all in minor positions. To hasten the change-over, the military government reopened the old Japanese Police Academy in Seoul on 15 October and gave a one-month basic training course to new recruits.[10]

By November a new National Police organization for South Korea began to take shape. Most of the Japanese were gone, and U.S. officers sought earnestly to eliminate the vestiges of their despotic methods. But the country was beset by postwar restlessness and agitation that the fledging Korean National Police Bureau still could not handle without assistance from U.S. troops. The foundation for an agency that could be respected by the people of Korea had been laid, however, and a basis for internal security was emerging.

Establishment of a National Defense Agency

Almost from the beginning, occupational authorities recognized that a rehabilitated police force would not be adequate to meet the needs of Korean national defense. As early as 31 October General Schick informed General Arnold that provision "for the National Defense is one of the primary functions of government." [11] If the government being sponsored by the United States were to endure, it would have to have a more effective means for quelling internal disturbances and defending its borders than the civil police organization. A governmental bureau, on the same level as those for Finance and Justice, for establish-

---

[9] Hist of USAMGIK, pt. II, p. 77.
[10] (1) Supreme Commander for the Allied Powers (SCAP), *Summation of Non-Military Activities in Japan and Korea,* No. 1, September and October 1945, pt. V, p. 12. Hereafter cited as *Summation.* (2) Hq, Far East Command, History of Occupation of Korea, pt. III, ch. IV, pp. 9–10, MS in OCMH files. (3) Interv with Col Argo, 21 Nov 51. Unless otherwise cited, all interviews, letters, and notes are in OCMH files.
[11] Memo, Schick for Arnold, 31 Oct 45, sub: Plan for the National Defense of Korea.

ing and co-ordinating Korean national defense forces was clearly in order.[12]

Since there was no framework for such an agency within the structure of the old Japanese Government-General, Headquarters, United States Army Forces in Korea, appointed a board of U.S. officers on 10 November to make a study of military and political conditions in Korea in order to determine the need for a national defense program.[13] In order not to delay the establishment of an agency until the board had completed its study, the military government on 13 November created an Office of the Director of National Defense with jurisdiction over the Bureau of Police and over a new Bureau of Armed Forces comprising Army and Navy Departments.[14] General Schick became the director on the day following.[15] Shortly thereafter a staff for the office was organized with the USAFIK board of officers as a nucleus.

The study produced by this group recommended a modest development of Korean national defense forces to supplement a projected 25,000-man police force. For the Army and Air Force, there would be one corps of three infantry divisions supported by essential service troops and one transport and two fighter squadrons, together with ground components, totaling 45,000 men. The Navy and Coast Guard would be limited to 5,000 men.[16]

Since the strength contemplated for the police and defense forces would be comparatively low, based on a population total of over 15,000,000 in South Korea, the plan for recruiting volunteers called for the acceptance of only those that could meet the highest possible physical and mental standards. Quality would compensate in part, it was hoped, for the lack of quantity.

---

[12] Schick recommended in this memorandum that the Korean police force be augmented and redesignated a *constabulary.*

[13] SO 26, Hq USAFIK, 10 Nov 45, as amended by SO 28, Hq USAFIK, 13 Nov 45, as further amended by SO 29, Hq USAFIK, 16 Nov 45.

[14] Ordinance 28, Hq USAMGIK, 13 Nov 45. According to Col. Loren B. Thompson, who in 1945 attended the School of Military Government at the University of Virginia and the Civil Affairs Training School at Yale University, the concept of national defense as a function of military government or civil affairs was not considered at either school. Ltr, Apr 52.

[15] Appointment Orders 31, Hq USAMGIK, 14 Nov 45.

[16] (1) Ltr, Hq USAFIK, 18 Nov 45, sub: Report of Proceedings of Board of Officers, USAFIK files. (2) Notes furnished by Col Schick, 5 Feb 52.

The forces would be organized in accordance with modified United States Tables of Organization and Equipment and equipped from United States surplus stocks, with a three-year reserve. Recruiting for the Coast Guard would begin without delay; the police would be brought to full strength as soon as possible; the remainder of the plan would be implemented progressively and systematically during the following twelve months.

General Hodge approved the plan on 20 November, but General MacArthur felt that the question of armed forces for South Korea lay outside his purview. In referring the matter to Washington, he recommended that the police, in any case, be equipped with U.S. arms and equipment and be developed to the point where they could relieve U.S. tactical forces of civil police functions.[17]

While the policy makers in Washington debated the pros and cons of the proposal, General Schick's staff attacked some of the problems that would have to be overcome if approval were granted. One of the most formidable of these was the language barrier. Since few U.S. personnel understood Korean and qualified interpreters were difficult to come by, they decided to open an English language school at the Methodist Theological Seminary in Seoul. The purpose of the school, which began classes on 5 December, was to teach English basic military expressions to potential Korean officers.[18]

Many of the students enrolled in the school came from the numerous private armies that had sprung up around the time of the Japanese surrender. Some fourteen unofficial quasi-military organizations had been established to preserve order in different areas of South Korea. Although their personnel had become an embarrassment to the U.S. forces in many instances, no attempt had been made to disband them during the fall of 1945. Potentially, these groups could provide a partially trained nucleus for the Korean defense forces, if and when such forces

[17] (1) Incl to Ltr, Hq USAFIK, 18 Nov 45, sub: Report of Proceedings of Board of Officers, USAFIK files. (2) Rad, CAX 55238, USAFPAC to War Dept, 26 Nov 45.

[18] (1) History of D.I.S. (Department of Internal Security) to 1 July 1948, Hq Provisional Military Advisory Group, APO 235, Unit 2, p. 20, copy in USAFIK files. (2) Historical Report, Office of the Chief, U.S. Military Advisory Group to the Republic of Korea, period 1 July to 31 December 1949, p. 1. Hereafter, the latter source will be cited as HR–KMAG.

were authorized.[19] General Hodge believed that the most practical way to control this source of manpower was to divert its energies into a national channel, specifically into Korean national defense forces.[20]

In any case, pending a definite policy regarding the private armies, the military government invited six of the groups to send candidates to the language school. Qualifications were high so that only the best men would apply. Each candidate, besides having to show previous military experience, had to be a graduate of a secondary school; and, because the purpose of the school was not to teach the Koreans English, but to teach them basic military expressions *in* English, candidates were required to possess some knowledge of the English language. Over sixty applicants attended the first class.[21]

Creation of the Korean Constabulary

Despite the plans and preparations made by the military government staff for the establishment of the Korean defense forces, the outlook for their fruition was hardly encouraging in late 1945. In December the Foreign Ministers of the United States, the U.S.S.R., and the United Kingdom had agreed at Moscow that a provisional Korean democratic government should be set up for all Korea. They also arranged for a joint U.S.-U.S.S.R. commission to meet in Korea to work out the details of organizing a provisional government.[22] Thus, when the State-War-Navy Coordinating Committee (SWNCC) in Washington considered the plan for building up Korean armed forces, it recommended in late December that a decision be postponed until after the joint commission's negotiations were held. Apparently the United States did not wish to risk a misunderstanding with the Soviet Union. SWNCC did agree that the Korean National Civil Police should be furnished U.S. arms and equipment so that eventually

---

[19](1) *Summation,* No. 2, 1945, p. 185. (2) Ltr, Hq USAFIK CG to CG's, 6th, 7th, and 40th Infantry Divisions, 24 Nov 45, sub: National Defense of Korea, copy attached to Col Schick's notes, in OCMH files. (3) XXIV Corps, G–2 Summary, No. 21, 27 Jan 46 to 3 Feb 46, p. 7, G–2 files.

[20] See Rad, CAX 55238, quoted in JCS 1483/20, 30 Dec 45, Incl B.

[21] Notes, Col Schick, 5 Feb 52.

[22] Department of State, *Korea, 1945 to 1948,* (Washington, 1948), p. 3.

U.S. tactical forces could be relieved of their civil police functions.[23]

The action taken by the Washington policy makers was not entirely unexpected. General Hodge had called in Brig. Gen. Arthur S. Champeny, who had succeeded General Schick on 20 December as Director of National Defense, and, as Champeny later recounted the interview, "told me that [the] plan for an army was entirely too elaborate and would not be approved. He asked me to develop something more practical and smaller. I came up with a plan of a police reserve consisting of 25,000 to be trained along infantry lines . . . This plan was submitted and approved by XXIV Corps." [24] Therefore, when word arrived that SWNCC had postponed a decision on the establishment of a full-fledged defense force, Champeny's alternate plan, called BAMBOO, offered another way of providing South Korea with increased internal security forces.

BAMBOO envisaged a constabulary-type police reserve established on a fixed post-camp-station basis under the Bureau of Police and was to be used as a supporting force and during periods of national emergency.[25] Initially, one company would be formed in each of the eight provinces of South Korea and organized as infantry (U.S. style), less weapons platoons. Complements would consist of 225 Korean enlisted men and 6 officers, the latter to be furnished by a centralized officers' training school.[26] The plan was to send out to each province a United States Army training team of two officers and four enlisted men who would select initial activation and training areas and begin recruiting and organizing. In each area a company would be

[23] JCS 1483/20, 30 Dec 45. JCS approved the recommendations on 9 January 1946 and informed MacArthur the same day. SWNCC recommended that equipment be furnished the police on the same basis as tools provided to indigenous civilians employed in projects for U.S. forces, to be (1) returned on completion of mission or at the time the U.S. forces evacuated Korea, or (2) sold or otherwise transferred to the Korean administration at the time of establishment of an international trusteeship or of a completely independent Korean government.
[24] Ltr, Gen Champeny to author, 7 Mar 52. By "XXIV Corps," Champeny probably meant Hq USAFIK.
[25] Notes, furnished by Col Thompson, former G–3 and later Director, Department of National Defense, dated Apr 52.
[26] Seoul English Language School until 1 May 1946, when the Korean Constabulary Training Center was established. Office of the Military Attaché, Seoul, Rpt R–26–49, 12 Aug 49, G–2 Doc Lib, DA, ID 584449.

formed overstrength by approximately 20 percent. After a short
period of training, a second company would be built around the
surplus of the first, in another location. The new company would
likewise be recruited overstrength, to provide a cadre for a third.
At that time a battalion headquarters and a headquarters company would be formed, and thereafter second and third battalions activated in a gradual expansion to one regiment of
Constabulary in each province.[27]

A Constabulary recruiting station opened at the English language school in Seoul on 14 January 1946 under the direction
of three military government officers. A publicity campaign followed. The Korean police were notified, as were the private
armies; pamphlets, radio announcements, and notices in local
newspapers helped to spread the word. Candidates flocked to
enlist. After a brief interview with an American officer, applicants filled out questionnaires and were examined by Korean
doctors from a nearby mission hospital. The United States Army
furnished vaccine for inoculations. Selected Koreans were transported to a former Japanese barrack area northeast of Seoul on
the Ch'unch'on road, where a Constabulary garrison had been
established.[28]

Earlier, Lt. Col. John T. Marshall had selected the site, which
consisted of a large drill field and physical fitness course, several
two-story barracks, a typical Japanese kitchen with cooking
bowls and sinks, Japanese-type baths, and a boiler room. Nearly
all windows had been broken and the buildings were filled with
straw and debris. In addition, the kitchen, boiler room, and baths
had been stripped of all pipe and copper bowls. Before troops
could occupy the area, an extensive rehabilitation was necessary.

---

[27] (1) Ltr, Office of the Civil Administrator, Hq USAMGIK, to all Provincial
Governors in Korea, 9 Jan 46, sub: The Organization of the Korean Constabulary,
among Col Schick's notes, OCMH files. (2) Ltr, Gen Champeny to author, 7 Mar
52. (3) Hist of D.I.S. to 1 Jul 48, pp. 15–17.

[28] (1) Notes, Col Thompson. (2) Notes furnished by Lt Col John T. Marshall
(former member of the Bureau of National Defense and first American Chief of
Constabulary), 7 Jan 52. (3) Ltr, Col Harry D. Bishop to author, 6 Mar 52. (4)
Report of Military Government Activities, Hq USAMGIK, 14 February 1946, pt.
VIII, p. 5, OCMH files.

The military government arranged by contract for Korean labor to do this, and by 14 January the garrison had been established and was ready to feed and quarter troops.[29]

Initial recruiting greatly exceeded American expectations. By the end of January nearly three companies had been formed in the Seoul area alone.[30] The military government supplied limited amounts of clothing and equipment from abandoned and captured Japanese stocks.[31] As the units were organized, a basic training program began under the direction of United States Army officers.[32] At this time the first battalion of the 1st Regiment, Korean Constabulary, was activated, and Colonel Marshall became the first American Chief of Constabulary.[33] Because as yet there was no Korean counterpart to Marshall, the young Korean officers who were to command new companies were selected on the advice of Lee Hyung Koon, former Korean colonel in the Japanese Army then serving as an "advisor" to the Director of National Defense.[34]

On 24 January 1946 eighteen lieutenants came from the U.S. 40th Division, which was deactivating, to the military government's Bureau of National Defense.[35] After a brief period of orientation sixteen of these officers set out in pairs for the various

[29] (1) Notes, Lt Col Marshall. (2) Interv, Col Argo.
[30] (1) *Summation*, No. 4, Jan 46, p. 285. (2) Interv, Maj Gen Chang Chang Kuk, ROK Army (ROKA), 14 Oct 53. General Chang commanded one of these original companies.
[31] (1) *Summation*, No. 5, Feb 46, p. 287. (2) Rpt, cited n. 28 (4), above. (3) Notes, Col Thompson.
[32] According to Colonel Thompson (notes), the Japanese drill was used until 11 February, when it was replaced by United States Army drill. Adequate translations of American drill commands were not devised until 30 April, and these were a mixture of Japanese and Korean. In inclosure to a letter to Maj. Gen. A. C. Smith, Chief of Military History, 28 August 1953, Lt. Col. Clarence C. DeReus states that Japanese drill had not been entirely abandoned as late as July 1948. The idea was to incorporate some type of training to promote discipline.
[33] (1) Notes, Col Marshall. (2) Interv, Col Argo. (3) HR–KMAG, p. 1.
[34] (1) Ltr, Gen Champeny. (2) Interv, Col Louis B. Ely, former G–2, Bureau of National Defense, 17 Dec 51. Lee later became a lieutenant general in the Republic of Korea Army.
[35] Incl to Ltr, Col DeReus, cited above. General Champeny and Colonel Thompson stated that there were sixteen; Colonel Marshall wrote that there were only seven; HR–KMAG reported eight. However, USAMGIK rosters show sixteen second lieutenants and two first lieutenants being assigned in that period.

provinces, accompanied in each case by one American (Nisei) enlisted man who spoke Japanese. The teams, together with Korean graduates of the language school and a few picked Korean enlisted men from the 1st Battalion, were to set up regimental headquarters and organize regiments by local recruiting. With "funds, food, clothing and equipment for this adventure . . . almost nonexistent," the first training teams faced a prodigious task.[36] Factories and other buildings, formerly owned by the Japanese, had to be converted into billets for use by the Constabulary. Training areas had to be located and secured. When food supplies had been obtained from native sources, warehouses had to be bought or rented. Recruiting stations had to be set up. And since authority to arm the National Police had not extended to supporting the Constabulary, arrangements had to be made with local military government groups to procure abandoned Japanese weapons and equipment.

In the latter connection, United States tactical forces in South Korea were then in the midst of a program of destruction of Japanese armament. Occupation Instructions No. 2, issued by General MacArthur's headquarters in September 1945, had directed that Japanese equipment appropriate only for warlike uses be destroyed, except for what might be used for intelligence and research purposes or desired by American troops for trophies. However, 60,000 Japanese rifles along with fifteen rounds of ammunition for each weapon had been set aside by the Americans in storehouses pending the time when a Korean Army and Navy might have use for them. From this reserve the Americans issued rifles to Constabulary units as they were activated. The Constabulary later obtained a few Japanese light machine guns from American troop units that had collected them as souvenirs.[37]

The rate at which the Korean regiments were activated is not clear. Besides the regiment at Seoul, seven seem to have been formed by April 1946—at Pusan, Kwangju, Taegu, Iri, Taejon,

---

[36] HR–KMAG, p. 1.

[37] See: (1) "Demilitarization and Evacuation of Japanese Military Forces," History of United States Army Forces in Korea, pt. I (Tactical), ch. VII, OCMH files; (2) Notes, Col Thompson; (3) Incl to Ltr, Col DeReus, 28 Aug 53.

Ch'ongju, and Ch'unch'on.[38] In any case, the regiments must have been very small, for the total strength of the Constabulary at the end of April 1946 was slightly over two thousand men.[39] While not impressive, the force represented Korea's first national military effort in many years, and the National Police were assured of support if internal conditions got out of hand. Moreover, if and when circumstances permitted a bona fide Korean Army, the Constabulary would provide a nucleus for expansion.

The Korean Coast Guard

Along with the formation of the Constabulary, Americans helped the Koreans to establish a coast guard. Smuggling and piracy were plaguing the Korean coasts and waters after World War II and the need for this additional security force was obvious. Since a coast guard organization had existed under the Japanese in Korea, the military government transferred it on 14 January 1946 to the jurisdiction of the Director of National Defense as a framework for a Korean coast guard. American Army officers set up a training station at Chinhae on the south coast and on 8 February began recruiting in Seoul.[40]

The Coast Guard was slower in developing than the Constabulary. Scarcities in equipment and qualified personnel were universal problems in Korea. The matter of leadership in the Coast Guard was of special concern to the Americans, for Ko-

---

[38] (1) Incl to Ltr, Col DeReus, 28 Aug 53. (2) Republic of Korea, Military History of Korea (hereafter cited as MHK), translated by 500th Military Intelligence Service Group, Headquarters, United States Army Forces in the Far East (USAFFE), Chart 9–3, p. 151, copy in OCMH files. The latter source, while valuable, is in some respects highly biased and should be used with caution. The author found one brief reference to the establishment of these regiments in the History of USAMGIK (pt. III, vol. I, p. 52). The History merely mentioned the "first recruiting drive by the newly formed Constabulary . . . in Ch'unch'on on 27 March 46 . . ." and stated that a goal of 225 recruits had been achieved by the end of the month.

[39] GHQ, CINCFE, USAFPAC, *Summation of United States Army Military Government Activities in Korea*, No. 7, April 1946, p. 12. Hereafter this source will be cited as *Summation, USAMGIK*.

[40] (1) USAMGIK Ordinance 42, 14 Jan 46. (2) *Summation*, No. 5, Feb 46, p. 288. (3) Ltr, Gen Champeny. (4) Ltr, Col Bishop, 15 Apr 52. (5) *Summation, USAMGIK*, No. 14, Nov 46, p. 29, reported that the strength of the Korean Coast Guard at the end of November 1946 was only 165 officers and 1,026 enlisted men.

reans with experience in modern methods of seamanship were hard to find. Without competent Korean officers, the Coast Guard could not hope to operate effectively. Even more critical was the Korean Coast Guard's almost total lack of vessels. While there had been approximately fifty-two small craft at Chinhae at the beginning of the American occupation, they had been used by the U.S. 40th Division to repatriate Japanese and were unavailable when the Korean Coast Guard was formed. This was truly a handicap, as a later Republic of Korea publication noted, since vessels "are most necessary in a naval organization." [41]

In U.S. advisory personnel, too, the Coast Guard was not as well served as the Constabulary. Urgent requests by General MacArthur to the War Department for U.S. naval supervisory and training personnel make this clear.[42] During the eight months following its establishment, the Korean Coast Guard was headed successively by two members of the U.S. naval reserve and one U.S. Army officer who was a graduate of Annapolis. Bases at Inch'on, Mukhojin-ni, and Mokp'o, and the training station at Chinhae were set up and operated by junior U.S. Army officers who accomplished more than might have been expected under the circumstances, but lacked the experience necessary to build an effective naval organization. After considerable negotiations, fifteen U.S. Coast Guard officer and enlisted advisors arrived from the United States in September 1946 to provide the Korean service with the benefit of professional advice.[43]

Under the guidance of experienced U.S. coast guardsmen, the little Korean "navy" entered a period of relative progress. Together the Americans and Koreans organized a more efficient Coast Guard headquarters at Seoul, activated new bases at Kunsan, Pusan, and P'ohang-dong, initiated training programs, and

---

[41] (1) MHK, p. 33. (2) Ltr, Gen Champeny.

[42] (1) Rad, CA 55527, CINCAFPAC Adv, Tokyo, Japan, to War Dept, 3 Dec 45. (2) Rad, C 58428, CINCAFPAC Command, Tokyo, to War Dept, 4 Mar 46. (3) See also JCS 1483/42, 19 Sep 47.

[43] (1) Capt George E. McCabe, USCG, History of U.S. Coast Guard Detachment in Korea, 2 September 1946 to 25 February 1947, copy in OCMH files. (2) Interv, Capt James R. Chesler (who activated the Mokp'o Base), 21 Jun 52. (3) See MHK, p. 33.

laid the groundwork for a radio communications system. In the fall of 1946 they commissioned eighteen vessels of various types (loaned by the United States), which had arrived from Japan and the Philippines. By January 1947, Capt. George E. McCabe, the officer in command, reported that the Korean Coast Guard had been "placed afloat with reasonably well-trained personnel. . . ." [44]

On 2 July 1947, Mr. E. H. Foley, Jr., Acting Secretary of the Treasury, asked the JCS for approval to withdraw the U.S. Coast Guard advisory detachment from Korea no later than 15 September 1947. Mr. Foley pointed out that the officers and men were needed in the United States and stated that the intent of Congress as expressed in hearings on fiscal year 1948 appropriations did not justify keeping U.S. Coast Guard personnel overseas. [45]

General Hodge informed the JCS that he was willing to replace the U.S. Coast Guard advisors with qualified civilians provided that the change-over took place after 15 November 1947. The Korean Coast Guard was in the midst of important phases of organization and training and the introduction of new advisors before then might disrupt progress. On 2 September the JCS told the Secretary of the Treasury that it would probably require as much as ninety days to recruit the civilian replacements and that an additional thirty days would be needed for the transfer of advisory responsibilities after the civilians arrived in Korea. The Secretary agreed to delay withdrawal of the Coast Guard personnel until the new personnel were indoctrinated.

The recruitment of retired and reserve Coast Guard officers as civilians evidently took longer than the JCS anticipated. Special permission had to be secured for them to wear uniforms so that they could impress their Korean counterparts. Negotiations between the Coast Guard, the JCS, and USAFIK on

---

[44] (1) McCabe, cited n. 43 (1). (2) Hist of D.I.S. to 1 Jul 48, pp. 21–29. (3) MHK, p. 33. (4) See also ch. IV, below.

[45] See JCS 1483/39, 9 July 47, and JCS 1483/42, 19 Sep 47, for discussion.

the retention of the Coast Guard personnel until the civilians could take over the task lasted well into 1948.[46]

The Department of Internal Security

The spring of 1946 was a period of instability within the military government in Korea, largely because of the U.S. Army's postwar readjustment policies. New officers and enlisted men were assigned, accumulated sufficient points to make them eligible for discharge from the service, and then departed for home. In less than seven months there had been five Directors of National Defense, and three of the changes occurred in the 11 April– 1 June period.[47]

Changes also had occurred in the Korean defense structure, beginning with the removal of the Bureau of Police from the Office of the Director of National Defense. Since early 1946 some Americans had advocated an autonomous Korean police force; in their opinion, which was supported by Korean pressure, the police did not properly belong under the jurisdiction of the national defense agency. The military government recognized this on 29 March by establishing the National Police as a separate organization. Next, on 8 April, USAMGIK redesignated all major Korean governmental elements as departments, including the Office of the Director of National Defense.

Indications of Soviet sensitivity to the use of the National Defense designation apparently instigated the discard of the title in June 1946. General Hodge conferred in May with Maj. Gen. Archer L. Lerch, who had succeeded General Arnold as military governor, and they decided to substitute the concept of internal security for "national defense." On 15 June the Department of National Defense became the Department of Internal Security. The Bureau of Armed Forces with its sub-

---

[46] JCS 1483/48, 15 Jan 48. The author has not been able to ascertain from either U.S. Army or U.S. Coast Guard files exactly when the civilian advisors arrived and when the U.S. Coast Guard personnel left Korea. Probably the change took place about 15 August 1948, when the Republic of Korea was inaugurated. See Ltr, Comdr Clarence M. Speight, USCG, 16 Sep 53.

[47] Lt. Col. Lyle W. Bernard succeeded Champeny on 11 April; Colonel Thompson followed Bernard in May; and Col. Terrill E. Price became director on 1 June. In the Constabulary, Lt. Col. Russell D. Barros replaced Colonel Marshall as chief in March. See: (1) USAMGIK Appointment Orders, 89 (18 May 46), 99 (8 Jun 46), and 100 (21 Jun 46); (2) Notes, Col Marshall.

ordinate Army and Navy Departments was abolished, and instead new Bureaus of Constabulary and Coast Guard were set up. The effective date for the activation of the Constabulary and Coast Guard was given as 14 January 1946.[48]

Commenting on these superficial changes later on, General Hodge wrote:

. . . I was very interested in establishing a Korean Army from the beginning of the Occupation, not only to relieve American troops of many details in handling Korean security, but to get a start for the future when we accomplished our mission of setting up a Korean Government. I met with much opposition at higher levels apparently in the belief that at that stage of our relations such a move might be misunderstood by the Russians and be a source of difficulty when it came to the co-ordination of the American and Russian zones of Korea into a single nation.[49]

Still another change occurred in September 1946, when the Koreans had been free of Japanese rule for a year. For reasons already stated, Koreans in all branches of the new government had been functioning under the close supervision of American counterparts. To say that the latter actually governed South Korea is nearer the truth. The Koreans nevertheless learned quickly, and, with a year of instruction and observation behind them, General Lerch felt that they were ready to become less dependent upon American supervision. At his direction the Koreans became responsible for administration on 11 September 1946, and Americans in military government were ordered to assume a strict advisory status.[50]

---

[48] (1) Notes, Col Thompson. (2) USAMGIK Ordinances, 63 (29 Mar 46), 64 (8 Apr 46), and 86 (15 Jun 46).

[49] (1) Ltr, Gen Hodge, to Maj Gen Orlando Ward, 18 Mar 52. (2) See also: Notes, Col Thompson; Ltr, Col Joseph B. Coolidge to author, 30 Apr 53, Thompson recalled that, as Deputy Director and later Director of National Defense in the March-May 1946 period, he had favored a strong Korean defense organization. On 24 May, a visiting representative from MacArthur's headquarters informed him that the "outside" was disturbed by the use of the terms "army" and "navy" and that "they" considered an army and navy most unnecessary for South Korea. Later, Thompson said, the G–3, XXIV Corps, Colonel Coolidge, told him that the Soviet representatives on the Far East Commission in Tokyo had complained about the terms and that MacArthur had "felt obliged to comply." Coolidge did not recall . making such a statement, but he agreed that the shift in terms probably resulted from a U.S. desire to avoid a misunderstanding.

[50] (1) Dept of State, *Korea, 1945 to 1948*, p. 121. (2) Hist of D.I.S. to 1 Jul 48, pp. 14–15. (3) HR–KMAG, p. 2.

In the Department of Internal Security, the Director, Col. Terrill E. Price, stepped down to the role of advisor, and the Korean Director technically took over the power to make major decisions. American officers on duty with the Constabulary or at Coast Guard bases also had to make a switch from command to advisory positions. From this time on, official correspondence had to be forwarded through the Korean chiefs, in Korean, with English translations accompanying only the most important documents.

Despite this encouragement to the Koreans to operate more independently, the American advisors actually had to maintain much of their direct control.[51] Paper authority could not provide experience and technical ability overnight, and the Koreans had yet to shake the consequences of their long subservience to the Japanese, master staff procedures and organization, and acquire mechanical know-how before they could assume the task of exercising full control over their internal security.

The Constabulary as a Police Reserve

In the month of September 1946 the advisor to the 8th Constabulary Regiment at Ch'unch'on, Capt. James H. Hausman, was transferred to the Bureau of Constabulary in Seoul. This move was significant, for, as one authority later declared, Hausman "had more to do with the . . . arming, equipping, moves, expansions [of the Korean Constabulary] than anyone else." [52]

Officially at this time there was no Korean chief of Constabulary to advise. The Bureau of Constabulary consisted of Maj. Lee Hyung Koon, 2d Lt. Yim Soon Ha, and a Korean enlisted man. Major Lee actually functioned as the Constabulary chief without the title because of the possibility of an unfavorable press reaction to his Japanese service during World War II. The bureau occupied a few small rooms in the Department of Internal Secu-

---

[51] (1) Interv, Maj James H. Hausman, 21 Jan 52. (2) Ltr, Col DeReus to author, 23 Sep 52. According to Colonel DeReus, this applied especially to matters concerning recruiting and training. See Incl to Ltr, DeReus to author, 28 Aug 53.

[52] Ltr, Brig Gen William L. Roberts (Ret), first chief of KMAG, to Gen Ward, Chief of Military History, 9 Nov 51. Subsequent correspondence and interviews by the writer with former military advisors to Korea support this view. Hausman later served with distinction as the liason officer between the KMAG chief of staff and ROK Army Chief of Staff through 1951.

rity building. It had no general or special staff sections, and no technical or administrative services. In the provinces there were eight undersized regiments of quasi infantry, varying in size from one to three companies.[53]

Shortly after Hausman's arrival in Seoul, Colonel Barros, the chief advisor, directed him to commence building up a Constabulary headquarters organization and in general to try to accelerate the whole program. The following few months saw another Constabulary regiment activated (in November 1946 on the island of Cheju-do), and Lt. Col. Song Ho Seung installed as Korean chief of Constabulary. Facilities, equipment, and experienced Korean officers were still scarce, however, and the task of expending the Constabulary was to stretch over a period of another two years.[54] There also was a dearth of American supervision and advice. With redeployment and demobilization of the U.S. Army in full swing, the number of military government advisors with the Korean Constabulary diminished steadily. As American officers left Korea to be reassigned or separated in the United States, there were few if any replacements. The number of advisors to the Constabulary during the September 1946– April 1948 period varied between four and ten officers, with the average hovering around six. At the same time, there were approximately twenty American advisors on duty with the Department of Internal Security. All this left the inexperienced Korean commanders largely on their own, and without American assistance they made limited progress.[55]

The Americans who remained with the Constabulary during these months had much to keep them busy, and the response varied with the individual. Unless the advisors were stationed in the Seoul or Pusan areas, or near the larger United States military

---

[53] (1) Interv, Maj Hausman, 21 Jan 52. (2) Incl to Ltr, Col DeReus, 28 Aug 53. (3) MHK, p. 151. (4) *Summation, USAMGIK,* No. 14, Nov 46, p. 26, reported the total strength of the Constabulary at the end of November as being 143 officers and 5,130 enlisted men, a daily average of approximately seventeen enlistments for the ten-month period, following the organization's establishment.

[54] (1) Interv, Maj Hausman. (2) Hist of D.I.S. to 1 Jul 48, p. 21. (3) HR–KMAG, p. 2.

[55] (1) Interv, Maj Hausman. (2) Ltr, Col DeReus, 23 Sep 52. (3) Incl to Ltr, DeReus, 28 Aug 53. In a letter from General Roberts to the author, 22 January 1952, Roberts stated that there were "less than 20 officers" when he arrived in May 1948. (4) See also Ltr, Maj Ralph Mason (Ret) to author, 28 Mar 53.

installations, they were under very little supervision. Isolated as were the outlying Constabulary garrisons, almost total responsibility for all phases of Constabulary organization, from recruiting to administration and training, was in the advisors' hands. What they accomplished depended upon their knowledge and ingenuity.[56]

Each advisor was as a rule responsible for more than one regiment, and these were often many miles apart. In at least one case, the advisor had to drive a total of 350 miles through the mountains of South Korea in order to complete a circuit of the units under his supervision. Training was on a seven-day week basis, including classes every night for Korean officers and noncommissioned officers, and often lasted sixteen hours a day. Some advisors conducted additional schooling in the English language.[57] Training was limited, however, not only by the lack of American supervision, but by restrictions imposed on the type of training the Constabulary regiments could conduct. Since the Constabulary organization was officially but a reserve force for the National Police of Korea, training in weapons other than individual arms was prohibited by the Department of Internal Security.[58] According to U.S. Army G–2 records, members of the Constabulary were trained only in the use of small arms, basic drill, and "methods of internal security." [59]

Whatever "methods of internal security" was supposed to mean, it probably meant something different to each of the advisors working with the Constabulary regiments. As one advisor later put it, "a more realistic approach . . . indicated that [restrictions on training] might well be taken with the proper proportion of salt." [60] The possibility that the Korean Constabulary might one day emerge as the Korean Army was not discounted by the advisors in the field. In some cases, where Constabulary regiments were stationed near United States infantry regiments, advisors borrowed American weapons for training their Korean

---

[56] (1) Interv, Maj Hausman. (2) Ltr, Col DeReus, 23 Sep 52.

[57] Ltr, Col DeReus, 23 Sep 52.

[58] Ltr, Col DeReus, 23 Sep 52. The author has been unable to ascertain where this restriction originated.

[59] Quasi-Military Forces, Project 3996, 12 Mar 48, in files of ACofS, G–2, FE&Pac Br, DA.

[60] Ltr, Col DeReus, 23 Sep 52.

charges. Sometimes the loan included a U.S. Army enlisted man, or even a squad, for demonstration purposes. Thus, although Constabulary armament was limited to Japanese rifles (and a very few Japanese light machine guns), Korean soldiers were exposed to training with the M1 rifle, mortar, and machine gun months before American weapons were issued to them.[61]

Not all of the Constabulary's training was accomplished by formal training methods. Lt. Col. Clarence C. DeReus subsequently wrote that civil disorders and guerrillalike activities by Communist elements offered opportunities for tactical training. While engaged in quelling such incidents, Constabulary units learned many lessons including the necessity for control in military operations, and the principles of village fighting. During one operation, in late 1947, the units under Colonel DeReus's command combined the tactics of the raid with those of the battalion in a night attack. Wherever possible in these field excursions, he stressed tactical principles, "purposely" rotating units in order that all could take advantage of that type of training.[62]

Other factors helped to determine the effectiveness of the Constabulary's training. With American supervision limited, the influence of the Korean officers who had gained their military experience under the Japanese or Chinese was often in evidence. In the absence of American tactical training, these officers naturally employed principles learned elsewhere. Although their methods often conflicted with the doctrine later taught by the United States Army, as in banzai charges against an enemy position, the value of the officers was not wholly negative. They were not bound to road nets, nor did they expect much in the way of organic transportation; the Japanese- and Chinese-trained Korean officers were satisfied with horses or human carriers. In the rugged Korean terrain, this attitude was important.[63]

---

[61] (1) *Ibid.* (2) Interv, Maj Hausman. (3) Interv, Maj Russell C. Geist, Jr., 11 Jul 52.

[62] See Incl to Ltr, Col DeReus, 28 Aug 53.

[63] (1) Ltr, Col DeReus to author, 4 Oct 52. (2) Ltr, Maj William F. West to Gen Ward, Incl 3, 20 Nov 52. (3) Ltr, Gen Roberts to author, 22 Jan 52. (4) Ltr, Lt Col Lawrence S. Reynolds to author, 17 Sep 52. (5) Ltr, Maj West to author, 16 Sep 52. (6) Ltr, Lt Col Eugene O. McDonald to author, 3 Dec 52. (7) Ltr, Gen Roberts to Gen Ward, 9 Nov 51.

In principle, the Korean Constabulary remained a reserve force for the police during 1946 and 1947. But as it grew in strength and prestige, the Constabulary became seriously involved in a conflict with the police over jurisdictional matters. Ordinarily the Constabulary had no authority to arrest lawbreakers, but it consistently ignored this lack of legal right, making arrests at will and searching without warrants. The Constabulary's assumption of normal police powers quickly aroused resentment and retaliation. Ill feeling between the two groups reached the point where the police frequently arrested Constabulary soldiers simply for being off their so-called military reservations.

Although the disputes were deeply rooted in professional jealously, politics also fanned the fires of dislike and distrust. Some of the Constabulary units were composed almost entirely of members of the old private armies, whose political philosophies were far too extreme for the more conservative police. Furthermore, a number of agitators and malcontents had now joined the Constabulary—some infiltrated by the Communists and other dissident parties, others drawn by the ease of getting into the organization. Since the Constabulary had to operate on a shoestring basis, the recruiting standards remained low and reasonably healthy applicants had little difficulty in enlisting.

Following a particularly blood battle in 1947 between a company of Constabulary and the police of the little town of Yongam, in southwestern Korea, American military government officers exerted their influence and brought together officials from both organizations for a series of conferences. While the meetings did not immediately relieve strained feelings, discussion helped to define the functions of each organization. Later the Constabulary showed a willingness to co-operate by launching a campaign to rid its ranks of undesirables and by adopting a recruiting plan designed to prevent agitators from enlisting.[64]

---

[64](1) HR–KMAG, p. 3. (2) *South Korean Interim Government Activities,* (hereafter cited as SKIG), No. 25, October 1947, p. 135, prepared by the National Economic Board, USAMGIK. (3) Hist of D.I.S. to 1 Jul 48, p. 28. (4) Interv, Maj Hausman. (5) Ltr, Col DeReus, 23 Sep 52. (6) Incl to Ltr, Col DeReus, 28 Aug 53.

An Army Is Founded

While these internal events had been taking place, developments on the international front began to alter the Korean defense scene. The joint U.S.–USSR commission established by the Moscow Conference had met in early 1946 and had reached an impasse on the question of which Korean elements should be consulted on the formation of a provisional Korean government. The Russians wished to exclude all parties and organizations that had voiced opposition to the concept of a five-year, four-power trusteeship proposed at the Moscow Conference. Since, of all the major groups, only the Communists had failed to denounce openly a trusteeship arrangement, acceptance of the Soviet conditions would have paved the way for the establishment of a provisional government dominated by the Communists. The refusal of the United States to eliminate the opposition so cavalierly had led to adjournment of the joint commission in May 1946.[65]

A year later the joint commission reconvened, but neither the Russians nor the Americans would agree to change their stand and the meetings came to naught. Convinced by this time of the futility of further negotiations with the USSR on this score, the United States decided to bring the question of Korean unification and independence to the attention of the United Nations General Assembly. In September 1947 the General Assembly agreed to consider the problem and almost immediately the USSR launched an obstructive campaign. The Russians first proposed that the Soviet and American forces in Korea be withdrawn in early 1948, leaving the Koreans to organize their own government, but the United States countered with the suggestion that elections be held in both zones under the observation of the United Nations first. Once this was done, the new government could make arrangements for the withdrawal of the foreign armed forces when Korean defense forces were ready to take over the responsibility for national security. The U.S. draft resolution in the Central Assembly in October 1947 went on to propose the creation of a U.N. temporary commission

---

[65] Dept of State, *Korea, 1945 to 1948,* pp. 4–5.

on Korea to observe the election and to act as consultants to the Koreans in setting up the governmental machinery and in arranging for the end to the occupation.[66]

When the General Assembly adopted the U.S. resolution in principle, the Soviet Union served notice that it would not co-operate with the U.N. temporary commission. Efforts by the commission to enter the Soviet zone in Korea were fruitless, but, nevertheless, in February 1948 the commission decided that it would observe elections in those parts of Korea to which it had access. On 1 March General Hodge announced that elections would be held in South Korea in May.[67]

In anticipation of the eventual establishment of Korean independence, the U.S. military government had been gradually assigning more responsibility to Korean administrators during 1947 and 1948. A South Korean interim government had been set up in May 1947 in accordance with this policy.[68]

As the prospects for independence increased, interest in the future development of the Korean armed forces also mounted. The rapid demobilization of U.S. forces after World War II and the cutbacks in military expenditures had led to manpower shortages in the armed forces and a close scrutiny of U.S. commitments overseas. Thus, in October 1947, the Department of the Army asked Generals MacArthur and Hodge for their recommendations on Korean forces. Hodge proposed a South Korean army of six divisions, complete with headquarters and service troops, which could be equipped and trained by U.S. personnel within one year. But MacArthur felt that the establishment of Korean defense forces should be deferred until the United Nations General Assembly had an opportunity to express its wishes.[69]

Four months later General MacArthur still considered the formation of a South Korean army premature. On 6 February 1948 he informed the Washington policy makers that the lack of training facilities, the dearth of competent Korean military

---

[66] *Ibid.,* pp. 6–7.
[67] *Ibid.,* pp. 7–14.
[68] USAMGIK Ordinance 141, 17 May 47.
[69] (1) Msg, WAR 88572, 16 Oct 47. (2) Msg, CX 56266, CINCFE to DEPTAR, 22 Oct 47. (3) JCS 1483/47, 24 Nov 47.

leaders, and the diminishing capabilities of the XXIV Corps to provide the personnel and equipment for an army argued against such a move. Instead, he favored an increase in the Constabulary to 50,000 men and the provision of heavier infantry-type weapons—though not artillery—from U.S. sources in Korea. Other items, if they were necessary, could come from American stocks in Japan.[70]

A significant factor in General MacArthur's recommendations was his assertion that the augmentation of the Constabulary from its current strength of approximately 20,000 to 50,000 men would require 105 days.[71] With the South Korean elections scheduled for May, a quick decision on the matter was highly desirable. The Joint Chiefs of Staff therefore authorized the augmentation on 10 March 1948 along with the issue of infantry small arms, cannon (from 37-mm. to 105-mm. inclusive), and armored vehicles (including the tank, M24, and armored cars), as deemed appropriate.[72]

While the American political and military leaders debated the wisdom of building up the South Korean armed forces, the Koreans, both North and South, were moving ahead with their own plans. On 8 February the North Korean Provisional Government announced the official birth of the Korean People's Army. And in the Department of Internal Security recruiting for the Constabulary was quietly stepped up in the expectation that independence would require larger defense forces. By the time the U.S. support for the increase of the Constabulary to 50,000 men was revealed in March, the strength of the force already approximated that mark.[73]

Organizational expansion kept pace with recruiting. Early

[70] (1) Msg, CX 58437, 6 Feb 48. (2) See also JCS 1483/51, 10 Mar 48, app. B.
[71] Accurate strength figures for the Constabulary during this period (and later) are not available to the author. According to HR–KMAG, p. 3, as well as interviews and correspondence, the organization's strength in late 1947 seems to have been between 18,000 and 20,000 men.
[72] (1) WARX 97886, CSGPO to CINCFE, 10 Mar 48. (2) See also: JCS 1483/51, 10 Mar 48, apps. A and B, and Memo, CofS, U.S. Army, for JCS on augmentation and equipping of South Korean Constabulary, pp. 421–422; Memo for Maj Gen J. Lawton Collins from Brig Gen Thomas S. Timberman, Chief, Operations Group, P&O, 11 Mar 48, sub: Augmentation of the South Korean Constabulary, P&O File 091 Korea, sec. I, case I, pt. 11–A.
[73] (1) Ltr, Hodge to Ward, 18 Mar 52. (2) Interv, Maj Hausman, 24 Jan 52.

in the year military government advisors helped the Koreans establish three brigade headquarters—at Seoul, Taejon, and Pusan. These were patterned after the headquarters organization of a U.S. infantry division, though greatly reduced in strength and with minor changes to fit local conditions. Each brigade assumed control of three regiments, and the Korean Constabulary began to resemble an army more than a police reserve force. The spring of 1948 also saw the activation of embryonic technical services.[74]

On 8 April the Department of the Army directed Hodge to create conditions in Korea so that U.S. forces could be withdrawn at the end of 1948 and the Korean commitment be brought to a close. Lest the South Koreans use their armed forces in an aggressive manner that might involve the United States in a war, Hodge would train and equip the forces primarily for defense and internal security. The United States envisaged, after the withdrawal of the occupation forces, the establishment of a diplomatic mission, with a military advisory group attached if necessary, to administer economic and military aid to South Korea.[75]

Since the advisors then scattered about the provinces were too few to carry out such a mission, General Hodge authorized the assignment of additional U.S. Army officers to the military government and directed XXIV Corps units to set up schools to train the Koreans in the use of American equipment.[76]

Under the impetus the training of the Constabulary improved in both scope and content during the summer of 1948. As more advisors became available to the Department of Internal Security, regular training inspections became possible, and the

---

[74](1) HR–KMAG, p. 3. (2) Interv, Maj Hausman, 16 Jan 52. (3) Interv, Maj Geist, 3 Jul 52. (4) History of the Korean Army, (1 July–15 October 1948), unsigned MS in USAFIK files. (5) MHK, p. 20. (6) Incl to Ltr, Col DeReus, 28 Aug 53. Records are not clear concerning the establishment of these brigades and technical services. MHK shows that the brigades were formed on 1 Dec 47; Colonel DeReus writes that they were established in January 1948. In a letter dated 2 September 1952, Maj West states only that the three brigades and technical services were in existence in March 1948.

[75] Msg, WAR 99374 to CG USAFIK, 8 Apr 48.

[76] (1)HR–KMAG, pp. 3–4. (2) Intervs, Majs Hausman and Geist. (3) Ltr, Maj West to author, 16 Sep 52. HR–KMAG reported that "approximately 90" officers were authorized. West states that these were volunteers.

CONSTABULARY GROUP TRAINING WITH 81-MM. MORTAR *at the Korean Weapons School, Taegu.*

Constabulary entered its first standardized training program in July. At the same time the U.S. 6th and 7th Divisions, along with other XXIV Corps units, assisted the Constabulary by conducting schools for its officers and men. Noteworthy were a weapons school established on 1 July at Taegu by the 6th Division, and cannon schools established on 10 July at Chinhae and Seoul by the 6th and 7th Divisions, respectively. In this way Constabulary troops received valuable training in the use of the U.S. light and heavy machine guns, 60-mm. and 81-mm. mortars, 57-mm. antitank guns, and 105-mm. howitzers (M2).[77]

On 20 May 1948, meanwhile, Brig. Gen. William L. Roberts replaced Colonel Price as advisor to the Director, Department

---

[77] (1) HR–KMAG, pp. 3, 4. (2) History of the Korean Army, USAFIK files. (3) Ltrs, Maj West. (4) Intervs, Majs Hausman and Geist. (5) Incl 3 to Ltr, Maj West to Gen Ward, 20 Nov 52, p. 3. (6) Comments by Capt William R. Stroud, Dir of Training, 6th Inf Div Cannon School, Chinhae, Korea, Sep to Nov 1948, OCMH files.

of Internal Security.[78] At an orientation conference held shortly thereafter, Captain Hausman had an opportunity to express his dissatisfaction with the relationship between the Department of Internal Security and the Constabulary. The chief deficiency, in his opinion, lay in the direct control exercised by Internal Security over the staff and command functions of the Constabulary. Since 1946 nearly all decisions concerning it had been made by the higher headquarters, to the extent that the Constabulary staff was little more than a liaison group between the Department of Internal Security and the regiments. General Roberts subsequently described the situation in these words:

> I found two large Korean Headquarters running the constabulary . . . viz DIS and KA [sic]. Physically they were in two buildings nearly adjacent, and the offices of each were intermingled. There were many Korean officers being used in these headquarters who were unnecessary when the troops were woefully short of them. It was evident that one headquarters only was necessary and desirable for many reasons, such as—one office would veto what another office would OK; a supply officer would get turned down at one place but obtain what he wanted at the other . . . Furthermore, there were two chiefs of staff . . . one for DIS and one for KA [sic]. What had been done was to build up the top with little at the bottom. . .[79]

Thus, one of General Roberts' first actions was to de-emphasize the Korean Department of Internal Security and place more direct responsibility with the Constabulary. Following a reorganization, the former on 25 June 1948 ceased to function as a headquarters group and became simply the Office of the Director, Department of Internal Security.[80] This placed the two organizations in the relative positions of a war department and an army organization, leaving policy making to the Department of Internal Security and operational control with the Constabulary staff. The move improved the situation considerably and was an important step toward enabling the Korean Constabulary to function efficiently.

Despite Communist propaganda and acts of terrorism against the elections in South Korea, over 90 percent of the registered

[78] GO 15, Hq USAMGIK, 19 May 48.
[79] Ltr, Gen Roberts, 22 Jan 52. By "KA" General Roberts presumably meant Korean Constabulary, for the Korean Army was not officially established until 15 December 1948. See Ltr, Maj Mason, 28 Mar 53.
[80] (1) History of D.I.S. to 1 Jul 48 p. 15. (2) HR–KMAG, p. 4. (3) Ltr, Gen. Roberts. (4) Interv, Maj Hausman.

voters went to the polls on 10 May 1948 under the observance of the U.N. Temporary Commission on Korea. The representatives selected met at Seoul on 31 May as the National Assembly and elected Dr. Syngman Rhee chairman. By 12 July the Assembly had fashioned a constitution calling for a president, with strong executive powers, elected by the National Assembly. Eight days later the Assembly elected Dr. Rhee the first president of the Republic of Korea (ROK).[81] The formal inauguration took place on 15 August, three years after the liberation from Japanese rule.

The stage was set for the transfer of authority from the U.S. military government to the elected government of the Republic of Korea. As the American military command relinquished its control to Dr. Rhee and his associates, a new relationship had to be established between the two to provide for the maintenance of U.S. forces in South Korea and for their role in the defense of the country until final withdrawal could be effected.

[81] Dept of State, *Korea, 1945 to 1948*, pp. 14–18.

CHAPTER II

The Provisional Military Advisory Group

Transfer of Authority

The United States Army Military Government in Korea came to an end when the ROK Government took control on 15 August 1948. General Hodge immediately opened negotiations with President Rhee for a smooth and equitable transfer of authority to the new government. On 24 August Hodge and Rhee signed a military agreement whereby the ROK Government would gradually assume command of the nation's security forces. Until the task was completed and the American troops withdrew from Korea, the United States would retain operational control of the Korean forces. In the meantime, the United States would continue to train and equip the Constabulary and the Coast Guard and would also continue to use the facilities and base areas required for the maintenance of its forces.[1] The conclusion, on 11 September, of an initial financial and property settlement that arranged for the surrender of property and funds controlled by the United States under the occupation and for payment of Korean goods and services received during the period of occupation virtually ended the transfer process.

The shift from military to civilian control led to a number of personnel changes and a realignment of authority within the U.S. command structure in Korea. President Harry S. Truman appointed John J. Muccio as his Special Representative to Korea with the personal rank of Ambassador and gave him authority to negotiate for the withdrawal of U.S. forces. Muccio arrived shortly after the inauguration and established the U.S. diplomatic mission in Korea on 26 August. On the following day General Hodge left the country and was succeeded by Maj. Gen.

---

[1] For complete text, see House Report 2495, *Background Information on Korea*, Report of the Committee on Foreign Affairs, Union Calendar 889 (Washington, 1950), pp. 15–16.

John B. Coulter as Commanding General, USAFIK and XXIV Corps.[2]

The position of the American military advisors with the Korean forces also underwent a change after 15 August. Official justification for their presence ended with the deactivation of the military government, but by the terms of the Hodge-Rhee military agreement, their training functions were to continue. To cope with the new situation, all advisory personnel were assigned to the Overstrength Detachment, Headquarters, USAFIK, and organized as a Provisional Military Advisory Group (PMAG) under the command of General Roberts.[3]

During the remainder of 1948 PMAG grew from 100 men to 241. The increase permitted slightly more than the former perfunctory coverage of Korean units by the advisors, but the Korean forces were also expanding at this time and the demands for advisory personnel continued to mount. Since the organization was a makeshift group chiefly for administrative purposes and occupied an anomalous position, it had little official status.[4]

The Debate Over Withdrawal

Before the South Korean elections General Hodge had been instructed to make plans and preparations for the gradual withdrawal of American forces from Korea by the end of 1948. On 15 September the first phase of the approved plan was put into effect, and USAFIK units began to leave the peninsula. But the desire to end the Korean commitment and its drain upon manpower and resources now came into conflict with the political realities of the situation.

In September 1948 the North Koreans formed a government

---

[2] (1) Hq USAFIK, GO 34, 27 Aug 48. (2) Msg, ZPOL 1350, CG USAFIK to State Dept, 27 Aug 48. (3) Msg, ZGBI, USAFIK to DA, 28 Aug. 48. (4) Dept of State, *Korea, 1945–1948,* p. 20.

[3] (1) Hq USAFIK, GO 31, 15 Aug 48. (2) PMAG GO 1, 15 Aug 48. (3) GHQ, SCAP and FEC, Historical Report, 1 January–31 December 1949, II, 25. (4) Ltr, KMAG to Chief, Military Hist, 1 Sep 52, in OCMH files.

[4] (1) Interv, Maj Geist, 11 Jul 52. (2) Interv, Col Ralph B. White, PMAG Finance Advisor, 14 Jul 52. (3) GHQ SCAP and FEC, Hist Rpt, p. 25. (4) PMAG SO 1, 21, 24, 25, 29, 31–34. (5) Rpts, Weekly Activities of PMAG, Chief, PMAG, to CG USAFIK, 20 Sep 48, 11 Oct 48, 20 Dec 48. (6) Hq PMAG Staff Memo 1, 20 Aug 48, PMAG AG 314.7.

that claimed jurisdiction over all of Korea. Taking the title of Democratic People's Republic of Korea, it became the direct rival of the United Nations-sponsored ROK Government. The USSR and its satellites quickly recognized the Communist-dominated regime, and the Soviet Government announced on 19 September that it planned to withdraw all of its forces from Korea by the end of the year. Since the U.N. General Assembly was about to consider the Korean problem again, the United States refused to commit itself to matching the Soviet withdrawal.[5]

Thus, the rise of the North Korean Communist state and the Russian eagerness to have all foreign troops leave the peninsula cast doubts upon the sagacity of the U.S. withdrawal program. The possibility of the Communists using force to unify the country while the ROK Government was weak and conditions were un-settled argued against a quick evacuation of South Korea. In October a rebellion within the Constabulary sharply illustrated the domestic unrest and focused attention on the internal agita-tion seething beneath the surface of Rhee's government.[6]

Since the ROK defense forces were not properly prepared to resist invasion, the U.S. State Department came to the conclu-sion in November that the continued presence of U.S. forces would have a stabilizing effect upon the over-all situation. Syng-man Rhee sent a plea to President Truman, urging that the United States maintain an occupation force in Korea until the ROK forces were capable of dealing with any internal or external threat and that the United States establish a military and naval mission to help deter aggression and civil war.[7]

The flow of events on the peninsula in the fall of 1948 together with the U.S. desire to await the results of the U.N. General Assembly's deliberations produced a temporary slowdown in the removal of troops from Korea. When the General Assembly passed a resolution on 12 December calling for the complete withdrawal of American forces, more than 16,000 still remained

[5] Dept. of State, *Korea, 1945 to 1948,* pp. 21–22.
[6] See below, pp. 39–40, for a discussion of the October rebellion.
[7] See James F. Schnabel, Policy and Direction: The First Year, June 1950–July 1951, a forthcoming volume in the UNITED STATES ARMY IN THE KOREAN WAR series, ch. II.

on Korean soil.   The JCS directed General MacArthur to scale down this figure as quickly as possible to one regimental combat team of 7,500 men.[8]

On 15 January 1949 the XXIV Corps left Korea for deactivation in Japan, and personnel from the U.S. 32d Infantry Regiment, 48th Field Artillery Battalion, an engineer company, and the 7th Mechanized Cavalry Reconnaissance Troop were left behind to man the component units of the newly reactivated 5th Regimental Combat Team. General Coulter left the same day, and General Roberts assumed command of Headquarters, USAFIK while retaining his position as Chief, Provisional Military Advisory Group.[9]

The question of whether the regimental combat team should remain in Korea for an extended period led the JCS to seek General MacArthur's comments in January. He told them that the United States did not have the capability to train and equip Korean troops to the point where the Koreans would be able to cope with a full-scale invasion accompanied by internal disturbances fomented by the Communists. If a serious threat developed, the United States would have to give up active military support of the ROK forces, he went on. Under the circumstances, MacArthur recommended the remaining U.S. units be withdrawn on 10 May 1949, the anniversary of the Korean elections.[10]

In the meantime, the United States formally recognized the Republic of Korea on 1 January 1949, and the National Security Council (NSC) conducted a thorough review of U.S. policy with respect to Korea.[11] The President's advisors reached the conclusion in March that further support and assistance to the ROK should not depend upon the presence of American military forces in the country and that complete withdrawal, preferably

---

[8] *Ibid.*

[9] (1) Msg, WARX 92575, to CINCFE, 15 Nov 48. (2) Msg, CX 66800, CINCFE to DA for CSGPO, 4 Jan 49. (3) Msg, DA Rad CM–OUT 81599, 21 Dec 48. (4) See also: JCS 1483/58, 22 Nov 48, pp. 451–53; P&O File 091 Korea, sec. V; Incl to Ltr, GHQ FEC to Dir P&O GSUSA, 7 May 49, sub: Rpt on Dispositions, Strengths and Combat Capabilities of the Major Air and Ground Forces in Overseas Commands, Rpts Symbol WDGPO–6, P&O File 320.2 Pac, sec. I.

[10] Msg, CX 67198, CINCFE to DA, 19 Jan 49.

[11] Department of State, *Bulletin,* XX (January 9, 1949), 59–60.

by 30 June, was politically and militarily desirable. They also advised the President to seek legislative authority for continuing military assistance for the fiscal year 1949–50 and, if developments warranted, thereafter. To handle the training of the ROK Army, Coast Guard, and National Police and to assure that the U.S. military assistance would be effectively utilized, they recommended that a U.S. military advisory group be established. President Truman approved these recommendations on 23 March 1949.[12]

Ten days later the USAFIK headquarters received instructions from the Department of the Army to make preparations for withdrawal by 30 June. Between 28 May and 29 June the 5th Regimental Combat Team moved in four increments from Inch'on to Hawaii.[13]

The Infancy of the ROK Army

As the U.S. troops left Korea during late 1948 and the first half of 1949, they turned over part of their equipment to the ROK forces in accordance with the military agreement signed by Rhee and Hodge. By November 1948 between 60 and 80 percent of the Constabulary's small arms and automatic weapons were American, but there was a dearth of mortars and heavy machine guns. Although only 52 of an allotted 90 105-mm infantry cannon (M3) had been received, a full issue of 37-mm anti-tank guns was on hand. Unfortunately, spare parts and all types of sighting and aiming equipment were in extremely short supply.[14]

During the spring of 1948, the South Koreans had added six infantry regiments to the original nine formed for the Constabulary and had created a fourth and a fifth brigade. They wanted to form a sixth brigade but were warned that the United

[12] See P&O File 091 Korea (1949), sec. I–A, bk. I, case 5/8.
[13] (1) Msg, DA 86379, CSGPO to CINCFE, 24 Mar 49 (sent to USAFIK on 2 Apr). (2) Hq USAFIK, Operation Order 3, 23 May 49, cited in Hq USAFIK, History of the G–3 Section, 15 January–30 June 1949.
[14] (1) Information on North and South Korean Army Forces, Incl 4 to Ltr, G–2, XXIV Corps, 23 Nov 48, sub: Ranks in Korean Military Forces, G–2 Documentary Library, DA, ID 513012. This source states that the Constabulary was 80 percent U.S. equipped, but another source affirmed 60 percent was a more correct estimate. (2) See Ltr, West to Ward, 20 Nov 52; Ltr, DeReus to Smith, 28 Aug 53.

THE PROVISIONAL MILITARY ADVISORY GROUP   39

States could not furnish equipment for further expansion at that time.[15]

In October 1948 the fledgling government and Army had undergone its sternest test. Domestic disturbances were common throughout South Korea, but the mutiny of the ROK 14th Regiment at Yosu on 19 October represented a serious threat. The uprising spread quickly to the towns of Sunch'on, Posong, Polgyo-ri, and Kwangyang. The American mission in Korea felt that Korea's future depended upon Rhee and his associates bringing the dissident elements under control quickly and firmly.[16]

The Yosu revolt appears to have been prematurely touched off by an order issued in October assigning the 14th Regiment to the island of Cheju-do to help quell disorders there. U.S. M1 rifles were issued to the regiment, though it retained its Japanese 99's as well. Among the high-ranking noncommissioned officers of the regiment were a number of Communists, and they apparently planned to use the extra rifles to arm fellow-travelers in the surrounding villages. Then came a second order instructing the regiment to move at once, and the Communist leaders had to act hastily or lose the opportunity for concerted action and for arming their coworkers. They fanned the antipolice sentiment among the troops of the 14th and incited an attack to take over the town.

As the rebellion spread to surrounding towns, loyal Constabulary units and police detachments were rushed from districts throughout southwest Korea. Brig. Gen. Song Ho Seung, the chief of the Constabulary, was placed in command of the government forces, and General Roberts sent Captain Hausman and two other advisors along to assist Song. The Korean general and the advisors set up headquarters at Kwangju. Soon five additional advisors joined the group, including two lieutenants who had been imprisoned by the rebels in Yosu and later escaped.[17]

---

[15] Information on North and South Korean Army Forces, cited in previous footnote.
[16] Dispatch 90, American Mission in Korea, 16 Nov 48, sub: Political Summary for October 1948, G–2 Doc Lib, DA, ID 0509409.
[17] The account of the Yosu incident is based upon: (1) HR–KMAG, p. 5; (2) The Truth About the Yosu Incident, paper loaned by Maj John P. Reed, who was one of the three advisors originally sent by Roberts (copy in OCMH files); (3) Interv Maj Hausman, 22 Apr 53; (4) Ltr, Col W. H. Sterling Wright to Gen Smith, 26 Aug. 53.

216–985 O–66—4

As the operation grew in scope and seriousness and because of the extremely poor communications between dispersed Constabulary units, a need for additional advisors arose. Coulter and Roberts sent a senior officer, Col. Hurley E. Fuller, to take over the responsibilities.

In the meantime, Captain Hausman and Capt. John P. Reed managed to round up part of a Constabulary regiment and on 21 October halted the rebel drive until loyal reinforcements could arrive. A counterattack rewon Sunch'on on 22 October, and two days later the loyal forces entered Kwangyang and Posong. Polgyo-ri fell on the 25th, and the rebels then made their final stand at Yosu. After two days of fierce fighting, the opposition ended, many of the mutineers slipping off to the rugged mountains to the north. Here, in the Chiri-san area, the rebel remnants became guerrilla fighters and a constant thorn in the side of the government.

The effort made by Captain Hausman and his fellow advisors in rallying the Constabulary and aiding in the conduct of the campaign was first rate. Without their assistance the revolt might well have become far more serious. The Yosu rebellion was also important in providing a training ground for the commanders, staff, and units of the Constabulary. Although anti-guerrilla activity earlier in 1948 at Cheju-do had given the Constabulary valuable experience, the Yosu affair allowed units to be employed for the first time on something approaching a major scale.[18]

Almost immediately after the fall of Yosu, repercussions began throughout the ROK forces. A purge to eliminate Communist influence in the Constabulary got under way and, according to General Roberts, over 1,500 were uncovered and removed from the service.[19] Except for a brief outbreak of Communist activity at Taegu that was soon brought under control, the Constabulary remained loyal.

In an interesting sidelight to the Yosu affair, the ROK leaders abolished the 14th Regiment on 28 October for its shameful conduct and burned its colors. All units bearing the number *4*,

---

[18] (1) HR–KMAG, p. 5. (2) Hist of the Korean Army, MS, USAFIK files. (3) The Truth About the Yosu Incident.
[19] Ltr, Roberts to Smith, 26 Feb 54.

either alone or in combination, were redesignated and the use of the number was henceforth abandoned.[20]

There were organizational changes as well in the post-Yosu period. Since 15 August the ROK officials had been referring to the Constabulary as the National Defense Army, despite the refusal of the United States to recognize the validity of the term. In late November the ROK Armed Forces Organization Act was passed, and on 15 December a complete ROK

CAPTAIN HAUSMAN

national defense organization, including a Department of National Defense, Army, and Navy, was set up. Brig. Gen. Lee Hyung Koon became the first ROK Army (ROKA) Chief of Staff.[21] At this time the ROK Constabulary brigades emerged as Army divisions, and fourteen Army branches were established.[22]

The transfer of U.S. arms to the Korean defense forces continued during the winter and so did the ROK recruiting program. Despite the fact that the United States had only authorized the transfer of infantry-type weapons and equipment for 50,000 men, the ROK forces in March 1949 totaled about 114,000—65,000 in the Army, 4,000 in the Coast Guard, and 45,000 police.

---

[20] See: (1) MHK, Chart 9–3; (2) Ltr, West to author, 16 Sep 52. In an interview on 14 October 1953, General Chang stated that the numeral 4 means ill fortune to many Koreans, much as the numeral 13 seems unlucky to many Americans. The Yosu revolt merely proved this to the Koreans, and thereafter 4 was not used as or within a ROK unit designation.

[21] (1) MHK, pp. 21–22. (2) Ltr, West to author, 2 Sep 52. (3) Comments, Captain Stroud. Because the United States evidently was anxious to avoid any inference that it would support a ROK Navy, U.S. recognition of the Coast Guard's redesignation was withheld. The Korean "Navy" will be referred to as the Coast Guard in this study.

[22] HR–KMAG, p. 5. According to the translation of MHK (page 22) in the possession of OCMH, this act simply authorized the formation of divisions, which were officially designated as such by President Rhee on 12 December 1949. However, since American sources refer to ROK Army "divisions" throughout 1949, they will be so called herein.

Approximately one-half of the Coast Guard and police were equipped with American side arms and carbines; the rest carried Japanese weapons. When the National Security Council in March recommended withdrawal of U.S. forces, it also suggested that the United States furnish minimum essential equipment for the additional 15,000 men in the Korean Army. Minimum equipment included a carbine, helmet, field pack, and six-month supply of carbine ammunition for each man. To strengthen the Coast Guard and police, the NSC urged that additional arms and vessels be provided the Coast Guard and that small arms support and ammunition be accorded a 35,000-man police force. A six-month stockpile of maintenance supplies to cover replacement and consumption requirements should be made available to all Korean security forces, the NSC concluded. Approval of the National Security Council's recommendations by the President led to the issuance of orders in late March for the transfer of the supplies and equipment before the U.S. forces withdrew from Korea.[23]

The American troops were also able, before their departure, to help train ROK soldiers in tactics and in the use of the weapons and equipment that they were turning over to the new Army. The 5th Regimental Combat Team prepared and staged demonstrations during its closing days in Korea to show the tactics employed by the squad, platoon, and company in both offense and defense. In addition, battalion demonstrations were mounted for the benefit of ROK officers and noncommissioned officers.[24]

The Expansion of the Advisory Group

On the same day—2 April 1949—that USAFIK received its orders to prepare for the withdrawal of U.S. forces from Korea, the Military Advisory Group received instructions to expand its organization. Previous experience had indicated that a successful advisor effort in Korea would have to reach down to the battalion level, where the advisors could supervise training closely and correct faulty methods before they become ingrained

---

[23] DA Rad, WARX 86359 to CINCFE, 29 Mar 49.
[24] (1) Notes attached to Ltr, Roberts to Smith, 26 Jan 54. (2) Hq USAFIK, Hist of the G–3 Sec, 15 Jan–30 Jun 49.

in the new recruits. Thus, the Army decided to expand the group sufficiently to participate in advisory activities to the battalion headquarters level in the Republic of Korea Army, the district headquarters level in the National Police force, and to any level of the Korean Coast Guard.[25] A week later a message from Washington established an over-all military ceiling of 500 spaces for the advisory group and directed that a Table of Distribution be prepared on that basis.[26] As submitted on 11 April, the proposed T/D called for 182 officers, 4 warrant officers, a nurse, and 293 enlisted men—or a total of 480. The Far East Command forwarded the table on 30 April, with a recommendation that 18 additional signal personnel (2 officers and 16 enlisted men) be included to help the diplomatic mission in Seoul with its communications facilities until civilian technicians could be recruited.[27]

Since the strength of the group at that time was only 92 officers and 148 enlisted men, a board of three PMAG officers began screening the units still under United States Army Forces in Korea.[28] The board experienced little difficulty in obtaining enlisted personnel; these were recruited as volunteers and had only to hold certain MOS's and be recommended by their officers for assignment to the group. Obtaining officers proved to be a difficult task. Except for a few volunteers, they had to be levied for duty as advisors. "Korea was considered a very undesirable assignment," wrote Lt. Col. Matthew J. Bartosik, a member of the board, later on. "Those [officers] on duty in Korea wanted to get out." [29]

The board at first considered only officers in the grade of captain or higher who still had a year to serve overseas. When meetings at ASCOM City,[30] USAFIK Headquarters, and the 5th

---

[25] (1) DA Rad, 86379, CSGPO to CINCFE (info CG USAFIK), 24 Mar 49. (2) DA Rad, 86425, CSGPO to CINCFE, CG USAFIK, CG USAFPAC, 30 Mar 49. (3) Hq USAFIK, Hist of the G–3 Sec, 15 Jan–Jun 49.

[26] DA Rad, WX 86933, 9 Apr 49.

[27] AC of S G–3 GHQ FEC, Historical Report, 1949, I, 45.

[28] HR–KMAG, an. 5.

[29] Ltr, Bartosik to author, 2 Jan 53.

[30] ASCOM (Army Service Command) City, so christened on 16 September 1945, was a former Japanese arsenal area west of Seoul used by the American occupation forces. ROKA later used it for technical services installations. See Hist of USAFIK, pt. I, ch. IV, pp. 31, 32.

Regimental Combat Team failed to turn up enough officers thus qualified, the board relaxed its requirements to permit the selection of first lieutenants while lowering the service requirement on overseas tours to six months. When the board still was unable to meet its quota, it took a few officers who had less than six months to serve overseas. Even so, before the advisory group obtained sufficient advisors for its Table of Distribution, fifteen officers had to be requisitioned from the Far East Command. "The board," recalled Colonel Bartosik sadly, "was a very unpopular group of people."

Considering the method used to procure additional advisors, the officers and enlisted men obtained by the PMAG board represented a fair cross-section of those available in Korea. The levy did bring to the advisory group many officers who were young and inexperienced. Although excellent and promising otherwise, all were not qualified to advise Korean regimental and division commanders, who by culture and training were prone to regard youth as callow and beneath notice.[31]

On 7 June the Department of the Army tentatively approved the Table of Distribution for the advisory group at 480 troop spaces, to be included within the Far East Command ceiling for 30 June and 31 December 1959.[32] Later changes reduced the total number of troop spaces to 479, as the Army deleted or lowered the number of finance, mess, and security personnel on the grounds that there was no justification for them under the Table of Distribution. On the other hand, the Department of the Army had approved Far East Command's recommendation that 18 signal personnel be assigned temporarily to the group for duty with the diplomatic mission and, in addition, had authorized 5 enlisted postal clerks on the same basis. Though authorized temporarily, the 23 spaces were included within the 500-space ceiling, putting the advisory group's initial military strength at 186 officers, a warrant officer, a nurse, and 288 enlisted men.[33]

---

[31] (1) Ltr, Col Bartosik, 2 Jan 53. (2) Ltr, Wright to Smith, 26 Aug 53.
[32] DA Rad, W 89646, 7 Jun 49.
[33] (1) DA Rad, WX 90559, 24 Jun 49. (2) DA Rad, WAR 90771, 28 Jun 49. (3) Ltr, DA AGAD–I 322 (KMAG) (24 Jun 49), CSGOT–M to CINCFE, 29 Jun 49, sub: Establishment of KMAG.

When the 5th Regimental Combat Team left for Hawaii in May and June and the surplus personnel who were scheduled for transfer to Japan moved out, PMAG moved into more spacious quarters on the southern edge of Seoul near Camp Sobingo, where the U.S. 7th Division had formerly been quartered. Real property belonging to the Republic of Korea was returned except for the building and land used by the diplomatic mission and PMAG.[34] On 30 June when Headquarters, USAFIK, was deactivated, the interim military agreement signed by Rhee and Hodge lapsed and the Koreans assumed complete and full control of their armed forces.[35]

With the departure of Headquarters, U.S. Army Forces in Korea, the Provisional Military Advisory Group emerged on 1 July 1949 as an official entity called the United States Military Advisory Group to the Republic of Korea (KMAG).[36] The group became an integral part of the American Mission in Korea (AMIK), along with the U.S. Embassy at Seoul, the local agency of the Economic Cooperation Administration (ECA), and a service organization called the Joint Administrative Services (JAS). Barring unforeseen circumstances, and restricted only by the limits of Korean economy and the continued support of its own government, KMAG hoped to help develop a more efficient Korean military establishment.

---

[34] Technically, all such property had been returned in the settlement concluded the previous September. However, USAFIK post engineers had retained the records pending actual evacuation by U.S. Forces. History of the Engineer Section, USAFIK, 15 January–29 June 1949, USAFIK files.

[35] (1) JCS 1483/72, 21 Jul 49. (2) U.N. Doc A/936, add. 1, II, Annexes, 36. (3) Incl 2 to Dispatch 455, 26 Jul 49, American Embassy, Seoul, to Chairman, Subcommittee, U.N. Commission on Korea, Seoul, 25 Jul 49, G–2 Doc Lib DA 581109. (4) Progress Rpt by the Secy of State on the Implementation of the Position of the U.S. with Respect to Korea 19 Jul 49, P&O File 091 Korea, sec. II, case 40/2. (5) Msg, KMAG X89, CG USAFIK, sgd Roberts, to DA, 30 Jun 49.

[36] (1) DA Rad, WAR 90771, to CINCFE, 28 Jun 49. (2) DA Ltr, AGAO–I 322 (24 Jun), CSGOT to CINCFE, sub: Establishment of KMAG, 29 Jun 49. (3) DA Rad 90992, CSGPO to Chief, KMAG, 1 Jul 49. KMAG often is erroneously called the "Korean Military Advisory Group," or "Korea Military Advisory Group." The correct title is as indicated in the text. (4) See Memo for Rcd, P&O Div GSUSA, FE&Pac Br, sub: Guidance for Answering Queries Relating to Withdrawal From Korea, 1 Jul 49, P&O File 091 Korea (1 Jul 49).

CHAPTER III

KMAG: The Instrument and the Challenge

Command Relationships

Originally the Department of the Army had intended to place KMAG under Ambassador Muccio's administrative direction while permitting General MacArthur to exercise operational control. However, MacArthur's experience with the Joint U.S. Military Advisory Group to the Republic of the Philippines (JUSMAGPHIL) made him reluctant to accept a similar arrangement for KMAG. In the case of JUSMAGPHIL, the JCS had laid out the group's missions and MacArthur's role had been limited to minor matters having little to do with the major task of advising the Philippine forces. Unless he were granted authority to assign the objectives for KMAG, MacArthur felt that the group should be controlled by the U.S. Ambassador. To safeguard military interests KMAG could be granted the right to communicate directly with the JCS on military matters, MacArthur continued, and he recommended that KMAG forward all military messages and reports through the Far East Command.[1]

Thus KMAG's relationship to Ambassador Muccio and the American mission in Korea underwent a quick change. Since Muccio had the responsibility for carrying out U.S. policy in Korea and KMAG was an element of AMIK, he was given operational control of the group. For administrative purposes KMAG was established as an Army Administrative Area, Foreign Assignment Activity, directly under the Department of the Army. The Far East Command's responsibility was limited to the logistic support of KMAG to the water line of Korea and to the emergency evacuation of U.S. personnel from the country

[1] Msg, CX 69456, CINCFE to DA, 23 Apr 49, in GHQ, SCAP and FEC Hist Rpt, 1949, vol. II, incl 27. General MacArthur wore three hats at this time (April 1949): Supreme Commander for the Allied Powers (SCAP) for his command of the forces occupying Japan; Commander in Chief, Far East (CINCFE), for his regional command of all U.S. Army, Navy, and Air Force units in the Far East; and Commanding General, U.S. Army Forces, Far East (USAFFE), for his command of all Army forces in the Far East.

if the need arose.[2] Since the Far East Command was the only U.S. military command in the area, KMAG did maintain close liaison with MacArthur's headquarters. KMAG representatives made periodic visits to Tokyo to discuss and co-ordinate evacuation plans and to keep the Far East Command informed on political and military developments in Korea.[3]

Although the KMAG operated under the control of Ambassador Muccio, the internal direction of the group was entirely in General Roberts' hands. The relationship between AMIK and KMAG centered on U.S. military assistance to Korea. All matters relating to the means, methods, and degree of such aid were of mutual interest and were carefully co-ordinated by the two agencies either at formal meetings or on a personal basis. On most other matters, particularly those involving military command or administration, the advisory group reported directly to the Pentagon.[4]

Direct logistic support for the American mission (including KMAG) came from AMIK's Joint Administrative Services. JAS was a civilian organization designed to relieve other AMIK elements of housekeeping duties. Under American JAS supervisors, Korean employees maintained buildings and utilities, operated billets and messes, and performed a multitude of similar tasks. With the Far East Command furnishing logistic support only as far as Korean ports, the Joint Administrative Services also was the link between KMAG and U.S. Army supply installations in Japan. The various segments of the mission submitted periodic requests for supplies to JAS, which in turn requisitioned the supplies from Japan and delivered them upon their arrival at Pusan or Inch'on.[5]

[2] GHQ SCAP and FEC, Hist Rpt, 1949, II, 26, 51.

[3] DA Rad, WARX 90992, 1 Jul 49. (2) KMAG Relationship With FEC, Orientation Folder (OFldr), sec. I. This folder, undated, was compiled in the spring of 1950 by General Roberts for his successor. Copy in OCMH files.

[4] Interv, Col Wright, former CofS, KMAG, 5 Jan 53. (2) Advisor's Handbook, 17 October 1949, an. 3 to Semiannual Report, Office of the Chief, U.S. Military Advisory Group to the Republic of Korea, period ending 31 December 1949. Hereafter this semiannual report and the KMAG Semiannual Report, dated 15 June 1950, will be cited as SA Rpt, KMAG, and will carry appropriate date.

[5] (1) Interv, Col Wright. (2) Interv, Lt Col Robert E. Myers, former Director of Supply, KMAG, 7 Jul 52. (3) Joint Administrative Services, OFldr, sec. I. JAS furnished all supplies to KMAG except Class II (equipment prescribed by Table of Equipment).

The legal status of KMAG and its personnel was settled by agreements between the United States and the Republic of Korea, which granted the KMAG staff and their dependents the same immunity accorded to AMIK diplomatic personnel. Some Koreans had felt that the U.S. military advisors should be subject to the laws of the Republic of Korea, but the inclusion of KMAG under the American Mission in Korea paved the way for the establishment of diplomatic immunity.[6]

Internal Arrangements

Shortly after the military advisory group began operations in July, General Roberts asked reconsideration of the Department of the Army's earlier reductions of finance, mess, and security personnel from KMAG's Table of Distribution. He reminded his superiors that the advisory group was the sole U.S. financing agency in Korea; that Korean mess stewards could not maintain the standards required for the four widely separated messes in operation; and that the security of KMAG areas would be left in the hands of the Korean military police, since JAS could provide few American supervisors because of personnel limitations.[7]

The Department of the Army restored the mess and security spaces later in the month, but pointed out that the Department of State and the Economic Cooperation Administration had agreed to furnish their own finance personnel. Under the circumstances, the Army felt that two additional enlisted men would be sufficient for KMAG's needs, including the finance advisory program. This revised the advisory group's personnel authorization for 31 December 1949 to 186 officers, 4 warrant officers, a nurse, and 304 enlisted men—495 in all.[8] Later in the year KMAG lost 23 enlisted spaces, some of which were replaced by civilians,

---

[6] HR–KMAG, an. 15, pp. 14, 15. According to this report, from 1 July 1949, when the interim military agreement expired, to the end of 1949 (and presumably until the KMAG agreement was signed on 26 January 1950), the advisory group "continued with the status of diplomatic immunity [previously] existing."
[7] KMAG Msg, ROB 017, Chief, KMAG, to DA, 5 Jul 49.
[8] Msg, WARX 91952, DA to KMAG, 26 Jul 49. (2) See also Ltr, Dir, O&T, OACofS, G–3, to TAG, Assignment Br, DAAA Sec, 26 Jul 49, sub: T/D KMAG, CSGOT.221 (5 Jul 49).

CHART 1—KMAG TABLE OF DISTRIBUTION, 1949

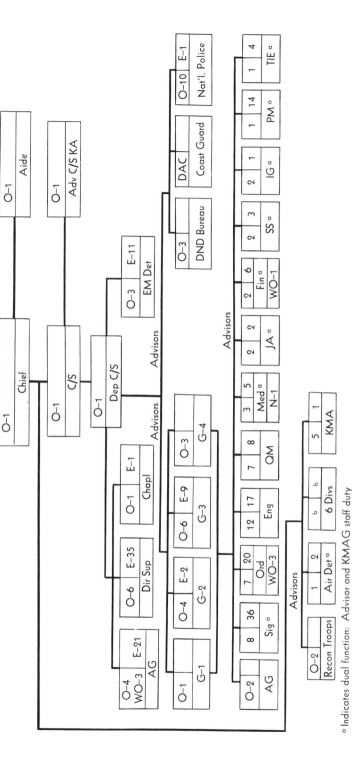

a Indicates dual function: Advisor and KMAG staff duty

ᵃ Indicates dual function: Advisor and KMAG staff duty
ᵇ Thirteen officers and fourteen enlisted men with each ROK Army division
Source: Adapted From Semiannual Report, Period 1 July–31 December 1949, United States Military Advisory Group to the Republic of Korea

TABLE 1—UNITED STATES MILITARY ADVISORY GROUP TO THE REPUBLIC OF KOREA

	Gen.	Col.	Lt. Col.	Maj.	Capt.	1st Lt.	Total Off	Nurse	WO	Enl
Total	1	3	28	40	100	9	181	1	7	283
Office of the Chief	1	1	2	3	6	5	18	-----	3	68
Department of National Defense Bureaus			3				3			
Chief of Staff Korean Army		1					1			
G–1			1				1			
G–2			1	1	2		4			2
G–3			1	2	3		6			9
G–4			1	2			3			
Finance			1		1		2		1	6
Inspector General			1		1		2			1
Judge Advocate			1		1		2			2
Adjutant General			1	1			2			
Special Services					1	1	2			3
Provost Marshal					1		1			14
Troop Information and Education					1		1			4
Medical			1		1	1	3	1		5
Ordnance			1	1	5		7		3	20
Signal			1	1	4	2	8			36
Engineer			1	1	10		12			17
Quartermaster			1		6		7			8
Reconnaissance Troops				1	1		2			
Air Base Detachment				1			1			2
Korean Military Academy			1	2	2		5			1
Korean Army Divisions (6)			6	18	54		78			84
National Police		1	3	6			10			1

Source: Compiled from Revised Table of Distribution No. 400–1734, effective 31 December 1949.

and the military strength authorization stabilized at 472 officers and men.[9] (*Table 1* and *Chart 1*)

The advisory group also was authorized 20 Department of the Army civilians. Of these there were nine advisors to the Korean Coast Guard, one interpretor-translator for the Korean National Police, 5 secretary-stenographers for various KMAG

[9] (1) DA Rad, WAR 95373, CSGOT to Chief, KMAG, 13 Oct 49. (2) DAAA Personnel Authorization 2, 19 Oct 49. (3) Ltr, Dir, O&T, OACofS, G–3, DA to TAG, 13 Oct 49, sub: Rev Personnel Authorization for KMAG, File CSGOT.2. (4) Rev T/D 400–1734, effective 31 Dec 49, copy in DA Rpt, KMAG, 31 Dec 49, an. 1.

staff sections, 2 special service hostesses, a Troop Information and Education programmer, and a civilian personnel officer. In addition, KMAG employed 2 hostesses and 4 post exchange workers from nonappropriated funds. Because Korea was considered an undesirable area in which to work, KMAG's civilian members were difficult to recruit and it usually took several months to obtain a replacement from the United States.[10]

Since most of the major installations of the Republic of Korea Army were located in the general vicinity of the Capital City, two-thirds of all KMAG personnel worked and lived in the Seoul-Inch'on area.[11] KMAG headquarters was located in the ROK Army headquarters building in Seoul, near the edge of town where the highway ran south to Yongdungp'o. Members of the advisory group working in or around Seoul lived in Camp Sobinggo, a compound containing 109 western-style houses, a dispensary, a chapel, officers' and service clubs, and barracks. Seven miles to the south at Yongdungp'o was another compound, containing thirty-two houses. At ASCOM City, nineteen miles west of Seoul and the site of many of the Korean Army technical services installations, a third compound housed sixty U.S. military and civilian members of the American mission and their dependents. The remaining KMAG advisors were scattered throughout South Korea in approximately eighteen locations.[12]

Bachelor officers assigned to Seoul either lived at the KMAG Officers' Club or made arrangements with AMIK's Joint Administrative Services for billets at hotels maintained by the mission. The nurse and other female members of the group lived in a hostess billet at Sobinggo, and enlisted personnel were quartered in the barracks there. For dependents of married KMAG personnel near Seoul the advisory group used 96 of the 109 houses at Camp Sobinggo and 17 of the 32 at Yongdungp'o, largely one-story frame and stucco buildings with from one to four bedrooms. The same type of housing was available at most field stations, but because there were few American schools in Korea and limited medical, post exchange, and commissary fa-

---

[10] (1) Civilian Employees, KMAG, OFldr, sec. I. (2) HR–KHAG, an. 5.
[11] SA Rpt, KMAG, 31 Dec 49, sec. I, p. 2.
[12] Quarters and Billeting, OFldr, sec. I.

cilities, dependents normally accompanied principals only to
Taejon, Taegu, Pusan, and Kwangju. Bachelor officers and enlisted men at field stations lived in dependent houses in com-
pounds near Korean Army division or regimental headquarters.[13]

As mentioned earlier, Korea was not a popular assignment
for U.S. Army personnel. KMAG was a small outpost far removed from what Americans called "civilization," in a country
where high prices, substandard housing, limited transportation,
and political disturbances were the order of the day.[14] To balance
the adverse conditions there were, nevertheless, features tending
to make duty in Korea desirable—for example, a comparatively
short service tour. As against a full thirty months for members
of the Far East Command in Japan, the tour in Korea for military personnel without dependents was only eighteen months;
while those who had their dependents with them were required
to remain for only twenty-four months. Of equal inducement,
military personnel in Korea drew in addition to their regular pay
a per diem station allowance. Military personnel serving in areas
where adequate subsistence and quarters either were not available or were obtained at unusually high prices were entitled to
such an allowance. In Korea this amounted to three dollars per
day for subsistence and seventy-five cents per day for quarters;
since quarters were available at all KMAG stations, only the
subsistence portion of the station allowance was paid to members of the advisory group.[15]

The additional ninety dollars per month was useful in Korea
in defraying such expenses as the prices in effect at the mission-
operated commissary, which was the only source of groceries
for both individuals and organized units.[16] Because of freight and
handling charges and the costs of maintaining the commissary,
prices there were 30 percent higher than in the commissary in
Tokyo. In any case, the station allowance was well received by

[13] (1) *Ibid.* (2) KMAG Staff Memo 108, 27 Dec 49. (3) Ltr, Col Bartosik, 2
Jan 53.
[14] Morale, OFldr, sec. I.
[15] (1) Morale; Length of Tours and Extensions; and Station Allowance, OFldr, see I.
(2) KMAG Staff Memo 108. (3) Station Rpt, Office of the Army Attaché, American
Embassy, Seoul, 1 May 50, p. 20, in G–2 Doc Lib, DA, ID 66620.
[16] The subsistence allowance was raised to $3.75 per diem on 1 April 1950, totaling
$112.00 per month in addition to regular pay.

all members of the advisory group and undoubtedly had much to do with the fact that a surprising number requested extensions to their tours of duty with KMAG.[17]

For the medical and dental care of KMAG personnel and their dependents, the KMAG Medical Section operated a small general dispensary at Camp Sobinggo. A staff included full-time medical and dental officers, six enlisted men, and a nurse who spent part of her time teaching modern nursing methods to Korean girls. Being the only U.S. Army medical facility within several hundred miles, the KMAG dispensary was equipped to handle most types of routine and emergency cases. When necessary, the staff had recourse to a field-type x-ray machine and a small laboratory. An ambulance borrowed from the Republic of Korea Army stood ready for emergencies. Serious cases were hospitalized eight miles away at a Seventh Day Adventist missionary hospital or transported by air to Japan. Since many officers and enlisted men were far removed from even the small KMAG dispensary, enlisted aidmen were detailed to five of the larger field installations. Each was supplied with a footlocker containing medical supplies and medicines. These aidmen all had had experience as medical and surgical technicians and were able to render first aid and treat minor injuries. For remote detachments, air evacuation was available in emergencies, although this was not always possible in the Kangnung area which was sometimes isolated by snow during winter months.[18]

To provide for the religious needs of the group, KMAG had a Protestant chaplain and also arranged for the services of a Catholic priest from a cathedral in Seoul. There was no Jewish chaplain because there were too few of that faith in KMAG at any one time.[19]

Radio communication was of great importance to KMAG. With advisory personnel outside the Seoul-Inch'on district located in widely separated areas, radios were the only means of day-to-day contact. As a provisional organization the group's radio network had consisted of a net control station at Seoul

[17] Station Allowance; and AMIK Commissary, OFldr, sec. I.
[18] (1) Ltr, Col Bartosik, 7 Aug 52. (2) HR–KMAG, an. 18. (3) KMAG Dispensary and the VD Program, OFldr, sec. I.
[19] HR–KMAG, an. 14, p. 1.

(SCR–399), a station at Taegu (SCR–399), and mobile stations at Taejon, Kwangju, Wonju, Kangnung, and Ch'unch'on (SCR–193's). Additional mobile stations had been established for special operations, as when U.S. advisors accompanied Korean Army units in campaigns against guerrillas. This network expanded after the establishment of KMAG, and by the end of 1949 there were twelve stations on two separate nets with a common net control station at KMAG headquarters. One net maintained contact with advisors in the interior of South Korea; the other served advisors with ROK Army units at Wonju, on the Ongjin Peninsula, and at other locations generally along the 38th Parallel.[20]

Enlisted radio operators assigned to the Signal Section manned the KMAG net control station. At field stations, because of insufficient signal advisors, operators often served dual roles as radio operators for their advisory detachments and assistant signal advisors to Korean Army signal companies. All stations worked on a definite schedule, twice daily, while the net control station in Seoul maintained a continuous watch on both nets. Besides transmitting tactical and operational messages, the radio net also served as a substitute telephone system over which groceries could be ordered, medicine practiced, services contracted for, and families contacted.[21]

The majority of KMAG concentrated on advisor functions, but there were certain administrative duties that could not be avoided. Supply, transportation, communications, and personnel administration fell into this category. In some cases administrative functions could be carried out in addition to advisory duties, but others required the full-time attention of members of the group.[22]

Personnel administration and logistics both demanded the entire effort of a number of officers and enlisted men. In the former category all administration was centralized under the

---

[20] HR–KMAG, an. 10, including Incl A.

[21] Ltr, Col Bartosik to Lt Col Richard J. Butt, 28 Apr 50, sub: Orientation, OFldr, sec. I.

[22] (1) Interv, Col Wright, 5 Jan 53. (2) Interv, Capt Kevin G. Hughes, 6 Oct 52. (3) Interv, Capt Howard Erwin, 6 Oct 52. (4) Ltr, Col Bartosik, 7 Aug 52. (5) KMAG Staff Memo 108.

Adjutant General's Section to conserve personnel. This permitted the KMAG G–1 advisor to devote all his attention to the counseling of his ROK counterpart.

When the advisory group was a provisional organization under U.S. Army Forces in Korea, supply and other logistical matters had been the responsibility of the G–4 advisor, Maj. Russell C. Geist, Jr. As the day of USAFIK's withdrawal drew near, handling the advisory group's supply problems and at the same time assisting the expanding Korean forces became increasingly difficult. Logistical problems accumulated to a point where there sometimes was confusion about which subject—KMAG supply or Korean Army supply—was under discussion at any given time. Geist also was responsible for assigning and maintaining dependent homes, a duty that demanded much attention. Late in the spring of 1949 General Roberts designated Maj. Thomas MacConnell III a headquarters commandant in order to relieve Major Geist of dependent housing problems, but with other matters being shifted from departing USAFIK units to the advisory group this was not enough. The G–4 advisor still had all he could do to help the expanding Republic of Korea Army, much less carry out normal operational support for KMAG.[23]

The final solution was a separate agency called the Director of Supply, established on 28 June 1949 to handle all logistical matters pertaining to the U.S. Military Advisory Group.[24] Lt. Col. Robert E. Myers was the director, leaving Major Geist free to devote his time to the Republic of Korea Army G–4. The Headquarters Commandant became the Assistant Director of Supply, bringing in dependent housing, and thereafter all of KMAG's housekeeping activities were concentrated within one section. It was this agency that linked KMAG with AMIK's Joint Administrative Services.[25] Other full-time KMAG staff activities were the dispensary, a headquarters group for the enlisted detachment, post exchange and club officers, and the chaplain's office.

---

[23](1) HR–KMAG, an. 4, p. 2, an. 6, 1. (2) Interv, Maj Geist, 3 Jul 52. (3) Interv, Lt Col Robert E. Myers, 7 Jul 52. (4) Interv, Lt Col Lewis D. Vieman, 14 Jul 52.
[24] KMAG Staff Memo 33, 28 Jun 49.
[25] Director of Supply, OFldr, sec. I.

With the exception of KMAG's G–2 Section, the remaining staff advisors had few duties pertaining to the advisory group. The G–2 Section was not officially an intelligence collecting agency until the revised Table of Distribution went into effect, but it functioned in that capacity to some degree from the beginning.[26] When information of potential value to the United States Government was reported by the Korean Army, the senior G–2 advisor, Captain Reed, naturally passed it along to General Roberts. As time went by, the scope of KMAG G–2 duties increased, requiring daily and weekly intelligence estimates and reports, briefings for visiting officials, investigations of political incidents, and other routine tasks. In addition, as the sole overt U.S. intelligence agency in Korea, the KMAG G–2 Section acted as liaison between certain covert (U.S.) intelligence agencies, and even acted for them on occasion.[27]

KMAG G–3 activities amounted to little. With the Americans scattered around Seoul and throughout South Korea's 36,700 square miles,[28] and in view of the nature of the group's mission, a program of training was not feasible. Except for the group's evacuation plan (CRULLER), which was under contant study by G–3, and an occasional round of familiarization firing of weapons by all personnel, the G–3 Advisory Section concerned itself with the training of the Korean Army.[29] The duties of the KMAG Provost Marshal, Inspector General, and Public Information Officer were equally limited. The little organized recreation for members of the group was arranged by civilian Special Services personnel; the military members of the section worked with Korean Army Special Services.[30]

---

[26] WARX 90992, CSGPO to Chief, KMAG, info CINCFE, sub: Terms of Reference for Chief, KMAG, 1 Jul 49. Par. 8 of this message states that KMAG, while not an intelligence collecting agency, had the same responsibility as all other U.S. armed forces for reporting information that might affect the security or interests of the United States.

[27] (1) Ltr, Maj John P. Reed, 9 Jan 53. (2) Ltr, Capt Frederick C. Schwarze, 6 Jan 53. (3) HR–KMAG, an. 3. (4) See also G–2 Organization and Operations, OFldr, sec. II.

[28] SCAP, *Summation,* No. 1, Sep and Oct 45, p. 1.

[29] (1) Ltr, Maj West, 16 Sep 52. (2) Ltr, Col Reynolds, 17 Sep 52. (3) Ltr, Col Ralph W. Hansen, 2 Aug 52.

[30] See HR–KMAG, ans. 13, 16, 17, 20.

Operating Procedures

A few days after reporting in, new arrivals attended a formal orientation by the KMAG staff. At this briefing the mission, staff procedures, and problems of the advisory group were presented. According to the terms of reference sent to General Roberts on 1 July 1949, KMAG was to help the Republic of Korea, within the limitations of the Korean economy, to develop internal security forces by advising and otherwise assisting the South Koreans in organizing and training their Army, Coast Guard, and National Police and to ensure that U.S. military assistance was used effectively.[31] The mission, therefore, placed the emphasis upon the development of "internal security" forces, essentially defensive in training and weapons, rather than upon the formation of a dual-capability army.

After General Roberts' introductory remarks, the chief of staff, Col. W. H. Sterling Wright, and the G–1, G–2, G–3, and Director of Supply discussed staff procedures, aspects of their particular duties that were noteworthy, and advised the new officers on what they could expect during their Korean tour. An "Advisor's Handbook" and a procedure guide were issued for later reading. This orientation contrasted sharply with that given to the early military government advisors, who usually received, a manila folder containing a mimeographed sheet of general instructions and a form letter of introduction to the military governor of the province where their regiments were located.[32]

New officers further attended one of the weekly KMAG staff meetings, if possible, before departing to their assigned posts. These meetings took place every Saturday morning and were attended by all advisors in the Seoul, ASCOM, and Inch'on areas. Here representatives of the general and special staff sections, and those advisors working with Korean Army units in the vicinity, reported to the chief of KMAG. The meetings were very useful in orienting members—new and old—of the advisory group on policy and current activities.[33]

---

[31] DA Rad, WARX 90992, CSGPO to Chief, KMAG, 1 July 49.

[32] (1) Orientation—Newly Arrived Officers, OFldr, sec. I. (2) Interv, Maj Hausman, 21 Jan 52.

[33] Staff Meetings, OFldr, sec. I.

Theoretically each division, regimental, and battalion commander in the Republic of Korea Army now had an American officer at his side, aiding him in executing his duties. This was the so-called counterpart system. Advisors likewise worked hand in hand with the Korean Minister of Defense, Army Chief of Staff, members of all general and special staff sections at Army headquarters, and the heads of all technical and administrative services. On a smaller scale, the Korean Coast Guard and National Police were similarly assisted.[34]

In practice, the U.S. Military Advisory Group never attained such a comprehensive coverage of the Korean Army. Moreover, though the advisory group reached its full, authorized strength by the end of 1949, KMAG never was able to assign advisors to all Korean battalions—infantry and otherwise—at any one time.[35] For despite the 65,000-man limit set in March as the maximum to be equipped by the United States, and in the face of KMAG opposition, the ROK recruiting machine had continued to function at a rapid rate. By 1 July 1949, when KMAG was established, the ROK Army had risen to a strength of more than 81,000; a month later it was nearly 100,000 strong.[36] The Koreans meanwhile activated 2 new divisions in June, the Capital and the 8th, so that while KMAG's Table of Distribution was based on a Korean Army of 6 divisions, the advisory group after 1 July 1949 actually was training 8 divisions.[37] Nor did the revised Table of Distribution of 31 December provide for advisory coverage of more than 6 Korean divisions. The situation was further aggravated by the table's failure to include advisors for the ROK Army school system. As schools were reorganized and new ones established, KMAG had to divert advisors from T/D positions.[38] The picture was far from hopeless, however, and when the group reached full strength most ROK battalions had the benefit of U.S. Army advice and assistance, if only on a

[34] An. 3, Advisor's Handbook to SA Rpt, KMAG, 31 Dec 49.
[35] (1) Ltr, Gen Roberts, 22 Jan 52. (2) Ltr, Roberts to Ward, 9 Nov 51. (3) Ltr, Col Hansen, 2 Aug 52.
[36] HR–KMAG, an. 2.
[37] (1) Ltr, Roberts to Ward, 9 Nov 51. (2) Ltr, Roberts, Nov 52. (3) Ltr, Col Hansen, 14 Nov 52.
[38] See ch. IV, below.

KMAG Signal Advisor *with Signal Section of the ROK Capital Division.*

part-time basis. Where two or more battalions were located in the same area, as in the case of the ROK Capital Division at Seoul, it often was possible for units to "share" advisors.[39]

General Roberts was of the opinion that the system could not be effective unless counterparts had desks in the same office, inspected troops together, and otherwise shared intimately daily tasks and problems.[40] This was why the U.S. Military Advisory Group had no separate headquarters building of its own. KMAG staff advisors worked beside their Korean opposites in the headquarters building of the Republic of Korea Army. The Koreans

---

[39] Ltr, Col Hansen, 14 Nov 52.

[40] (1) SA Rpt, KMAG, 31 Dec 49, sec. I, p. 3 (see also an. 3, Advisor's Handbook, pp. 1–5). (2) 1st Lt. Martin Blumenson *et al.,* Special Problems in the Korean Conflict (hereafter cited as Blumenson, Special Problems), Hq EUSAK, III, pt. 14, ch. I, 2, in OCMH files. (3) Ltr, Col Hansen, 2 Aug 52.

set aside a few rooms for the exclusive use of KMAG—private offices for General Roberts and Colonel Wright, administrative offices, and a conference room. Elsewhere throughout the building Americans and Koreans shared offices, the advisor to the Korean G–1, for example, occupying a desk in his counterpart's office. At Korean Army schools, at technical services installations, and at field stations, counterparts maintained the same close working relationship.[41]

There were two exceptions to this rule. Because of heavy administrative and operational responsibilities, General Roberts confined his counterpart relationship with the ROK Minister of National Defense to correspondence and occasional meetings. For the same reason, KMAG's Chief of Staff seldom dealt directly with the ROK Army Chief of Staff. In this case Captain Hausman had been detailed as a liaison between Colonel Wright and his counterpart and occupied a desk in the latter's office. Hausman's years of experience in Korea made him a valuable staff officer for this purpose. However, when important issues were pending, as the annual defense budget estimate or legislation affecting the Korean security forces, meetings between counterparts at this level became more frequent.[42]

Under KMAG's counterpart system, advisors exercised no direct authority over their counterparts. They were expected to control training or operations by influence, suggestion, and guidance. "Advisors do not command," the KMAG Advisor's Handbook proclaimed, "they ADVISE!" What they accomplished depended largely upon their powers of persuasion and on the esteem in which they were held by their Korean counterparts.[43] All was not always smooth sailing. Advisors sometimes encountered opposition from senior Korean officers who used their rank to disregard the advisor's advice. This was particularly true in the administrative, supply, and fiscal and financial management fields. Fortunately, the Korean Minister of Defense had asked

---

[41] (1) Interv, Lt Col Martin O. Sorensen, 17 Dec 52. (2) Interv, Col Wright, 5 Jan 53.

[42] Conferences With the Minister National Defense; Relationship With the Chief of Staff, KA, OFldr, sec. II.

[43] (1) Advisor's Handbook, 17 Oct 49, an. 3 to SA Rpt, KMAG, 31 Dec 49, pp. 2, 3. (2) SA Rpt, KMAG, 31 Dec 49, sec. I, p. 3. (3) Ltr, Lt Col John B. Clark, 26 Dec 52. (4) Ltr, Capt Schwarze, 6 Jan 53.

General Roberts to report un-co-operative ROK officers, an action that usually effected a quick improvement in the situation. Another powerful lever the advisors had at their disposal was the fact that the United States was furnishing the money, supplies, and equipment for the Korean forces. "Keep this in mind," advisors were instructed, "but use it seldom." [44]

Not that most Korean officers opposed their advisors; on the contrary the majority welcomed American assistance and tried diligently to put into practice what they were taught.[45] Nor should it be inferred that American methods were in all cases forced upon the Koreans. While the U.S. advisors usually had no choice but to suggest that American methods be employed, the wise advisor gave his counterpart latitude when the latter's ideas did not conflict radically with U.S. Army doctrine.[46] One advisor recalls that he "allowed the Korean commander to have his way [in small matters] and utilized this point to gain concessions of importance." [47] And sometimes, as in the case of discipline, where Korean methods were often at complete variance with those practiced in the U.S. Army, it turned out that the Korean officers' approach was the method best understood by Korean soldiers. Oriental ways of exacting military discipline were in every sense of the word punitive, but many former advisors to Korean security forces agree that, if not carried to extremes, they probably worked best with Korean troops.

In some cases where friction arose between counterparts, the fault lay on the side of the American advisor. While the majority of KMAG personnel were conscious of the importance of their positions and carried out their duties accordingly, the meager replacement pipeline to Korea sometimes left officers and men who were not suited to the advisory role. One misfit habitually threatened his counterpart with courts-martial and even used physical violence in imposing his "advice." [48] But such extreme

---

[44] (1) Advisor's Handbook, p. 5 cited n. 43 (1), above. (2) Conference With the Minister National Defense, OFldr, sec. II. See also Ltr, Col DeReus, 4 Oct 52.
[45] (1) Ltr, Col Hansen. (2) Ltr, Col Reynolds. (3) Ltr, Col McDonald. (4) Interv, Col Sorensen. (5) Ltr, Col Clark. (6) Interv, Capt Schwarze, 6 Apr 53.
[46] Advisor's Handbook, cited n. 43(1), above, pp. 2, 3.
[47] Ltr, Col DeReus, 4 Oct 52.
[48] Ltr, Col Hansen, 2 Aug 1952.

cases were rare, and the offending Americans did not remain long with KMAG.

Special Problems

There were certain problems that complicated the task of the American advisors in Korea. Some arose from the unsettled course of Korea's history, others had their roots in the post-World War II political upheaval. The customs and practices peculiar to the Orient were often difficult for the Americans to comprehend, yet they had to be taken into consideration in working out feasible solutions to the matters at issue. And then there was the problem of communication.

Although there had been a short-lived attempt to establish a language school for Americans after the war, it had soon ended for lack of sufficient interest. As one former KMAG officer later remarked: "There was good attendance initially, but the poor quality of instruction caused a rapid fall-off of attendance and eventual abandonment of the project." General Roberts did encourage the advisors to learn Korean, but few made the attempt; the majority was content to accept the situation passively. Those that did try usually limited their efforts to a smattering of Korean words and phrases. If social intercourse had been the sole requirement, the language barrier would have been relatively minor, for professional interpreters were available and a sufficient number of Koreans spoke some English.[49]

The real difficulty lay in the fact that written and spoken Korean lacked expressions and terms necessary to an understanding of modern military lore.[50] Koreans who had served in the Japanese Army during the war might well have been instructed in Japanese, which had all the necessary terminology, had not sev-

[49] (1) Language Problem and Dictionary, OFldr, sec. I. (2) Advisor's Handbook, cited n. 43(1), above, p. 2. (3) Station Rpt, Office of the Army Attaché, Seoul 1 May 50, p. 2, G–2, Doc Lib, DA, ID 666120. (4) Ltrs, Col Hansen, Col McDonald, Capt Schwarze, Maj Reed.
[50] (1) Language Problem and Dictionary, OFldr, sec I. (2) Ltr, Col McDonald, 3 Dec 52. (3) Interv, Col Wright, 5 Jan 53. (4) Interv, Col Sorensen, 17 Dec 52. (5) Interv, Capts Erwin and Hughes, 6 Oct 52. (6) See also Communications Procedures in Allied Operations, prepared by the Signal School, Fort Monmouth, N.J., pp. 36–52, copy in OCMH files.

eral factors argued against such a procedure. In the first place, less than 15 percent of the Koreans understood Japanese and the remaining 85 percent would still have had to be taught in Korean.[51] And secondly, the Koreans, and particularly President Rhee, strongly opposed the use of the Japanese language in Korea.

Since the Korean military and mechanical experience under Japanese rule had been extremely limited, terms such as *machine gun* and *headlight* had not found their way into the language and, along with such expressions as *phase line, zone,* and *movement by bounds,* were impossible of literal translation into Korean. Even a simple term such as *squad* had to be explained exhaustively before a Korean soldier knew what was meant. His language simply contained no equivalents for words and concepts of that nature. In order to bridge this gap, the Koreans resorted to descriptive phrases: a machine gun become a *gun-that-shoots-very-fast;* a headlight might be called *candle-in-a-shiny-bowl.* But because the accuracy of those descriptions depended upon the imaginations of individual linguists, even this device did not solve the problem. Interpretations were inconsistent and ranged from the ingenious to the inadequate. Where one interpreter referred to a machine gun as above, another might call it a *gun-of-many-loud-noises.* U.S. advisors sometimes used two interpreters at once, in hopes that together they might arrive at precise meanings, but more often than not the linguists merely argued at length, so that Korean listeners did not know at all what was being discussed.[52]

The situation was further compounded by the Oriental custom of circumlocution. Koreans use more words in expressing themselves than do Westerners and usually approach their subject on a tangent. Carrying over the habit into the interpretation of military words and phrases—which did not exist in their language—merely added to the basic problem. Thus, it might have helped if all the advisors had spoken Korean fluently, but it would not necessarily have solved the matter. What ROKA

---

[51] See Grajdanzev, *Modern Korea,* p. 269.
[52] (1) Ltr, Col Hansen. (2) Ltr, Col McDonald. (3) Interv, Col Wright. (4) Ltr, Col Albert L. Hettrich, 17 Nov 53.

needed badly was a standardized terminology for its equipment and doctrine.

Before December 1949, efforts to evolve a simple dictionary of terms suitable for Koreans and advisors alike had been on a hit-or-miss basis and advisors handled the language problem individually. Some had learned enough Korean to get their meaning across, others had relied on their interpreters.

In December the G–3 Advisory Section began compiling a simple dictionary of military terms. Selecting 500 U.S. Army phrases in common usage, the G–3 advisors submitted them to a committee of five Korean officers and twelve civilian translators. This group, called the Korean Army G–3 Editing Committee, worked for several months, translating the terms into appropriate Korean characters and phonetic spellings. The finished product met with continuing criticism from Koreans who felt that certain terms had been translated incorrectly.[53] In March 1950 the Korean Army assigned fifteen additional English-speaking officers to the Editing Committee, for the ambitious project of translating the entire *Dictionary Of United States Army Terms.*[54] When completed, the Korean version was to be standard for the Republic of Korea Army, superseding the more or less accurate dictionaries already in use. This project was still under way in June 1950.

Besides the Army's efforts to relieve its language problem, a civilian organization in Seoul called the Korean-American Society worked on a Korean-English dictionary that included military terms. Specifically, the society devised written Korean characters for new military terms as they were accepted by the Army. In addition, a Korean civilian named Mister Oh, and his son, worked closely with the Army on a separate military dictionary, in what appeared to be a "labor of love." Although 73 years old, Mr. Oh carried the honorary title of interpreter and was permitted to wear an Army uniform. He and his dictionary both were lost during the early days of the war.[55]

---

[53] (1) Ltrs, Col Hansen, Col Reynolds. (2) Interv, Col Wright, 5 Jan 53. (3) Interv, Col McDonald, 8 Apr 53. (4) Editing Committee, OFldr, sec. III.

[54] (1) Editing Committee, OFldr, sec. III. (2) Interv, Col McDonald.

[55] (1) Interv, Col McDonald. (2) Blumenson *et al.,* Special Problems, MS, p. 23. According to the latter source, at least one copy of Mr. Oh's work may be extant.

The alternative to the confusion and disagreement attendant upon the invention of a Korean military language, as General Roberts suggested, would have been the acceptance of English as the universal language of the ROK security forces. Many Koreans, especially among the officer corps, already knew some English, and the language had up-to-date military terminology and literature easily available. In addition, the task of the U.S. advisors would have been greatly simplified if their charges had all learned English.[56] But this solution was not adopted, probably primarily because of the lack of time and instructors.

Another problem of some concern to the Americans was the role of the ROK Government in the development of the armed forces. In a young democracy, where the military experience level was low, the appointments to high command and staff positions were often based upon political connections rather than ability. In a number of cases the political appointees were not qualified for the positions they held and, in addition, were apathetic or even hostile to the advisors' teachings. Since KMAG lacked legal authority, it was important that key positions be occupied by Koreans who were receptive to American advice. Usually KMAG pressure served to eliminate the incompetent and inimical ROK officers.[57]

The Americans also had to deal with the problem of prestige or "face," which was of great importance to the Koreans. As previously mentioned, the ROK officers were very sensitive about rank and often refused to co-operate with KMAG officers junior to them, despite the U.S. officers' excellent qualifications. Senior ROK officers disdained in many instances to consult with their staffs, since they were inferior in grade or in years, and were hesitant in changing or canceling orders lest this indicate that they might have been wrong in their original diagnosis of a situation or problem. For the same reason, subordinate commanders and staff officers were reluctant to present unfavorable news to their superiors or to the KMAG advisors. The unwillingness to admit mistakes or errors in judgment led to a lack of accurate

---

[56] (1) Language Problem and Dictionary, OFldr, sec. I. (2) Interv, Col McDonald.
    [57] Ltr, Roberts to Ward, 9 Nov 1951. (2) See also Ltrs, Col Hansen, Col Reynolds.

information or even to supplying misinformation to preserve face.[58] How to deal with this question subtly and with tact posed a major challenge to each advisor. The most efficacious course of action required a great deal of patience and understanding and the development of mutual trust and respect between an advisor and his counterpart.

Another facet of the prestige problem appeared in the Korean use of armed forces for parades and escorts. The Koreans were very fond of parades, and whenever visiting dignitaries came to Seoul the ROK Army cavalry regiment, which was the show-piece of the Army, was called upon to display its horses and equipment. The ceremonies disrupted the troops' training schedule, damaged the horses' hooves on the pavement, and used up valuable gasoline. As for escorts, every Korean commander seemed to feel that he needed a large number of bodyguards when moving about the countryside to protect himself from guerrillas. Although there was some possibility of assassination, the escorts provided an expensive prestige factor since the vehicles and troops were diverted from more important tasks.[59] These were minor matters, it was true, but they helped to deprive the ROK forces of valuable training time.

---

[58] (1) Ltrs, Col Hansen, Col Clark, Maj Reed. (2) The Road to Ruin, lecture delivered at Korean Army Staff School, 20 Feb 50, by Col Vieman, transcript in OCMH files. (3) Incl 3 to Ltr, Lt Col Walter Greenwood, Jr., to Gen Smith, 26 Jan 54.
[59] (1) Interv, Col Sorensen. (2) Ltr, Col Hansen.

CHAPTER IV

Training the ROK Forces

A detailed and accurate record of the organization of the ROK Army in mid-1949 is not available since neither the KMAG advisors nor the Koreans themselves maintained complete files. It is certain that a U.S. Army-type headquarters and eight infantry divisions—in various stages of organization—were in existence. The advisory group devoted most of its time and effort during the year that followed to the improvement and strengthening of this ROK Army core and to the development of its supporting forces.

ROKA Organization and the Adoption of a Training Program

Of the eight divisions—the 1st, 2d, 3d, 5th, 6th, 7th, 8th, and Capital—only the last was close to full strength. There was the nucleus of a cavalry regiment at Seoul and a small air liaison detachment at Kimp'o airfield. Artillery consisted of six battalions of 105-mm. light howitzers (M3) and three battalions of 57-mm. antitank guns, all grouped at the Korean Army Artillery School near Seoul. For technical services there were a signal, a quartermaster, and two ordnance battalions, and an engineer construction group, all at different levels of organization. The ROK Army had eight schools operating in the vicinity of the capital city.[1]

Four of the infantry divisions and one regiment of a fifth were located close to the 38th Parallel in late 1949, and three divisions were in southern Korea campaigning against guerrillas and guarding mines, railways, and other installations. (*Map I—inside back cover*) With practically all of the Army either on frontier duty or safeguarding internal security, the training problem promised to be a difficult one.

General Roberts sent out KMAG survey teams in May and June 1949 to assess the current training and organizational status

---

[1] Compiled from: (1) HR–KMAG, with annexes; (2) MHK, ch. II, pp. 14–29; (3) Ltrs, Intervs, on file in OCMH.

KOREAN CAVALRY

of the ROKA units so that a program of development could be fashioned. The teams contained representation from each KMAG staff section, and their task was to inspect the units and review their dispositions. Proceeding from outfit to outfit with mimeographed check sheets, the teams observed training in both combat and technical services.[2]

The inspection of ROK 2d Division elements at Taejon probably was typical. Here a KMAG team observed Korean troops making an approach march. When the troops had bivouacked, the advisors moved in to check such fundamentals as sanitation, cover and concealment, and security. Later the Americans went to the 2d Division's barrack areas to observe living conditions, inspect equipment, and watch training demonstrations. Korean

---

[2] (1) SA Rpt, KMAG, 31 Dec 49, sec. IV, p. 12. (2) Gen Roberts, Commander's Estimate, 1 Jan 50, copy loaned by Capt Harold S. Fischgrund. (3) Interv, Col McDonald, 8 Apr 53, New York. (4) Interv, Capt Fischgrund, 20 Nov 52. See also: KMAG G–3 Opns Rpt 10, 3 Sep 49; Ltr, Gen Roberts to Lt Gen Albert C. Wedemeyer, 2 May 49, P&O File 091 Korea, sec. III, case 51.

commanders had been notified in time to prepare for the team's visit. KMAG teams were careful to visit ranges and observe Korean soldiers on the firing lines, for earlier reports of weapons qualification by Republic of Korea troops had conflicted widely. Where one unit reported itself 100 percent qualified in a weapon, another would rate but 20 percent of its personnel as having successfully completed the required firing. Even in view of the fact that some units had spent much time in the field, away from the ranges, differences were striking.[3]

From KMAG's inspections there emerged a clearer picture of the immensity of the task ahead. In the opinion of one U.S. officer, the Republic of Korea Army in June 1949 "could have been the American Army in 1775."[4] Except for its intense national pride, there was little to recommend the ROKA as a military force. While most combat units seemed to have completed a full cycle of basic training at one time or another, not all had participated in platoon and company problems. The technical service units were embryonic, having developed but little since their activation just over a year before. Training facilities in general were scarce and inadequate, and at all levels there were deficiencies emphasizing a need for better trained officers and noncommissioned officers, more equipment, and all kinds of technical specialists. Furthermore, the inspections revealed that South Korean soldiers needed training in weapons and markmanship, a fact that helped to explain why Korean Army task forces operating against guerrillas were expending thousands of rounds of ammunition while inflicting remarkably few casualties among the enemy.[5]

The conditions brought to light by the inspection teams appeared to argue for the adoption of a flexible program of training for the ROK Army in 1949. While soldiers who had served since the days of the Constabulary could not fail to benefit by reviewing basic training, to compel them to do so would be to retard the progress of the Army as a whole. Units engaged in

---

[3] (1) Interv, Col McDonald. (2) Interv, Capt Fischgrund.

[4] Ltr, Col McDonald, 3 Dec 49.

[5] (1) Marksmanship, OFldr, sec. III. (2) Roberts, Commander's Estimate. (3) Ltr, Col Hansen, 2 Aug 52. (4) Ltr, Col Clark, 26 Dec 52. (5) Ltr, Col Reynolds, 17 Sep 52.

small unit training would gain most by continuing on that level. Still, KMAG inspections had shown serious deficiencies everywhere, regardless of the level of training. Members of units displaying a fair ability to operate as platoons or companies also revealed defects in individual training. How to strike a balance between the need for training in basic subjects and the desirability of permitting qualified units to continue on higher levels was the question.[6]

The answer lay in a program based on the U.S. Army's Mobilization Training Program (MTP) 7–1, formulated in September 1943, which provided for the progressive training of each type of unit within the infantry regiment, from individual training through battalion problems (with one regimental command post exercise following the battalion training, during the twelfth week). From his preceding assignment as S–3, U.S. 5th Regiment, Maj. Eugene O. McDonald (G–3 Training Advisor) had brought with him to KMAG some training literature, including old lesson plans from the Infantry School at Fort Benning and a copy of MTP 7–1. "It sometimes took months for units in Korea to obtain training material from service schools in the United States," recalled Major McDonald later, "so we decided to use my copy of MTP 7–1 as the basis for the Korean Army's program." That particular series, moreover, suited the organization of the Republic of Korea Army, which had none of the later weapons, such as recoilless rifles.[7]

KMAG's version of MTP 7–1 was a six-month program divided into two phases: Phase I, from 21 June to 15 September 1949, for individual squad, platoon, and company training; and Phase II, from 16 September to 31 December 1949, for battalion and regimental training. Korean regiments would be introduced at points consistent with their weaknesses and capabilities, with some reverting wholly to individual training, others repeating specific phases, and those qualified continuing with small unit tactics, devoting only a part of their daily training hours to a review of selected basic subjects. Korean Army artillery units would train as field artillery batteries and cannon companies in

---

[6] Interv, Col McDonald.
[7] Interv, Col McDonald.

GENERAL ROBERTS INSPECTS ARMS *of the ROK 1st Cavalry Regiment, Seoul.*

Phase I, and as battalions in the role of direct support artillery in Phase II. The cavalry regiment would carry on individual training concurrently with small unit training. The technical services would train as prescribed by the chief of the service concerned. Divisional engineers, then consisting of small pioneer units in each division, would begin by reviewing basic and individual training. However, engineer combat battalions were to be formed in July in the four infantry divisions along the 38th Parallel, for which cadres of pioneers and demolitionists were already in training; a separate, eight-week training program for the battalions would begin early in August.[8]

---

[8] (1) Training Memo 6, Hq Korean Army, Seoul, 21 Jun 49, in KMAG File, FE&Pac Br, G–3, folder 20. (2) Training Program, Korean Army, OFldr, sec. III. (3) SA Rpt, KMAG, 31 Dec 49, sec. IV, pp. 13–14, 24–25. (4) Roberts, Commander's Estimate. (5) Ltrs, Col Hansen, 2 Aug 52 and 14 Nov 52. (6) Ltr, Col Reynolds. (7) Interv, Col McDonald.

Since the need for training in marksmanship was common to all elements, General Roberts insisted that all ROK soldiers, regardless of the level at which they otherwise trained, undergo intensive preliminary rifle instruction. All would then fire familiarization and qualification courses—first with the M1 rifle, then with other individual and crew-served weapons. It should be noted in this connection that much of the Korean soldier's weakness in marksmanship could have been due to the length and weight of the United States Army rifle since for the slightly built Orientals the weapon undoubtedly was long and heavy. The KMAG G–3 training advisors took this into consideration by allowing the Koreans additional time on rapid fire exercises and by lowering the qualifying scores.[9]

The advisory group further modified Mobilization Training Program 7–1 to conform with the Republic of Korea Army's facilities and equipment. The activation of the Capital and 8th Divisions, for instance, had worsened an already critical shortage of weapons and other equipment. Like KMAG's Table of Distribution, U.S. matériel support for the Korean Army was based on 65,000 men or six divisions, and the establishment of these additional divisions necessitated a wider distribution of that support.[10] This meant that troops and units had to rotate in order to receive certain training, or that training in some subjects had to be omitted entirely.[11]

Following the inspections by KMAG teams, and while units carried on individual training, Major McDonald drew up a master training program for all combat units. Regimental advisors then came in from the field for conferences with the KMAG G–3 Section, to help decide whether the units under their guidance could manage what had been scheduled for them.

---

[9] (1) Interv, Col McDonald. (2) Training Memo 6, Hq Korean Army, cited in preceding footnote. (3) Marksmanship, cited n. 5(1). (4) SA Rpt, KMAG, 31 Dec 49, sec. IV, p. 13. (5) Roberts, Commander's Estimate. The Americans had encountered similar problems in training the Filipino soldiers. The stock of the rifle was too long for them, and they had difficulty in reaching the bolt and the trigger.

[10] The Koreans tried to alleviate the situation by producing 20,000 Japanese rifles they had hidden when U.S. forces were destroying Japanese arms in 1945 and 1946. However, most of these weapons were unserviceable as well as without ammunition.

[11] (1) Training Program, Korean Army, cited n. 8(2), above. (2) Ltr, Gen Roberts, 22 Jan 52.

Schedules were adjusted in line with the advisors' recommendations if possible, but final levels of training usually fell short of
the points recommended in order to compensate for the possibility of an advisor's judgment being influenced by a natural pride
in his Korean unit. When the program was ready, it went for
approval to the Senior G–3 Advisor, Col. Ralph W. Hansen, to
General Roberts, and finally to the ROK Army G–3. By 1 July
the Korean Army had—as much as possible—settled into its
training program for 1949.[12]

Obstacles to Training Progress

As the training program got under way, military action along
the 38th Parallel began to increase. The artificial barrier between North and South Korea had long been the scene of
incidents, but until May 1949 the clashes had been isolated and
local in nature. On 3 May, however, North Korean troops made
a sortie towards Kaesong and initiated a rash of armed actions.
During the next six months more than 400 separate engagements
took place along the frontier.[13] While the majority were small
arms skirmishes between patrols, some actions (at Kaesong,
Ch'unch'on, and on the Ongjin Peninsula) resulted in heavy
casualties on both sides.[14]

Concurrently, guerrilla activity was increasing in the interior
of the country. Civil disorders and acts of sabotage had been
common in South Korea since 1945, but after April 1948 such
incidents gradually gave way to what appeared to be an organized guerrilla movement. Beginning with a series of uprisings
on the isle of Cheju-do, off the south coast of Korea, guerrilla
activity spread to the mainland in October 1948 when men
who had taken part in the Yosu rebellion escaped to the Chiri-
san area.[15] Other bands formed when deserters from ROK Army
units joined with trained guerrillas from the north who infil-

---

[12] Interv, Col McDonald.
[13] OACofS, G–2, DA, Weekly Intelligence Report (WIR), No. 49, 27 Jan 50, p. 16.
[14] (1) SA Rpt, KMAG, 31 Dec 49, sec. IV, p. 22. (2) HR–KMAG, p. 6. (3)
MHK, pp. 57–60. KMAG reported that some of the bloodiest engagements were
caused by South Korean units securing and preparing defensive positions that were
either astride or north of the 38th Parallel. This provoked violent action by North
Korean forces.
[15] See ch. II, above.

KOREAN POLICE ARREST A COMMUNIST RIOTER IN SEOUL

trated down the mountain chains into South Korea. By late 1949 these dissident elements were attacking villages and installations and becoming a serious problem.[16]

Quite apart from constituting a grave threat to the internal security of the Republic of Korea, the hostile activity had a definite effect upon the training of the Korean Army and, consequently, upon the mission of the U.S. Military Advisory Group. In the six-month period from July to December 1949 alone, Korean Army units were compelled to mount 542 separate counterguerrilla actions, an average of nearly three a day.[17] The practical benefits of actual contact with an opponent insofar as tactics and field experience were concerned could not be denied. But it created much the same situation that would have existed if a football coach had permitted his team to enter competition before it had mastered the fundamentals of the game or learned the proper signals. Being in the field a great

---

[16] (1) Capt. Harold S. Fischgrund, Summary of Operations, Korean Army, undated MS loaned by the author. (2) Interv, Capt Fischgrund, 29 Oct 52.
[17] OACofS, G–2, DA, WIR, No. 49, 27 Jan 50, p. 16.

part of their time, and thus away from the training areas, many units did not acquire the basic training they badly needed to cope with the foe on even terms.[18]

The disruptions to the training schedules caused by the border incidents and guerrilla activity, coupled with the ROK Government's removal of some key personnel through anti-Communist purges and the continuing expansion of the ROK Army from 65,000 to 100,000 men during mid-1949, prevented the completion of Phase I by September. Phase II therefore had to be revised to include additional platoon and company training.[19]

During the fall, KMAG unit advisors gave training in tactics and terrain appreciation to Korean officers to prepare them for battalion-level exercises. The training consisted of lectures and sandbox problems and often took place at night. The majority of Korean officers took on the extra work willingly ("hungrily," according to one advisor) and seemed to be enthusiastic about improving themselves and their proficiency in military skills. The Americans sometimes delivered their lectures without the aid of interpreters, using drawings and sign language to get their messages across—a surprisingly successful feat. General Roberts directed his advisors also to conduct battalion command post exercises. In view of the scattered troop dispositions and the necessary cutbacks to basic training in many units, this was about the only way to give training in staff procedures and at the same time train unit commanders who had no opportunities to participate in field problems. But since most KMAG advisors were many months removed from the time when they, themselves, had taken part in a command post exercise, the KMAG G–3 Advisor in November and December first conducted two all-KMAG refresher exercises for their benefit at the Korean Army Infantry School.[20]

---

[18](1) Ltr, Roberts to Ward, 9 Nov 51. (2) Ltr, Gen Roberts, Nov 52. (3) Ltr, Col Hansen. (4) Ltr, Col Reynolds. (5) KMAG G–3 Opns Rpt 29, 16 Jan 50. (6) Intervs, Maj Hausman, Maj Geist, and Capt Fischgrund. (7) See also KMAG SA Rpts, 1949 and 1950.

[19] See Supplement to Training Memo 6, Hq Korean Army, 8 Aug 49, KMAG File, FE&Pac Br, G–3, folder 20.

[20] (1) Interv, Col Sorensen. (2) Command Post Exercises, OFldr, sec. III. (3) See also Supplement 1 to Training Memo 6, Hq Korean Army.

Only 30 of the Republic of Korea Army's 67 battalions [21] had completed company training by the end of 1949. Of these, but 20 had begun the battalion phase. Eleven battalions had not yet finished their platoon training. Twenty-eight battalions had completed qualification firing of the M1 rifle, but the remaining 39 recurrently engaged in counterguerrilla activities, were from 20 to 90 percent qualified. ROKA's 6 artillery battalions had concluded Phase I of their training on 1 October, carrying units through battery tactics; Phase II, stressing the artillery battalion's role as a direct support arm, was under way. The 3 antitank battalions had finished their training, and an antitank company was assigned to each of 14 infantry regiments while 4 companies remained at the artillery school. All technical services, though hampered by a lack of skilled personnel, tools, and equipment, were expanding slowly through training programs, schooling, and on-the-job training. Each division now had its own engineer combat battalion and ordnance and signal companies.[22]

KMAG plans at this time, embodied in the Republic of Korea Army Training Directive No. 1 for 1950, called for four training phases, each of three months duration, during the coming year. If all went well, Korean Army units would have completed the battalion phase by 31 March 1950, including an eight-day series of field exercises, and the regimental phase by 30 June. Combined arms training, division problems, and finally maneuvers on a varying scale, would follow. Future plans also prescribed that Korean soldiers who had not fired basic weapons for record in 1949 would do so in 1950. Those who had already qualified would fire short familiarization courses.[23]

In early 1950 KMAG officials met with representatives of the Korean Army and National Police to formulate antiguerrilla plans for the coming spring. The Army and police had worked together closely in combatting dissident elements, but the Americans wanted to devise a method whereby the majority of Army

---

[21] Including the three squadrons of the cavalry regiment.

[22] (1) SA Rpt, KMAG, 31 Dec 49, ans. 9, 10. (2) HR–KMAG, ans. 7, 9, 10, 11, 18. (3) Roberts, Commander's Estimate.

[23] (1) SA Rpt, KMAG, 31 Dec 49, sec. IV, p. 15. (2) Interv, Col McDonald. (3) Marksmanship, OFldr, sec. III.

units could be released from security missions for training. From the meetings came a plan to organize approximately 10,000 Korean policemen into companies of 112 men each, forming a total of twenty-two combat police battalions. These battalions, each with a small staff and four companies, would be armed with U.S. carbines and Japanese rifles and scattered throughout South Korea as an antiguerrilla force. If heavy weapons support were required, Army units would be attached for that purpose. The plan went into effect in January 1950 and a cadre of 120 police officers was sent to the Korean Army Infantry School for a special course in basic tactics. This and a following group were to comprise the bulk of the officers for the new battalions and, upon graduation, the officers were to staff combat police schools at Inch'on, Taegu, and Pusan in order to train battalions as they were activated.[24]

Desirable as was the objective in organizing combat police battalions, its achievement was another matter. There was very little money or equipment for the venture.[25] Despite the urgency of getting Army units into garrison, organizing and training the police was agonizingly slow. Only one police battalion took to the field during the first five months of 1950.[26] To make matters worse, the Korean Minister of Home Affairs in May could not or would not allocate funds from the police budget to continue the program. In the meantime, the Army could not maintain the schedule outlined in Training Directive No. 1 for 1950. While certain regiments along the 38th Parallel managed to keep pace, others, notably in the south, were still tied down by counter-guerrilla operations. By the middle of March only one battalion each of the ROK 5th Division's three regiments had been able to come in from the hills and resume training; that even the one battalion could come was due in part to a lull in guerrilla activ-

[24] (1) OACofS, G-2, DA, WIR, No. 49, 27 Jan 50. (2) WIR, No. 51, 10 Feb 50, pp. 9, 11. (3) National Police, Combat Battalions and Police Schools, OFldr, sec. V. (4) Interv, Lt Col Harold K. Krohn (Advisor to Korean National Police, Feb 50-Dec 51), 3 Jun 53. See also KMAG G-3 Opns Rpts 29 (16 Jan 50), 30 (21 Jan 50), 31 (28 Jan 50), 33 (11 Feb 50).
[25] (1) Interv, Col Krohn, 3 Jun 53. (2) See also Ltr, Chief, KMAG, to the Hon Paik Sung Wook, ROK Minister of Home Affairs, 15 Mar 50, OPS file 091 Korea, sec. I, case 3/2.
[26] SA Rpt, KMAG, 15 Jun 50, sec. IV, pp. 12, 13. Colonel Krohn states that, to his knowledge, no combat police battalions were fielded before June 1950.

ity. Hopes that all units would complete the battalion phase by 31 March 1950 diminished, and then vanished. On the 14th of that month the ROK Army published a second training memorandum. This was a concentrated, thirteen-week schedule to bring all units through the battalion phase by 1 June and the regimental phase by summer.[27]

But by 15 June 1950 only the ROK Capital Division's 9 battalions, 6 battalions of the ROK 7th Division, and a battalion of the ROK 8th Division had completed the battalion phase of training. Thirty others were through the company phase, and 17 had not yet finished the platoon phase. Two battalions had had 75 percent of their platoon training and 50 percent of their company training. Seventeen battalion staffs and 5 regimental staffs had participated in command post exercises; 14 battalions had taken the 8-day maneuver exercises; and 6 battalions had taken Tank Hunting Team training. All Korean troops had fired for record with the M1 rifle, however, and qualification firing of other individual arms and of crew-served weapons was well along. The technical services were progressing satisfactorily despite the difficulty with which Korean Army personnel absorbed and applied technical instruction.[28]

Earlier in June, after directing the Minister of Home Affairs to get police units into the field, President Rhee had approved a supplemental budget for the National Police in the amount of 1,000,000 won (approximately $1,100). During the following two weeks fourteen police battalions took over internal security duties in South Korea. Army battalions began returning to their bases for training. At this point the U.S. Military Advisory Group postponed the target date for completing the ROK Army's battalion level training to 31 July 1950, and the regimental phase to 31 October 1950.[29]

[27] (1) OACofS, G–2, DA, WIR, No. 61, 10 Feb 50. (2) KMAG G–3 Opns Rpts 38 (18 Mar 50), 40 (1 Apr 50), 46 (13 May 50), 50 (10 Jun 50). (3) Training Program, Korean Army, OFldr, sec. III. (4) Office of the Chief, KMAG, Highlights of Weekly Staff Meeting, 18 Mar 50, par. 5, copy in OCMH files.

[28] Compiled from SA Rpt, KMAG, 15 Jun 50, an. V. Section IV of this report (page 8) states that only two regiments had completed the battalion phase; the charts in Annex V shows that sixteen battalions had finished the phase.

[29] SA Rpt, KMAG, 15 Jun 50, sec. IV, pp. 8–12.

The School System

Along with the training of Korean troops and units, the U.S. Military Advisory Group founded a military school system. Though designed to raise the proficiency of the Army as a whole, this system was for the particular benefit of Korean officers. The Americans had long been aware that the ROK Army's greatest weakness was in leadership. Many Korean officers did not appreciate or accept the responsibilities inherent in their commissions, and commanders and staff officers at all levels were deficient in professional knowledge. Few understood the mechanics of staff work or troop leadership and control. A great many were more interested in maintaining positions in the officer "class" than in performing their duties as officers. Much of this stemmed no doubt from Korea's historical background, but it is likely that the Constabulary's early years, which had been marked by restrictions on training and by a poverty of equipment and American advisors, also were responsible. Reasons notwithstanding, these deficiencies had to be rectified if ever the Republic of Korea Army was to function effectively and without foreign advice.[30]

Before the establishment of KMAG, American military advisors had set up eight military schools in South Korea: a combat intelligence school, schools for the constabulary's signal, engineer, artillery, ordnance, military police, and band personnel, and a so-called Korean Military Academy. These had been formed with a minimum of facilities, trained Korean instructors, and American advisors, and, according to later KMAG estimates, had not produced graduates who were qualified by acceptable standards. One great problem had been the lack of appreciation on the part of senior Korean officers of the value of military schooling. Faced with the grim realities of guerrilla warfare, Korean commanders had been understandably reluctant to spare officers and men for what they considered

---

[30] (1) Korean Army School System, OFldr, sec. III. (2) Blumenson *et al.,* Special Problems, III, pt. 14, ch. I, 24–25. (3) Ltr, Roberts to Ward, 9 Nov. 51. (4) Ltr, Gen Roberts, 22 Jan 52. (5) Ltr, Col Reynolds, 17 Sept 52. (6) Interv, Col Vieman, 12 Oct 53. (7) See also Office of the Army Attaché, Seoul, Rpt R–43–52, 25 Jan 52, G–2 Doc Lib, DA, ID 871087.

to be less urgent matters. It had required constant and vehement high-level American advice merely to persuade them to assign personnel as students and instructors at the school.[31]

Only after the advisory group had begun to expand, and in the light of expected further military aid from the United States, was schooling for the Korean Army given a high priority. On 15 April 1949 General Roberts transferred Lt. Col. Lewis D. Vieman from the ROK 5th Division to advisory group headquarters, designated him Schools Advisor, and directed him to draw up plans for putting a schools program into effect.[32]

Colonel Vieman was of the opinion that the objective of the schooling program should be to raise the military educational level in the Korean Army to a point where by January 1952 the Army could stand alone. To attain this, he recommended that the existing schools be strengthened and improved, and that a Command and General Staff College and Infantry, Adjutant General, Quartermaster, Medical, and Finance Schools be established. He proposed further that courses and curriculums at existing and new schools be co-ordinated and integrated into a master program for military schooling, and that the Korean Military Academy be reorganized along the lines of the U.S. Military Academy. Finally, Vieman drew up a program by which, with all of these schools in operation under a sufficient number of qualified advisors and Korean instructors, 13,850 officers and officer candidates and 16,474 enlisted men could be graduated by 1 January 1952. Under this program:

All company-grade officers would attend basic courses at their branch schools.

Thirty percent of all officers (including all field-grade officers) would attend advanced courses at branch schools. Advanced courses would include basic subjects until it was possible to make graduation from basic courses a prerequisite for attending advanced schools.

Three hundred selected officers would attend the staff college.

Three thousand regular army officer candidates would be trained and commissioned.

Officers and enlisted men would attend specialist courses in sufficient numbers to provide two trained persons for each T/O specialist or technician position.

---

[31] (1) Korean Army School System, OFldr, sec. III.   (2) SA Rpt, KMAG, 31 Dec 49, sec. IV, p. 15.

[32] (1) Interv, Col Vieman, 16 Dec 51.   (2) Ltr, Col Clark, 26 Dec 52.

In addition, as many Korean officers as the U.S. Department of the Army would allow would attend schools in the United States.[33]

Oldest among the schools in operation was the Korean Military Academy, a direct descendant of the English language school set up by the U.S. Military Government in December 1945 and later the Korean Army's officer candidate school. The language school had been renamed Korean Constabulary Training Center on 1 May 1946, had served as the Constabulary's OCS until 20 August 1948, and then was redesignated as the Korean Military Academy.[34] The Constabulary had been expanding, however, and there were urgent demands for Korean officers in the field. KMA, as the Americans called it, was compelled to turn out officers quickly, and plans for long-term schooling faded into the background. Throughout the fall and winter of 1948 and spring of 1949 the academy continued to function as the ROK Army's officer candidate school.[35]

The Korean Military Academy's failure to fulfill its academy role had also been due to the lack of a Korean faculty. The pressures of officer candidate training and the Army's need for experienced officers in the field had left the school's advisors little time and material for building a competent Korean staff. The advisors had done the instructing through interpreters. A conversion of KMA to actual academy status had to be prefaced by measures for correcting, or at least improving, this condition. After the graduation of an OCS class on 23 May 1949, Maj. Russell P. Grant, senior advisor to the academy, requested permission from General Roberts to delay the entrance of the next class for several weeks. This granted, Major Grant also asked that several high-ranking Korean officers who possessed a good knowledge of English be assigned to the school. The

[33] (1) Korean Army School System, OFldr, sec. III. (2) SA Rpt, KMAG, 31 Dec 49, sec. IV, pp. 15–17. (3) Interv, Col Vieman, 12 Oct 53.

[34] In a letter, 2 June 1953, Lt. Col. Russell P. Grant (Senior Advisor, Korean Military Academy, 4 August 1948–5 June 1950) states that the school was called the Officer Training School (OTS) for a very brief period before its redesignation as an academy.

[35] (1) Ltr, Col Grant, 2 Jun 53. (2) Ltr, Col Reynolds, 17 Sep 52. (3) Office of the Military Attaché, Seoul, Rpt R–26–49, 12 Aug 49, G–2 Doc Lib, DA, ID 584449.

ROK Army acquiesced, and the academy advisors spent five weeks in June and July training these officers as instructors.[36]

When the military academy reopened on 15 July it was still an officer candidate school. Though the school was better organized than it had been, and now had a minimum of Korean instructors, there were not yet enough Korean instructors qualified in military or academic subjects to institute a four-year program. Moreover, there was still an acute need for junior officers in the field, a need other schools could not supply. A one-year course began at this time, nevertheless, with instruction in English, economics, and mathematics; and, while all candidates were to attend the military academy during the first six months of this course, they were scheduled to be assigned to the various branches of the Army and complete the year at branch schools. Two other officer candidate courses began in July: a six-month standard course, and a short "Special Course" for candidates in the engineer and finance branches, emphasizing technical and general subjects rather than purely military subjects. These courses were not duplicated at the Korean Military Academy.[37]

Over a period of several months, KMAG advisors meanwhile helped the Koreans reorganize the other military schools. First was the year-old Combat Intelligence School. The Koreans renamed this the Nam San Intelligence School on 25 June 1949 and instituted a new, improved course. By then enough students had graduated from the original course to permit a selection of the best for instructors, and these formed the teaching staff. Courses were 6 weeks in length, but whereas earlier classes had ranged from 9 to 35 students, each now enrolled about 80. The American advisors realized that the Korean Army eventually would need intelligence specialists, but until Korean divisions had enough trained personnel for their S–2 and G–2 Sections, they insisted that the Nam San School schedule instruction in combat intelligence through the division level only.[38]

---

[36] (1) Ltr, Col Grant, 2 June 53. (2) Ltr, Col Reynolds, 17 Sep 52. (3) Rpt R–26–49, cited in preceding footnote.

[37] (1) Ltr, Col Grant, 2 Jun 53. (2) Rpt R–26–49, cited n. 35(3) above.

[38] (1) Nam San Intelligence School, OFldr, sec. III. (2) See also Ltr, Maj Reed, 9 Jan 53.

The Engineer School reorganized next, on 26 June 1949, with a five-month officer candidate course. For this, students attended the Engineer School for one month, went on to the military academy for two months of instruction in nonengineering subjects, and returned to the Engineer School for the remaining two months. The class of seventy-eight students that graduated on 1 December 1949 was the first group of Korean officers to be commissioned directly into the Korean Army Corps of Engineers. Concurrently, the Engineer School conducted courses for enlisted riggers, carpenters, construction foremen, and toolroom keepers, who were to become cadres for engineer combat battalions in each infantry division upon graduation. On 12 December 1949 the school instituted a three-month basic engineer officer's course.[39]

The Signal School reorganized on 1 August 1949. The school had been established in July 1948 by a special team of U.S. Army Signal officers and men sent from Japan. By 1 July 1949 the school was conducting courses for linemen, switchboard operators, wire chiefs, technical noncommissioned officers, radio repairmen, and message center personnel, as well as short (one-month) courses for Korean officers. The reorganization established separate officer and enlisted departments, with a basic signal course for Korean officers and the above courses, plus an additional course for communication chiefs, for enlisted men. As in the other schools, KMAG advisors prepared the lesson plans and other study materials and had them translated into Korean by the Korean instructors who were to conduct the courses.[40]

The Ordnance School closed in July 1949 to permit preparation for improved courses to begin on 4 September 1949. KMAG ordnance advisors determined what tools, equipment, and instructors were needed and drew up class cycles through December 1950. When the school opened in September it offered automotive, artillery, and small arms maintenance courses, and on-the-job training in the receipt, storage, inventory, and issue of ordnance supplies and ammunition. Later the Ordnance

[39] (1) HR–KMAG, an. 11. (2) The Engineer School, OFldr, sec. III.
[40] (1) The Signal School, OFldr, sec. III. (2) HR–KMAG, an. 10, Incl 3, Incl F.

School instituted an officer candidate course (branch material), and basic and advanced courses for Korean ordnance officers.[41]

Following the completion in October 1949 of the first phase of training for the ROK Army's artillery battalions and anti-tank companies at the Artillery School, an artillery battalion became organic to the Capital Division and to each of the divisions along the 38th Parallel, and fourteen antitank companies were assigned to infantry regiments. One artillery battalion and four antitank companies remained as school troops for the Artillery School. The school then instituted basic and advanced courses for officers, a noncommissioned officer's course for the first three enlisted grades, and specialist courses for both officers and noncommissioned officers. Later, artillery officer candidates who graduated from the Korean Infantry School's branch immaterial course [42] attended the Artillery School for further training. The instructors for all courses were Korean, and all had previously completed identical courses given by American advisors.[43]

Several of the new schools recommended by Colonel Vieman came into being during this same period. A Quartermaster School opened on 4 July 1949, with a 5-week basic quartermaster officer's course. Two months later the school instituted a 4-week basic administration and supply course for noncommissioned officers, and in October a 13-week course for special graduates of the Korean Military Academy. During August a Korean Army Medical School opened at ASCOM City, with officer and nurse orientation courses, a medical administrative officer course, and a basic medical course for enlisted men; previously, Korean medical personnel had trained with U.S. Army medical units and hospitals located in Korea. A separate Finance School opened on 19 October 1949. Before the establishment of this school, Korean quartermaster and fi-

[41] (1) The Ordnance School, OFldr, sec. III. (2) Ltr, Col Hettrich, 17 Nov 53. (3) HR–KMAG, an. VII. Branch material training consisted of instruction in subjects pertaining to arm or service specialization. Branch immaterial training was devoted to general subjects without arm or service specialization.

[42] See below.

[43] (1) The Artillery School, OFldr, sec. III. (2) SA Rpt, KMAG, 31 Dec 49, an. 10, pp. 1–2.

nance personnel had received identical training according to the Japanese system. The KMAG Finance Advisor, Lt. Col. Ralph B. White, had been trying since 1948 to separate the two functions, and this school was the first real step in that direction.[44]

Early in August 1949, General Roberts directed Maj. John B. Clark to set up an Infantry School. The Infantry School, said KMAG's chief, should be set up to qualify Korean company-grade officers as platoon leaders, company commanders, and battalion staff officers and, in addition, include a course to prepare junior field-grade officers for posts as battalion commanders and regimental staff officers. If possible, it should be open by November 1949.[45]

For this task Colonel Vieman assigned five United States officers as assistant advisors to Major Clark. Following the selection of a site at Sihung, near Seoul, the Republic of Korea Army assigned officers and men to the Infantry School as permanent school troops. The Americans then prepared schedules and lesson plans, using the U.S. Army Infantry School as a model. Major Clark later wrote that most of the Korean Infantry School advisors were recent graduates of the Infantry School at Fort Benning, and that that was a great advantage. The plan was to conduct concurrently four basic courses of twelve weeks each and two advanced courses of eight weeks each. A KMAG directive during this planning stage ordered an officer candidate school organized in conjunction with and at the Infantry School, as a step toward the eventual removal of officer candidate training from the Korean Military Academy. For this, the Infantry School advisors recommended a fourteen-week branch immaterial course followed by a twelve-week branch material course at one of the other branch or service schools. General Roberts approved the plan.[46]

Preparations took less time than anticipated, and the In-

[44] (1) Quartermaster School; Korean Army Medical School; and Finance School, OFldr, sec. III. (2) Interv, Col White, 17 Dec 51.

[45] Ltr, Col Clark to author, 26 Dec 52.

[46] (1) *Ibid.* (2) The Infantry School, OFldr, sec. III. (3) Interv, Col Vieman. 12 Oct 53.

Col. Min Ki Sik, *Commandant of the Korean Infantry School, and Major Clark, senior advisor to the school.*

fantry School opened in late September 1949.[47] Phasing in all courses, including those for officer candidates, reached a peak by the end of the year. In addition to the regular curriculum, the Infantry School later conducted special courses, such as the basic tactics course for combat police officers early in 1950 and a course in conjunction with the Command and General Staff College for senior Korean commanders.

Another new school was the Korean Army's Command and General Staff College, which opened in September 1949 with a class of twenty-nine majors and lieutenant colonels attending a three-month course. American advisors gave all of the instruction. The need for the school was great, for the manner in which

---

[47] Col Clark writes that the school opened on 23 September 1949. KMAG G–3 Operations Report 14, 1 October 1949, reported that the school opened on 26 September 1949. OFldr states that the school "was organized" on 1 August 1949.

Korean staffs operated was unsound. Most staff officers did not function as advisors and responsible assistants to commanders but as aides and "yes men." This was due in part to the inefficiency of staff officers, who did not know their jobs, and in part to the ignorance of commanders, who did not know how to use their staffs; some commanders punished and relieved staff officers who did not give them the answers they wanted to hear—if, indeed, they consulted their staffs. The Staff College therefore was designed not only to instruct Korean officers in the performance of general staff duties, but also to orient commanders on the proper employment of staffs.[48]

Colonel Vieman, in addition to his position as KMAG Schools Advisor, was also the senior advisor at the Staff College. Soon after the first course got under way, he realized that it would take several years at the current rate to expose all senior Korean officers to staff training. He therefore set up a special senior officers' course for regimental and division commanders and their executive officers and for the chiefs and executives of Army staff sections, to run in eight-week cycles beginning in December 1949. The officers would attend the Infantry School for three weeks and the Staff School for five weeks, thus receiving a bare minimum of instruction on tactical doctrine and staff procedure. To insure that senior officers would attend, Colonel Vieman and other members of the KMAG staff exerted as much pressure as possible upon the Korean Army staff.[49]

Thirteen major schools were in operation by the end of 1949, with the greatest advisory effort being devoted to the Infantry and Staff Schools. On 20 December Colonel Vieman became KMAG's G–4 Advisor, replacing Major Geist, who returned to the United States. At this time the position of Schools Advisor was abolished and responsibility for the schools fell to the KMAG G–3 Training Section.[50] The Schools Advisor had been the driv-

---

[48] (1) The Staff School, OFldr, sec. III. (2) The Road to Ruin, lecture given by Col Vieman at the ROK Army Staff School on 20 Feb 50, transcript loaned by Col Vieman.
[49] (1) Interv, Col Vieman, 12 Oct 53. (2) Korean Army School System; The Infantry School; and the Staff School, OFldr, sec. III. (3) See also KMAG G–3 Opns Rpts 28 (9 Jan 50) 34 (18 Feb 50).
[50] (1) Intervs, Col Vieman, 18 Dec 51, 25 Nov 52. (2) Interv, Col McDonald, 8 Apr 53.

ing force behind the schools program. With the program under way, matters relating to budget, procurement of facilities, the assignment of students and instructors, and schedules were less pressing and could be handled more or less routinely by the G–3 Section.[51]

Besides attending their own schools in Korea, Korean officers were also studying at service schools in the United States. A colonel and five lieutenant colonels had left Korea on 14 August 1948 to attend the advanced course at the Infantry School, Fort Benning. A second group, consisting of two colonels, a lieutenant colonel, a major, a captain, and a first lieutenant, followed nearly a year later, on 18 July 1949. The latter two colonels attended the Ground Forces School at Fort Riley for six months and then went to Fort Benning for the basic infantry course. The remainder of the second group went directly to the Artillery School at Fort Sill to take the advanced course.[52]

In the opinion of the chief of KMAG, this program was well worth while. The original group of Korean officers to study in the United States were advanced quite rapidly after they returned to Korea in July 1949. One became a division commander, another the commandant of the Korean Infantry School, the third an assistant commandant at the Infantry School, the fourth an assistant commandant at the Korean Military Academy, and the fifth the commandant of the Korean Staff School. These officers did much to raise the standards of instruction and doctrine in the Korean service school system. In May 1950 the Department of the Army allotted to the Republic of Korea Army a total of twenty-seven spaces, with quotas in the Command and General Staff College, and the Infantry, Artillery, Signal, Ordnance, Medical, Adjutant General, Quartermaster, Finance, Military Police, and Transportation schools, for the fiscal year 1951 under Mutual Defense Assistance Program (MDAP) funds.[53]

---

[51] See: (1) Ltr, Col Grant, 2 Jun 53; (2) Ltr, Col Clark, 26 Dec 52; (3) Ltr, Col Hettrich, 17 Nov 53.

[52] HR–KMAG, pp. 4, 7.

[53] (1) SA Rpt, KMAG, 31 Dec 49, sec. VII, p. 39. (2) SA Rpt, KMAG, 30 Jun 50, sec. IV, p. 10. The latter report cites WAR 82586, sub: FY 51 MDAP Training, Foreign Nationals, 6 May 50, and WAR 83000, same subject, 16 May 50.

Another KMAG program approved by the Department of the Army involved sending thirty-three Korean officers to Japan as observers with Eighth U.S. Army units. The purpose of this program was to provide Korean officers with an opportunity to observe over a period of time the administrative and training methods employed by American units. In this way they could see for themselves the results of thorough planning, correct staff procedures, good leadership, and proper training methods, all of which had been stressed by KMAG advisors. For control the group of thirty-three officers was divided into four teams, each consisting of three infantry officers, and one officer each from the artillery, engineer, medical, ordnance, and signal branches, with one team having an extra infantry officer. Thus organized, one team was attached to each of the four U.S. divisions in Japan. The group arrived in Yokohama on 15 April 1950 and was scheduled to remain away for three months. Still another KMAG plan called for sending twenty-eight Korean officers to attend U.S. service schools in Japan, but the Department of the Army had not given its permission by 25 June 1950.[54]

Early in 1950 the chief of KMAG appointed a board of three advisors to consider the advisability of moving the Korean Military Academy to another location. The board advised against the move, then went on to recommend that the academy secure instructors from Seoul National University and begin a four-year academic course in June 1950 patterned closely after the U.S. Military Academy's curriculum. For military training, the board recommended that cadets take a three-month basic course during the first summer, a three-month advanced course during the second summer, and a three-month course to include battalion tactics during the third summer. In event of war during the four years, all cadets thus would have had at least the equivalent of a regular officer candidate course. The chief of KMAG, the Korean Army G–3, and President Rhee approved these recommendations, and a class of 350 cadets entered the

---

[54] (1) SA Rpts, KMAG. (2) Training of Korean Army Officers in Japan, OFldr, sec. III.

academy on 6 June 1950. Upon graduation they were to be awarded bachelor of science degrees and commissioned as second lieutenants in the Republic of Korea Army.[55]

The schools program promised to be KMAG's most successful enterprise. By 15 June 1950, ROK Army schools had graduated a total of 9,126 officers and 11,112 enlisted men, and had begun to produce graduates who could form an effective military organization. Nearly all officers in the rank of lieutenant colonel and higher had completed the advanced course at the Korean Army Infantry School, the command and general staff course, or the senior officers' course. More important, by attending school Korean officers had become aware of the value of schooling as a supplement to training and operations, and the concept had gained a more respected place in their thinking. The only real flaw in KMAG's plan, as later expressed by General Roberts, was that "... time ran out." [56]

Other KMAG Advisory Responsibilities

While the Korean Constabulary had been expanding and evolving toward its ultimate role as the Republic of Korea Army, the Korean Coast Guard had received little American or Korean assistance. To begin with, the ships and other equipment turned over to the Korean Coast Guard by the United States had been in poor condition. Many of the vessels had had to be towed to Korea and had required extensive overhauling before they became operable. A lack of spare parts and maintenance materials had made renovation a slow and difficult process. Then, delivery of the spare parts and materials authorized by the United States early in 1949 had not been satisfactory. This had been due partly to procurement difficulties in the United States and partly to the Korea Government's unwillingness to divert to the Coast Guard such supplies as were delivered in Korea. Finally, American ad-

---

[55] (1) Ltrs, Col Grant, 2 Jun 53, 20 Jul 53. (2) SA Rept, KMAG, 15 Jun 50, sec. V, p. 10. (3) See Korean Military Academy, OFldr, sec. III.

[56] (1) Ltr, Gen Roberts, 22 Jan 52. (2) Korean Army School System, OFldr, sec. III. (3) SA Rpt, KMAG, 15 Jun 50, sec. IV, pp. 9–10. (4) Ltr, Roberts to Ward, 9 Nov 51.

vice had been "woefully inadequate," even for such a small organization.[57]

When KMAG was established on 1 July 1949, the Korean Coast Guard had six U.S. civilian advisors. Three more arrived in the early fall of 1949, so that by the end of the year there were three in Seoul at Coast Guard headquarters and six at Chinhae, two at a Coast Guard academy there and four at the operating base and shipyard. For equipment, the Korean Coast Guard had approximately ninety vessels, ranging from Japanese mine sweepers to picket boats, of which less than one-half were operational. A Coast Guard officer candidate school and various service schools were in operation.[58]

Ambassador Muccio on 19 October 1949 reminded the Department of State that American interests in Korea, both strategic and otherwise, were large and increasing daily. A weak Korean Coast Guard not only jeopardized these interests, but also lessened U.S. prestige because of the impunity with which pirates and smugglers operated in Korean waters. Even the ROK Army's operations were involved, insofar as the movement of troops, supplies, and arms by sea to Yosu, Ongjin, and islands off the coast of South Korea was concerned. Mr. Muccio recommended urgently that the Korean Coast Guard be strengthened, at the least expense to the United States, with obsolescent U.S. equipment, guns, ammunition, and planes. At the minimum this reinforcement should include four patrol craft vessels, five picket boats, five scout-observation seaplanes, and fifteen 3"/50-caliber guns to rearm certain vessels then equipped with 37-mm. guns. The Ambassador also urged that KMAG's Coast Guard advisory staff be expanded to a total of twenty-three advisors.[59]

Two months later, General Roberts reported that the Korean Coast Guard's requirements had been included among

---

[57] (1) SA Rpt, KMAG, 31 Dec 49, sec. I, pp. 6–7. (2) Roberts, Commander's Estimate. (3) See also Orientation on Korean Navy (Ships, Condition and Speed), OFldr, sec. IV.

[58] See HR–KMAG, an. 12, and Orientation on Korean Navy (Ships, Condition and Speed), OFldr, sec. IV.

[59] EMBTEL 1295, Muccio to State, 19 Oct 49, included as an. 4 to SA Rpt, KMAG, 31 Dec 49. This message refers to State Department telegrams 594 (15 July 1949) and 706 (21 August 1949).

KMAG recommendations for additional MDAP aid for Korea for fiscal year 1950.[60] In order to keep the program within a ceiling of twenty million dollars, it had been necessary to forego the aircraft requested by Ambassador Muccio in October and have the Koreans purchase with their own foreign exchange funds the hulls and main engines of three patrol craft (for which the United States had borne repair and refitting expenses) and one patrol craft complete. General Roberts also noted that the condition of the Coast Guard was "a matter of growing concern," and asked that the additional advisors requested by Mr. Muccio be sent without delay.[61]

In early April 1950 the chief of KMAG again pointed out the critical need for Coast Guard advisors and requested that twelve additional positions be authorized and provided for in the Army's budget for fiscal year 1951. The comptroller replied within three weeks that Department of the Army plans for fiscal year 1951 called for a scaling down of U.S. Army activity in Korea, with an attendant reduction in personnel allotments. In any case, the Secretary of Defense had directed the Army to transfer budget and fiscal responsibility for civilian Coast Guard advisors in Korea to the Department of State, so that action to procure the additional advisors would have to be directed through Department of State channels.[62]

There the matter rested. On 15 June 1950 the U.S. Military Advisory Group reported that the Korean Coast Guard could be considered but 70 percent effective. The group warned at that time that the transfer of civilian Coast Guard advisors to Department of State payrolls did not diminish the need for additional advisors.[63]

American assistance to the Korean National Police was also limited. The police force had grown by 1949 to a strength of approximately 48,000 and was distributed by divisions accord-

---

[60] See below, ch. V.

[61] SA Rpt, KMAG, 31 Dec 49, sec. VII, pp. 37, 38. One PC (Patrol Vessel, Submarine Chaser) vessel arrived in Korea in February 1950; the other three were en route on 25 June 1950. See also MHK, p. 34, and HR–KMAG, an. 12.

[62] Ltr, KMAG to DA, Attn: Comptroller of the Army, 1 Apr 50, sub: Request for Increase, Civilian Personnel Authorization, and 1st Ind, 20 Apr 50, in SA Rpt, KMAG, 15 Jun 50, an. XV.

[63] SA Rpt, KMAG, 15 Jun 50, sec. IV, p. 14, and sec. VII, p. 24.

ing to population and guerrilla activity throughout the eight provinces of South Korea and on the islands of Cheju-do and Ullung-do. Since the police force was a national organization, it nominally came under the Minister of Home Affairs; actually, each police division was directly responsible to the governor of its province for operational control. The police were equipped with a miscellaneous assortment of weapons, including the Japanese Model 99 rifle, a limited number of U.S. carbines, and pistols of various makes and calibers, all of which complicated enormously problems of supply and maintenance.[64]

For this organization, KMAG's Table of Distribution authorized ten American advisors—one for each police division and two for the main headquarters of the police in Seoul. As was the case with most other KMAG advisory elements, there were seldom, if ever, that many advisors on duty at any one time. Between February 1950 and 25 June 1950, for instance, there were only four KMAG police advisors, with each responsible for at least two provinces.[65]

A final, and reluctant, KMAG responsibility entailed nurturing a ROK Air Force. Acceptance of this responsibility was gratuitous on the part of KMAG, for the Department of the Army had made it clear that "the US [was] in no way committed to support a Korean Air Force with advisors or materiel." [66] Fourteen liaison planes turned over to the Koreans in 1948 had been intended for an air liaison detachment for the Korean Army, and nothing more. Nevertheless, while the Army, Coast Guard, and National Police organizations were developing, the Korean Government, against the strong advice of the U.S. Military Advisory Group, separated the liaison unit from the Army and established a separate Air Force in October 1949.[67]

---

[64] (1) National Police, OFldr, sec. V. (2) SA Rpt, KMAG, 31 Dec 49, an. 11. (3) SA Rpt, KMAG, 15 Jun 50, an. VII.

[65] Interv, Col Krohn, 3 Jun 53. According to Colonel Krohn (and also OFldr), only nine advisors were authorized—one for each police division and one for the Director of Police. However, KMAG's T/D allowed ten spaces for police advisors. See SA Rpt, KMAG, 31 Dec 49, an. 1.

[66] SA Rpt, KMAG, 31 Dec 49, sec. I, p. 5.

[67] (1) *Ibid*. (2) Ltr, Chief, KMAG, to Korean Minister of National Defense, Seoul, 7 Oct 49, P&O File 091 Korea, sec. I, case 18/2.

American opposition to this move was based primarily on the fact that the advisory group was not set up to advise an air force. The one officer and two (later five) enlisted advisors at Kimp'o Airfield were inadequate for such an undertaking. Although the Korean Government had contracted for the purchase of ten AT-6 trainer aircraft from a private firm in the United States, there was not sufficient equipment to warrant a separate air arm. Furthermore, the Republic of Korea economy was utterly incapable of supporting an air force. Still, during the preceding year the Soviet Union had furnished the North Korean Security Forces with both Russian and Japanese weapons and equipment, including 30 YAK-3 fighter planes, 5 IL-2 attack planes, and 30 training planes of miscellaneous types. These, coupled with a superiority in armor and artillery, and feverish activity known to be taking place in North Korean training areas, painted an ominous picture. Faced with the *fait accompli* of a Republic of Korea Air Force, the Americans decided to meet the question of how KMAG with its limited complement could advise and assist in developing the new organization.[68]

With all these factors in mind, the chief of KMAG on 7 December 1949 recommended through Ambassador Muccio that the advisory group in Korea be assigned two instruction pilots and eight enlisted specialists from the United States Air Force. In the KMAG semiannual report of 31 December 1949, General Roberts further urged that U.S. policy be reviewed, and, if necessary, revised to include assistance to the Korean Air Force. In addition, among recommendations for additional fiscal year 1950 MDAP aid to Korea, KMAG's chief requested 40 F-51 fighter aircraft, 10 T-6 trainers, 2 C-47 cargo planes, and nearly a quarter of a million dollars worth of supporting signal equipment.[69]

---

[68] (1) SA Rpt, KMAG, 31 Dec 49, sec. I, pp. 5, 6, sec. III, pp. 11, 12, sec. VII, pp. 36, 37. (2) Roberts, Commander's Estimate. (3) Ltr, Seoul 99, Muccio to Dept of State, 26 Jan 50, sub: Transmitting Semiannual Report of KMAG for Period Ending Dec 31, 1949.

[69] (1) SA Rpt, KMAG, 31 Dec 49, sec. VII, p. 36. This cites EMBTEL 1473, Muccio to Department of State, 7 December 1949. (2) See also SA Rpt, an. 17 and ch. V, below.

Roberts made further efforts in May and June to secure aid for the ROK Air Force. Through Muccio, he recommended that six officers and eleven airmen be sent to Korea "to be charged against [the] authorized strength of KMAG and to be an integral part thereof." [70]

But the Koreans' ambitions for an effective, defensive Korean air force were doomed. With the meager assistance that KMAG was able to furnish, the Korean Air Force expanded to a strength of but 1,865 officers and men during the first six months of 1950, organized into a single flight group. The ten AT-6 trainers purchased by the Korean Government arrived in April, and these, together with the L-4's and L-5's, constituted the Republic's air strength on 25 June 1950. [71]

---

[70] (1) DEPTEL 744, Muccio to Dept of State, 23 May 50, in SA Rpt. KMAG, 15 Jun 50, an. XIV. (2) See also Section VII, pp. 23-24, of the report.

[71] SA Rpt, KMAG, 15 Jun 50, sec. IV, pp. 11, 12, sec. V, p. 16.

CHAPTER V

Status Quo Ante Bellum

Military Assistance to the ROK

Before the Communist invasion, United States military assistance to the Republic of Korea was predicated upon the policy that the South Korean military establishment was an internal security force. Equipment furnished by the United States was to permit the development of an organization that could maintain security within the borders of the Republic while, incidentally, deterring attacks from the north of the 38th Parallel.[1]

The National Security Council established the basic American policy governing military aid to Korea in the spring of 1949. Enough equipment for 50,000 men already had been or was being transferred from United States forces in Korea to the ROK Government, under the Surplus Property Act of 1944 (through the Office of Foreign Liquidation).[2] This equipment had originally cost the United States about $56,000,000 and had a 1949 replacement value of approximately $110,000,000. In March, following a review of the United States policy with respect to Korea, the Security Council had concluded that the United States should complete the equipment of the ROK Army to its then current level of 65,000 men. In addition, certain arms and vessels should be turned over to the Korean Coast Guard and a six-month stockpile of maintenance supplies made available to the Korean Government. The estimate of the original cost of this supplemental equipment was about $1,000,000, and

---

[1] Except where otherwise indicated, this section is based on information contained in: (1) *The Conflict in Korea,* "Military Assistance," Department of State Publication 4266, FE Series 45, October 1951, pp. 8–11; (2) House Report 2495, 81st Congress, 2d Session, *Background Information on Korea,* Report of the Committee on Foreign Affairs, 1950, pp. 33–40; (3) *Mutual Defense Assistance Program,* A Fact Sheet, Department of State Publication 3836, General Foreign Policy Series 25, April 1950; (4) House Document 613, 81st Congress, 2d Session, *First Semiannual Report on the Mutual Defense Assistance Program,* 1950; (5) Semiannual Repts, KMAG periods ending 31 Dec 49 and 30 Jun 50; (6) Mutual Defense Assistance Program, OFldr, sec. II.

[2] See ch. II, above.

the replacement cost was approximately a half million dollars more. Delivery was virtually complete by the end of 1949.[3]

The National Security Council also concluded that legislative authority should be sought for continued military aid to Korea, as part of a general United States program of military assistance to free nations. On the basis of this conclusion, the Republic of Korea was included among those nations marked for U.S. military aid under the Mutual Defense Assistance Act (Public Law 329, 81st Congress) of 1949, signed by President Truman on 6 October 1949. Under this act a total of $1,314,010,000 was appropriated for the fiscal year 1950 program of military assistance, of which $10,200,000 was at that time allocated to South Korea, mainly in the form of maintenance materials and spare parts to supplement the military equipment turned over under the Surplus Property Act.

In arriving at a distribution of military aid, Congress took into account the needs and responsibilities of both the recipient countries and the United States. In the case of Korea, as already noted, the tiny Republic was faced with serious problems in maintaining internal security. Marauding guerrillas and Communist-inspired revolts were weakening the position of the government. Frequent incidents along the 38th Parallel, involving North Korean forces, posed grave threats. Over all, there rode the shadow of invasion from North Korea, supported to an unpredictable degree by Communist China or the Soviet Union or both. In addition, South Korea's economy was anything but self-supporting, inflation was rampant, and the country depended upon American economic aid for survival. Without military aid from outside, the Republic of Korea was incapable of supporting adequate security forces or of maintaining the complex modern weapons of war.

The United States, on the other hand, had to determine the extent and character of assistance to Korea not only by the de-

---

[3] In a letter to Ambassador Muccio dated 20 July 1945, General Roberts stated that $55,939,990.64 in military supplies and equipment had been turned over to Korea by that date. Of the total, $1,250,000 worth had been turned over after 1 July 1949. An estimated $700,000 in equipment was still due. Copy in OCMH files.

mands of the Korean situation, but in the light of world-wide commitments. Besides South Korea, militant communism threatened Greece, Turkey, Iran, the Philippines, countries in the vicinity of China, and certain European nations. What the United States could do to bolster the economy and security of Korea—or of any other country or area—depended upon the extent of requirements and the ability of American resources to meet them.

KMAG prepared South Korea's military aid program in consultation with the ROK Government and the U.S. Embassy in Seoul. Several factors had to be considered in determining the Republic's requirements. While the U.S. equipment already furnished or being delivered to Korea had been sufficient when computed, increases in the size of the Korean forces and consequent use of equipment at abnormal rates posed new problems. Equipment for 65,000 men was being used to support an army of approximately 100,000 men. Stocks of maintenance materials and spare parts in particular had been drained at an alarming rate and were nearly exhausted. Moreover, because the Korean Army had been slow to develop supply discipline and maintenance, hundreds of vehicles, weapons, and articles of individual equipment were now unserviceable. Ammunition, too, had been used in excess of U.S. Army experience tables; of more than 51,000,000 rounds of ammunition of all types, the bulk of which was delivered to the Republic of Korea in June 1949, only 19,000,000 remained at the end of the year.[4]

At the same time, the Americans had to recognize that the South Koreans were helping to keep their forces in operation. An intensive program of procurement from domestic sources had been under way since the establishment of a Central Procurement Agency in November 1948. This agency, composed of representatives of each of the ROK Army technical services, acted under G–4 advisory supervision according to regulations based on U.S. Army purchasing and contracting procedures. Through the co-operation of ECA technicians, the faculty of Seoul University, and the staffs of various industrial plants in Korea, the Central Procurement Agency during its first year had

---

[4] HR–KMAG, an. 7 (including an. B).

developed local sources of supply and manufacture to the point where the following ratios of Republic of Korea security forces requirements came from the Korean economy: [5]

	Percent
Quartermaster (except POL)	100
Medical	95
Engineer	45
Signal	25
Ordnance	15

In support of this effort was the Korean Army's own Quartermaster Clothing Factory, in operation since June 1949. The factory had begun with a limited production of clothing for the Army and was gradually developing the manufacture of many items of quartermaster equipment. By 25 June 1950 it was turning out 1,200 two-piece fatigue or 800 two-piece wool uniforms daily, as well as socks, mosquito nets, comforter covers, flags, caps, bandages, and hospital gowns. The Korean Army Quartermaster Corps also had in operation a section for the repair of shoes and clothing. Beginning in May 1949 with the daily repair of 50 pairs of shoes and 60 two-piece fatigue uniforms, the unit increased production until by 25 June 1950 it was repairing 1,200 two-piece fatigue uniforms and 500 pairs of shoes each day.[6]

The Koreans, with KMAG advice, were trying further to gear their military establishment to the Korean economy through a Military Materiel Mobilization Board, similar to the Munitions Board in the U.S. Department of Defense. One of this board's best-known projects was an arsenal program, whereby Korean manufacturers and ordnance personnel, under the supervision of KMAG advisors, produced ammunition and spare parts for the model 99 Japanese rifle. The program would have done much to alleviate the acute ammunition shortage in Korea, but powder and primers were not available in sufficient quantity to

---

[5] (1) Sa Rpt, KMAG, 31 Dec 49, sec. VI, pp. 30–31, and an. 15 (2) Mutual Defense Assistance Program, OFldr, sec. II.
[6] HR–KMAG, an. 9. See also Maj Ernest J. Skroch, QMC, "Quartermaster Advisors in Korea," *The Quartermaster Review,* September–October 1951, pp. 9, 118.

permit notable success. By the end of 1949 Korean manufacturers were producing approximately 30,000 rounds of cartridges per month, all components of the Japanese rifle except the barrel, and were experimenting with the manufacture of grenades, mines, fuses, and blasting charges.[7]

In view of all these factors, KMAG and Embassy officials gave top priority to materials for maintaining the equipment already in possession of the Koreans. Although there were serious shortages of major items, the Korean forces could function to some degree if the equipment on hand were serviceable. Second priority went to ammunition; internal disturbances and border incidents showed no signs of abating, and therefore continued expenditures could be expected. Third priority covered the normal replacement factor. Thus, about 90 percent of Korea's Mutual Defense Assistance Program (MDAP) was devoted to ordnance supplies and equipment, of which more than half pertained to ammunition and the remainder to spare parts, with a very small portion allotted to replacement items. The remaining 10 percent covered spare parts for engineer and signal equipment, powder and primers for the arsenal program, and spare parts for Korean Coast Guard vessels.

The Americans did not include tanks, 155-mm. howitzers, and certain other heavy items of equipment. The decision was made in part because the items could not be fitted within the dollar limitations of the military aid program for Korea,[8] and in part because the KMAG staff felt that the roads and bridges of South Korea did not lend themselves to efficient tank operations. There is evidence, too, based possibly on a remark by President Rhee to Secretary of the Army Kenneth C. Royall in February 1949, that some Americans feared the Republic of Korea would embark upon military adventures of its own into North Korea if it had "offensive-type" equipment. However, it is much more likely that terrain factors and dollar limitations were actually re-

---

[7] SA Rpt. KMAG, 31 Dec 49, sec. VI, pp. 30–31. For details concerning U.S. support of the arsenal program, see P&O File 091 Korea, sec. II–A, bk. I, and also JCS 1483/68, 8 Jun 49, pp. 530–37.

[8] Ltr, Wright to Collins, 28 Oct 49, P&O File 091 Korea, sec. I, case 18.

sponsible for the United States' failure to furnish this type of equipment.[9]

Under the terms of the Mutual Defense Assistance Act, bilateral agreements between the United States and each of the recipient countries had to be concluded before actual shipment began. To reach these agreements, MDAP survey teams visited all countries scheduled to receive United States military aid. The team detailed to survey the programs of both Korea and the Philippines arrived in Seoul on 14 December 1949.[10] Consultations proceeded without difficulties, and the Korean authorities, including President Rhee, agreed to the program recommended by KMAG and the Embassy. On 26 January 1950 the two countries signed a formal agreement.[11]

Even with this program fulfilled, the Korean forces would be in "very strained logistical circumstances." They would still lack weapons and other major items of equipment, and the repair and maintenance items called for under the program would only be sufficient to place in serviceable condition the equipment then unserviceable. The supply of ammunition would be satisfactory, but only "under present circumstances." [12] For this reason, General Roberts on 17 December recommended through Ambassador Muccio that Korea's MDAP aid be supplemented by part of the $75,000,000 made available to the President under the Mutual Defense Assistance Act for aid to the general area of China.

[9] See: (1) Rpt of the MDA Survey Team for Korea (KMACC D–31), 8 Feb 50, P&O File 091 Korea, sec. IV, case 74; (2) P&O Memo for Rcd, 12 Jul 49, sub: Shipments of Ammunition to Korea, P&O File 091 Korea, sec. I, case 15; (3) Ltr, Gen Roberts to Maj Gen Charles L. Bolté, Dir P&O, 13 Sep 49, P&O File 091 Korea, sec. III, case 60; (4) Memo of Secy Royall's Conversations, Conference at Hq USAFIK, Seoul, Korea, 8 Feb 49, KMAG File, FE&Pac Br, G–3.
[10] Army Msg ROB 708, American Embassy, Seoul, to Dept State, 16 Dec 49, sub: MDAP for Korea. See also Rpt of the MDA Survey Team for Korea (FMACC D–31), 8 Feb 50, copy in P&O File 091 Korea, sec. IV, case 74.
[11] Embassy official E. F. Drumright later observed, ". . . it is only fair to note that the Korean authorities, and especially the Air Force and the Coast Guard officials concerned, were deeply disappointed by the meager aid allotted to those branches of the Korean Security Forces." From Ltr, Foreign Service of the United States of America, Seoul, 25 Jan 50, sub: Transmitting Recommendations for Additional United States Military Aid to Korea During Fiscal Year 1950, signed E. F. Drumright, copy in files of G–2 Doc Lib, DA, ID 635333. See also: (1) HR–KMAG, an. 4. (2) First Semiannual MDAP Rpt, p. 36.
[12] (1) OFldr. (2) SA Rpt, KMAG, 31 Dec 49, sec. I, pp. 7–8 and sec. VII, pp. 40, 41.

The Ambassador agreed that strengthening the defenses of Korea would further the policies and purposes set forth in the act. At a minimum, sufficient funds should be allotted to bring Korea's total military assistance in the fiscal year 1950 to $20,000,000.[13]

On 31 December 1949 General Roberts outlined specific recommendations for such additional aid, falling within an approximate dollar limitation of $9,800,000.[14] The proposed supplemental program called for F–51, T–6, and C–47 aircraft, 3-inch guns for Coast Guard vessels, and more signal and engineer equipment, 105-mm. howitzers (M2A1), and additional machine guns and mortars (including 4.2-inch), for the Army. With this extra equipment, insisted KMAG's chief, the Korean security forces would be in a condition to insure the integrity of the Republic of Korea. MDAP aid to Korea for fiscal year 1951 could then be devoted to replacement, repair, and maintenance items to enable the Korean forces to maintain themselves during that period.[15]

Shortly after the request for aid was sent to Washington, the United States made public an important decision that could not fail to influence the course of events in the Far East. On 5 January President Truman announced that the United States would take no military action, direct or indirect, to help the Nationalist forces of Chiang Kai-shek hold Formosa against the expected attacks of the Chinese Communists. Despite heavy criticism from the Republican members of Congress, Secretary of State Dean Acheson followed this declaration with the statement a week later that the United States would fight to defend Japan, Okinawa, and the Philippines, but that the new nations of Asia were on their own. The patent establishment of a U.S. forward defense line based upon Japan, Okinawa, and the Philippines placed both Formosa and the Republic of Korea in the realm of open territory for the Communists and no doubt served to encourage them to make more ambitious plans for future action against these areas.

This decision did not mean that the United States cut off

---

[13] Ltr, Drumright, 25 Jan 50, cited previously. This letter cites EMBTEL 1519, 17 Dec 49, and EMBTEL 1521, 19 Dec 49.

[14] See SA Rpt, KMAG, 31 Dec 49, an. 17.

[15] (1) *Ibid.* (2) OFldr.

military assistance to the Republic of Korea or that it refused
to consider further military aid. But precious time was lost
while Congress further reviewed and revised the MDAP needs
in the Far East to bring them into line with U.S. policy. Other
reasons for the delay involved a desire to avoid wasting American resources on programs that did not reflect the real needs
of the countries concerned and the necessity for determining
the availability from American stocks of the items requested.
To help refine the programs, survey teams again visited the
recipient countries, including the Republic of Korea. The teams
met with military representatives of each country and discussed
with them in detail the programs they had submitted. The idea
was to eliminate all items not actually needed, and to determine whether substitutions could be made for certain items.

Congress finally approved Korea's program on 15 March
1950 in the amount of $10,970,000.[16] However, U.S. supplies
and equipment did not immediately begin to flow across the
Pacific Ocean. Under the priority assigned to Korea by the
Joint Chiefs of Staff, the major portion of equipment earmarked
for the Republic of Korea was not available from excess of
war-reserve stocks. It had to come from commercial sources
in the United States under new procurement contracts. Even
the limited amounts of equipment available from Department
of Defense stocks had to be reconditioned. All this took time.
By 25 June 1950 approximately $52,000 worth of signal equip-
ment and $298,000 worth of spare parts were en route to
Korea; less than $1,000 worth had arrived.[17]

This left the Korean security forces all the more unprepared
to secure the Republic against invasion. Their logistical situation, moreover, had deteriorated to a point where by June 1950
supply and service for combat units could be provided only

---

[16] U.S. Senate, 82d Congress, 1st Session, *Hearings Before the Committee on
Armed Services and the Committee on Foreign Relations, Military Situation in the
Far East*, pt. 3, p. 1993. Hereafter, this source will be called *MacArthur Hearings*.

[17] (1) Ltr, Roberts to Ward, 9 Nov 51. (2) Testimony of Secy of State Dean
Acheson, *MacArthur Hearings*, pt. 3, p. 1993. See also House Rpt 2495, *Background
Information on Korea*, p. 34. A former KMAG officer states that "wire" worth
approximately $250 represented the sole MDAP delivery to Korea before the war.
See testimony of Maj Gen Lyman L. Lemnitzer from Appropriations Committee
hearings, quoted in *MacArthur Hearings*, pt. 3, p. 1992.

on a bare subsistence basis. Spare parts in all categories were exhausted, and U.S. military advisors in Korea estimated that 15 percent of the Korean Army's weapons and 35 percent of its vehicles were unserviceable. With the equipment on hand, full-scale defensive operations could be supported for a period of no longer than fifteen days. "Korea," warned KMAG on 15 June, "is threatened with the same disaster that befell China." [18]

The Opposing Forces

While the Republic of Korea security forces were developing, intense activity was taking place in North Korea.[19] Both a border constabulary and an Army had been established there in 1946; the army, equipped with Japanese rifles, had reached a strength of 20,000 by the end of that year. Under the supervision of the Soviet Army the North Korean forces were organized and trained for combat.

When the Russian units began to withdraw from North Korea in February 1948, they turned over limited quantities of their weapons, including a few tanks and aircraft to their protégés. A rapid expansion of the North Korean forces followed after the Democratic People's Republic of Korea was established in September 1948. This Communist-dominated government commenced to divert an increasing amount of its national resources to industrial development and to the increasing of its armed forces.[20]

Russian advisors remained with the North Korean forces after the last Soviet troops withdrew in December 1948 and in some instances as many as fifteen officers served on a single North Korean infantry division staff. Thousands of conscripts were gathered, and Koreans formerly attached to Chinese Communist forces were brought back to Korea to swell the ranks. For technical proficiency, the North Koreans could count on pilots, aircraft mechanics, and experts in tank warfare and

[18] SA Rpt, KMAG, 15 Jun 50, sec. IV, p. 18.

[19] Unless otherwise specified, data on the development of North Korea forces may be found in Roy E. Appleman, *South to the Naktong, North to the Yalu,* UNITED STATES ARMY IN THE KOREAN WAR (Washington, 1961), ch. II.

[20] See Department of State, *North Korea: A Case Study of A Soviet Satellite,* 20 May 1951.

maintenance who had been training for three years in the Soviet Union.[21]

The pattern of North Korean armed expansion was similar to that of its southern counterpart: it quickly outstripped the original plans. In March 1949 the Russians had agreed to furnish arms and equipment for six infantry divisions, three mechanized units, and eight battalions of mobile border constabularly. In addition, when North Korea had sufficient trained air force personnel available, the Soviet Union was to provide 20 reconnaissance aircraft, 100 fighter planes, and 30 light and medium bombers.[22]

In the months that followed, the North Korean forces grew apace. In the spring of 1951 large shipments of arms flowed in from the Soviet Union, equipping the North Korean forces with heavy artillery, automatic weapons, and new propeller-driven aircraft. The North Korean economy supplemented Soviet deliveries with light arms and ammunition. By June 1950 the North Korean forces contained eight infantry divisions at full strength, two infantry divisions at half strength, a separate infantry regiment, a motorcycle reconnaissance regiment, an armored brigade, and five brigades of Border Constabulary troops. Including army and corps troops, the North Koreans had an estimated strength of slightly over 135,000 men in their ground forces.[23] The armored brigade was equipped with the excellent Russian-built T–34 medium tank. In addition, the North Koreans had about 180 aircraft supplied by Russia, of which about 40 were YAK fighters and 70 were attack bombers. According to KMAG intelligence estimates, all North Korean units except one division and certain battalions of the Constabulary brigades had completed training to include the battalion in the attack, rifle firing at moving targets, the assault of fortified

---

[21] *Ibid.*

[22] (1) Memo by C of S, USA, Implications of a Possible Full-Scale Invasion from North Korea Subsequent to Withdrawal of U.S. Troops From Korea, 8 Jun 49, P&O File 091 Korea, sec. I–A, bk. II, case 5/21. (2) See also JCS 1776/2, 11 Jun 49, pp. 10–26.

[23] The breakdown of this figure is as follows: infantry, 103,800; constabulary, 18,600; armored troops, 6,000; motorcycle troops, 2,000; army and corps troops, 5,000.

positions, and road marches. Combined exercises to regimental level had been in progress since the beginning of the year.[24]

South Korean forces in June 1950 totaled approximately 151,000 men. Of these about 95,000 were Army, 6,100 Coast Guard, 1,800 Air Force, and 48,000 National Police. The ROK Army's artillery consisted of 89 serviceable 105-mm. howitzers (M3) and 114 57-mm. guns (M1); in armor it could count 26 armored cars (M8) equipped with 37-mm. guns and 15 half-track vehicles (M2 and M3A2). The ROK Coast Guard had 105 vessels of all types, of which 58, including fishing vessels, were serviceable. The ROK Air Force had a total of 10 Harvard trainers (AT–10) and 12 serviceable liaison aircraft.[25]

The development of North and South Korean forces thus had paralleled each other in a very general way. The outstanding differences sprang from the halfhearted U.S. support of ROK forces as compared with the fuller assistance given North Korea by the Soviet Union. While the United States in 1946 was hedging about the terms *national defense* and *internal security* in South Korea,[26] the Communists were sending thousands of North Koreans to the USSR for specialized training. While a handful of U.S. military advisors were nursing the South Korean Constabulary through the years 1946–49, each North Korean division trained under scores of Soviet advisors. Where South Korean armament was limited to a few light howitzers and armored cars, with no combat aircraft or tanks, the North Korean forces boasted fighter planes, medium armor, and artillery of far greater range than that employed by Republic of Korea forces.

The mission of the South Korean forces was to maintain the internal security and sovereign rights of the Republic of Korea. KMAG's terms of reference contained authorization to furnish strategic, tactical, and technical advice to these forces. Since political and military conditions compelled the Koreans to defend the northern border of the Republic, advice and assistance to the Koreans in organizing their defenses were implicit in KMAG's mission.

---

[24] SA Rept, KMAG, 15 Jun 50, sec. III, pp. 5–7.
[25] *Ibid.,* sec. V, p. 16, and an. X.
[26] See ch. I, above.

For general defensive planning, the Americans divided the terrain along the 38th Parallel into six areas for analysis, and, without attempting to consider probability factors, assigned each zone a letter (A to F).[27] Area A was the Ongjin Peninsula, covering approximately twenty-six air-line miles of mountainous terrain along the parallel. That portion of the peninsula occupied by South Korean troops was an island insofar as the Republic of Korea was concerned, for it was bounded on three sides by water and on the north by the 38th Parallel. Strategically, the area was of value only in that the possessor had a third-rate warm water seaport and a secondary all-weather airstrip. Tactically, possession of Ongjin Peninsula would be of value to the North Koreans because it would release their troops from a mission of containment; moreover, the peninsula could serve as a base for a seaborne assault on the port of Inch'on. One ferry crossing connected the eastern edge of the peninsula to the mainland across Haeju Bay.

Area B covered approximately thirty-five air miles across the Ch'ongdan area from Haeju Bay to the Yesong River. This terrain was very mountainous along the 38th Parallel and northward, but south of the line were foothills and flatlands. The latter were suitable for the employment of armor, though tanks would be channelized except in winter when the rice paddies were frozen solid. The Yesong River, flowing from north to south, seldom froze sufficiently to support troops or vehicles. There was one good lateral road in this area (south of the parallel) and six fair roads running north and south. A ferry and a large double-track railroad and highway bridge spanned the Yesong River, connecting the zone with the Kaesong area to the east.

Area C stretched for about thirty-one air miles along the Parallel from the Yesong River to the Imjin River. The principal town in this area was Kaesong, ancient capital of Korea. The terrain was similar to that in the Ch'ongdan area and was suitable for armor under the same conditions. There were three fair

---

[27] SA Rpt, KMAG, 15 Jun 50, an. III, sec. I.   Also see SA Rpt, KMAG, 31 Dec 49, an. 5.

38TH PARALLEL IN THE KAESONG AREA

north-south roads and one good lateral road south of the parallel, as well as large numbers of foot-paths and ox trails crisscrossing the area. The primary railroad link between North and South Korea passed through here. If held by an enemy, the zone would provide an excellent tactical base from which to launch an assault into the Seoul district. Such an assault, would, however, be greatly impeded by the Imjin River; although the stream occasionally froze to a depth sufficient to support foot troops and vehicles, a successful attack would have to include the capture of two large single-lane railway bridges, one of which had been converted for the use of wheeled and light tracked vehicles.

Area D, called the Uijongbu area, extended for some twenty-two miles from the Imjin River eastward to include a north-south valley running between Seoul and Wonsan, important east coast seaport and rail center in North Korea. This ancient invasion route contained a road and railroad connecting the lowlands around Seoul with the flatlands in the vicinity of Wonsan. Although not in first-class condition, the corridor was the best approach to Seoul from the north and was militarily important. There was good observation both north and south of the Parallel in this zone. One poor lateral road and numerous mountain trails led east toward Ch'unch'on.

Area E ran from the Seoul-Wonsan corridor approximately thirty-six air-line miles to the eastern limitation of the Hongch'on River valley where it crossed the 38th Parallel at Pup'yong-ni. The terrain was mountainous and lent itself favorably to guerrilla action. On each flank of the zone, minor valleys ran north and south along the Choyang and Pukhan Rivers, which converged at Ch'unch'on to become a tributary of the Han River. Although a highway and railroad ran over the mountains from Ch'unch'on to Seoul, good roads in this zone were few. There was an improved airstrip in the valley containing Ch'unch'on. Laterally, a road wound deviously through the mountains toward Kangnung, on the east coast.

The remaining twenty-nine miles—Area F—contained the most rugged country along the 38th Parallel. Except for a few miles of coastal plain, the terrain was wild and completely mountainous. One good road ran along the coast; other roads in the zone were hazardous and practically impassable during the winter months. A railroad bed had been laid along the coast by the Japanese, but while tunnels and concrete abutments were complete, there were no tracks nor had bridges actually been built; the coastal road followed the roadbed. One second class seaport at Chumunjin and one airstrip at Kangnung posed the only strategic targets; tactically, the zone lent itself to guerrilla warfare.

In view of the terrain, the ROK Army's lack of equipment and need for training, and the guerrilla activity in South Korea, the Americans felt that it would not be practicable for ROK divisions to deploy in formal defensive positions across the width of the peninsula. It was likely, moreover, that any thrusts from the north would occur in certain predictable areas; zones B, C, and D all contained good avenues of approach. ROK Army officers believed that the Uijongbu area was the key to the city of Seoul, and that an invasion, if it came, would be concentrated there. The United States advisors therefore recommended a series of strong outpost positions blocking probable avenues of approach as the best defense along the 38th Parallel.[28]

As Korean units replaced U.S. Army units along the border in late 1948 and 1949, the ROK Army assigned sectors on the mainland to the 1st, 7th, 6th, and 8th Divisions, and stationed the Capital Division's 18th Infantry Regiment (later the 17th) on the Ongjin Peninsula. These units organized and maintained strategic strongpoints, and covered less important areas within each sector with foot or motorized patrols. As noted earlier, the majority of units in each of these divisions remained well south of the line, engaged in training or guarding installations. The remaining ROK Army divisions—the Capital (less one regiment) at Seoul, and the 2d, 3d, and 5th in the south—and the cavalry regiment, constituted the Republic of Korea Army Reserve. In the event of invasion, the units on the Ongjin Peninsula and west of the Imjin River would withdraw, leaving the western sector with a natural defense line along the Imjin River north to where the stream crossed the 38th Parallel. The reserve would then: (1) counterattack; (2) reinforce the ROK 1st and 7th Divisions; (3) reinforce the ROK 6th and 8th Divisions; or (4) suppress guerrillas in the interior of South Korea, in that priority. The U.S. Military Advisory Group believed that the ROK Army could contain and repel an invasion, unless Chinese Communist Forces participated, if it abided by this plan.

Like other U.S. installations throughout the world, the American Mission in Korea had an alert and evacuation plan ready for emergencies. This plan,[29] labeled CRULLER, was designated to safeguard the persons and property of all U.S. citizens and certain designated foreign nationals in Korea in the event of internal disturbances or of invasion from North Korea. It also provided for their evacuation along with their property, if time permitted. The plan was so drawn that it could be implemented as a joint AMIK–KMAG plan or used by either element separately. The senior KMAG G–3 Advisor was responsible for keeping the plan up to date.

---

[28] See: (1) SA Rpt, KMAG, 31 Dec 49, sec. IV, pp. 24–25; (2) SA Rpt, KMAG, 15 Jun 50, sec. IV, p. 15.
[29] P&O File 381 CR (14 Jul 49) R/F 7–28/867.

For the purposes of the plan, emergencies were classed as minor, limited, and major. A minor emergency would exist during riots and local uprisings, when the Republic of Korea Government seemed capable of handling the situation. A limited emergency would exist under the same conditions, if agencies of the Korean Government had ceased to function in certain areas. A major emergency would arrive upon the complete failure of the ROK Government to function on a national scale, and when an invasion from North Korea was imminent or in progress. The declaration of a state of emergency was the responsibility of the U.S. Ambassador to Korea, Mr. Muccio.

Under CRULLER, neither AMIK nor KMAG were to take any action during a minor emergency other than to recognize the situation. If the emergency became "limited," the Ambassador, in co-ordination with the chief of KMAG, was to help advise ROK governmental agencies until law and order were restored. He would also secure the safety of Americans and their property in the affected areas. Should the emergency become a major one, the Ambassador, after declaring the emergency, was to alert all U.S. nationals in Korea, procure such elements of the Korean security forces (under Korean command, but with KMAG advisors) as were necessary for protection, and, if he felt that conditions were sufficiently critical, order the evacuation portion of CRULLER into effect.

In this event, an alert in the form of a code word—FIRESIDE— would be transmitted in the clear by any and all means to Americans throughout South Korea. A prepared radio message would be sent at once to General MacArthur, notifying him of the situation. Military personnel would join their commands immediately, and civilian workers would be transported to their quarters while dependents returned to their billets and prepared for movement to assembly areas. All would keep radios tuned to Station WVTP for further instructions. Upon transmittal of a second code word—HIGHBALL—another message would go to the Far East Command, and the actual evacuation would commence. Americans in the vicinity of Seoul would proceed to an evacuation center at ASCOM City for processing and transportation to either the port of Inch'on or Kimp'o Airfield. A similar evacuation center would receive Americans at Pusan. U.S. nationals in other areas of South Korea would make their way either to ASCOM or to Pusan, whichever was nearer.

The advisory group's responsibilities under CRULLER were many. Besides co-ordinating the protection furnished by ROK security forces, the chief of KMAG was charged with obtaining air and surface craft for the evacuation, as well as air and naval cover, from the Far East Command. The advisory group was responsible for establishing the evacuation centers at ASCOM and Pusan. In addition, it was to set up transportation pools for further evacuation to the ports of Inch'on and Pusan and to the airfields at Kimp'o and Pusan. If water and air facilities were not available near Seoul, KMAG had to insure that the rail line running from the capital city to Pusan remained open. In addition, the advisory group was responsible for searching for Americans who failed to check through the evacuation centers.

That the North Koreans eventually intended to attack southward was doubted by few South Koreans or KMAG advisors.[30] The signs and portents were clear. But Korea now lay outside the defense perimeter established by the United States in January, and, instead of strengthening and expanding the KMAG assistance to the ROK Army, the Department of Defense was ready to reduce the staff in Korea. The U.S. administration was economy minded in the spring of 1950 and was making an effort to cut military expenses in the 1951 fiscal year by reducing special duty groups throughout the world. Thus, in April the Department of the Army directed General Roberts to prepare a plan for the gradual curtailment of the KMAG.[31]

The situation in Korea in June 1950 was hardly reassuring. The overseas tours of Roberts and several of his chief assistants were at an end, and KMAG was entering a period of transition. Since the United States appeared to be losing interest in the

[30] (1) Interv, Gen Chang, former ACofS, G-3, ROKA, 14 Oct 53. (2) Interv, Capt Schwarze, former Asst G-2 Advisor, KMAG, 14 Oct 53.
[31] (1) DA Rad, WAR 81993, 18 Apr 50. (2) SA Rpt, KMAG, 15 Jun 50, an. I. (3) Ltr, Col Bartosik to Col Butt, 28 Apr 50, sub: Orientation, copy in OFldr, sec. I. (4) Key Officer Assignments, OFldr, sec. I. See also Memo for Sec of Defense (through Maj Gen J. H. Burns), from Gen Lemnitzer, 29 Jun 50, sub: Intelligence Aspects of Korean Situation, OCMH files.

military defense of the Republic of Korea, KMAG's future was at best dubious. From the north the threats of invasion mounted. Timed usually to coincide with a date of special significance to Koreans, such as a traditional holiday or a change of season, the word barrages had been emanating from P'yongyang for over a year. In the spring of 1950 the North Koreans intensified their campaign to discredit the government of Syngman Rhee and to disrupt the ROK elections. When this failed, they proffered two unification proposals in June that the ROK Government spurned. In the meantime, behind the political and propaganda campaigns, the North Koreans finished their preparations for a serious resort to military force to achieve unification on their terms. Evidently convinced by the U.S. policy declarations on Korea that only the ROK armed forces would have to be beaten, they, backed by Soviet aid, were now ready to carry out their threats.[32]

---

[32] For an interesting discussion of the possible effects of the U.S. declarations upon Soviet-North Korean plans, see Allen S. Whiting, *China Crosses the Yalu* (New York: Macmillan Co., 1960), pp. 38 ff.

CHAPTER VI

The Coming of War

The First Assaults

In spite of a year of continuous psychological and political pressure and a number of military false alarms, the actual invasion of South Korea on 25 June 1950 came as a surprise. Many of the KMAG advisors and ROKA officers and men were on passes and spending the weekend in Seoul and other towns. Of the four divisions and one regiment assigned to the defensive positions south of the 38th Parallel, only four regiments and one battalion were actually at the front. The remainder were located in positions well to the rear.[1]

Early on the morning of the 25th, elements of the ROK 17th Regiment stationed on the Ongjin Peninsula received heavy small arms fire from the North Korean Border Constabulary brigade facing them across the Parallel. (*Map II*) About 0400 high-explosive artillery and mortar shells began to fall on the ROK lines in increasing numbers.[2] For over an hour the North Koreans continued a tremendous barrage. After the initial stunning shock, the ROK defenders rallied and returned fire, but, as dawn broke with overcast skies at 0530, elements of the North Korean (N.K.) *6th Division* passed through the Border Constabulary and attacked in force. Soon they had annihilated an entire ROK battalion and had compelled the remnants of the 17th Regiment to fall back toward the sea.[3]

As the ROK 17th retreated, KMAG sent two L–5 aircraft to the peninsula to evacuate the five U.S. advisors still with the regiment. When it became apparent that the two remaining

---

[1] For a complete account of the situation and of combat operations in Korea during the June–October 1950 period, see Appleman, *South to the Naktong, North to the Yalu.*

[2] Time and dates are local. Seoul time is fourteen hours ahead of Eastern Standard Time. Thus, 0400 on 25 June in Seoul would be 1400 EST 24 June, in Washington D.C.

[3] See Hq FEC/UNC, History of the Korean War, 25 June 1950–30 April 1951, prepared by Maj. James F. Schnabel, vol. 1, pt. 2, ch. II, MS in OCMH files. Hereinafter this source will be cited as Schnabel, Korean War.

battalions would either have to be withdrawn or be wiped out, the ROK Army sent two landing ships, tank (LST's), to join the one already lying off the Ongjin Peninsula. Col. Paik In Yup, the regimental commander, loaded his troops and most of their equipment on board the LST's, and by 1730 on 26 June the North Koreans were in complete possession of the peninsula.

Other attacks in force developed simultaneously to the east at Kaesong, Uijongbu, Ch'unch'on, and along the east coast, serving notice that the North Koreans were mounting not minor raids, but a general offensive.

At the old capital of Kaesong, just south of the 38th Parallel, units of the North Korean Border Constabulary held positions on a hill overlooking the town. The only KMAG officer in Kaesong on 25 June was Capt. Joseph R. Darrigo, advisor to the ROK 12th Regiment. His assistant, 1st Lt. William E. Hamilton, had gone to Seoul to pick up supplies, and Darrigo was alone in their quarters on the north edge of town.

Darrigo awoke early on Sunday morning to the sound of artillery shells whistling over his head and landing in Kaesong.[4] As one of the more sensitive areas along the 38th Parallel, Kaesong had been subjected to intermittent Communist artillery fire for months; only a week earlier twenty South Korean civilians had been killed by shells. The barrage this morning was unusually intense, however, so Darrigo jumped from his bed and, clad only in his trousers, ran from the house. Outside, the captain and his Korean houseboy jumped into a jeep and drove south into Kaesong. They came under small arms fire upon reaching the center of town, for enemy troops were already entering the city, but they managed to escape without injury and continued southward to Munsan-ni. Darrigo remained there all day with Col. Paik Sun Yup, commander of the ROK 1st Division, who was bringing up his troops from their garrison points— some from the outskirts of Seoul. Kaesong was in enemy hands by 0900 that morning.

Farther to the east, the North Koreans launched an even more powerful attack. The N.K. *3d* and *4th Divisions,* supported by

[4] Based on Interv, Capt Darrigo with Lt Col Roy E. Appleman, 5 Aug 53, and ltrs from Darrigo to Appleman in OCMH files. See also Ltr, Hamilton to Appleman, 9 Jul 53, and Ltr, Lt Col Lloyd H. Rockwell to Appleman, 21 May 54.

strong units of the N.K. *105th Armored Brigade,* struck south
early in the morning on a wide front south of Ch'orwon. One
armor-infantry column stabbed at Uijongbu from due north, a
second moved relentlessly down the Kumhwa-Uijongbu highway from the northeast. Considering the enemy superiority in
men, armor, and heavy guns, the ROK 7th Division fought
well. The enemy took rather heavy casualties but pressed on
toward Uijongbu.

On the morning of 26 June three KMAG advisors left Seoul
for Uijongbu, ostensibly to verify or disprove reports that Russians were operating Soviet tanks within the Communist invad-
ing forces. The advisors actually went north to observe a scheduled counterattack by the ROK 2d Division, elements of which
had arrived from Taejon during the night. The counterattack
failed to develop, primarily because of the division commander's
procrastination but also because important elements of the 2d
Division failed to arrive in time. By noon Uijongbu was under
heavy enemy artillery fire. The town fell that night.[5]

In the Ch'unch'on sector, the enemy crossed the border in
two places and launched a double-barreled attack toward the
town. The N.K. *7th Division* came down from the northwest and
the N.K. *2d Division* moved in from the north. Elements of the
ROK 6th Division were forced to give ground, and the invaders
penetrated Ch'unch'on several hours later. Stubborn counterat-
tacks by the ROK 6th Division prevented the enemy from cap-
turing the town, however, and the North Koreans had to call
upon additional armor and artillery to bolster their attacks. In the
meantime, the withdrawal of the ROK forces to the west exposed the flanks of the ROK 6th Division, and the valiant defenders had to pull back on 28 June. Nevertheless, they had
delayed the enemy offensive for three days and inflicted heavy
losses on the North Korean *2d Division.*[6] And perhaps, more important, they were able to withdraw in an orderly fashion with
their units and equipment intact.

---

[5] (1) Interv, Col Wright, 24 Nov 53. (2) Interv, Schwarze with Schnabel, 13 Mar
51. (3) Ltr, Col James S. Gallagher, 5 Oct 53. (4) Incl 2 to Ltr, Col Greenwood,
22 Feb 54.
   [6] Ltr, Lt Col Thomas D. McPhail to Col Appleman, 28 Jun 54. See also Appleman,
South to the Naktong, North to the Yalu, ch. III.

On the remote east coast the ROK 8th Division's 10th Regiment also came under attack. The senior advisor to this division, Maj. Gerald E. Larsen, was at the division headquarters in Kangnung with two other KMAG officers and three KMAG enlisted men. Maj. George D. Kessler was at Samch'ok with the headquarters of the division's one other regiment, the 21st. Two battalions of the 21st Regiment were far to the south, engaged in counterguerrilla operations; the regiment's mortars, antitank guns (57-mm.), and heavy machine guns, however, were all at Samch'ok, where a regimental weapons school was in operation.[7]

Korean officers awakened Major Kessler at daybreak on 25 June, and delivered a radio message from Larsen. The message simply stated that the North Koreans were attacking the 10th Regiment on the 38th Parallel. At about the same time, Korean police brought word that ships were landing men at two points along the coast north and south of Samch'ok. Kessler and his counterpart quickly drove north to a hilltop near Mukhojin-ni, whence they saw junks and sampans lying offshore and several hundred men milling about on the coastal road. They then went south to the reported site of the other landing, below Samch'ok, where they observed much the same thing. When they arrived back in Samch'ok they saw ships circling offshore there, apparently preparing to land more men. ROK troops brought antitank guns to the coast and opened fire. When at least two boats had been sunk, the naval force withdrew.

At this point, Major Kessler did not realize that a full-scale invasion of South Korea was in progress since guerrilla infiltration of ROK territory had been going on for years. The troops that landed on the coast that day had acted like guerrillas rather than regular units. But the North Korean *5th Division* and two battalions of an independent unit were moving southward from the 38th Parallel at this same time.

Late on Sunday afternoon, the commander of the ROK 21st Regiment received orders to report to 8th Division headquarters at Kangnung. Kessler, still unaware of the general nature of the North Korean operations, decided to accompany his counter-

[7] Based on Interv, Lt Col George D. Kessler, 24 Feb 54.

part. Since the coastal road was apparently blocked north of
Samch'ok, the two officers decided to go inland to another north-
south road and circle around to Kangnung through the mountains. As often happened in Korea, however, the road shown on
the maps actually was not there. After traveling for some time
the two men were forced to abandon their vehicle and walk for
several miles to a rural police box, from which they called the
8th Division and arranged for a vehicle to be sent as far south
as possible along the route they intended to take. They arrived
in Kangnung late the following afternoon.[8]

There Kessler learned that attacks had been general all along
the 38th Parallel. Major Larsen was surprised to see him, having thought him captured by the enemy troops who had landed
the preceding day near Samch'ok. Larsen informed him at this
time that the senior advisor to the ROK 6th Division, Lt. Col
Thomas D. McPhail, had radioed instructions for the 8th Division advisors to join him at Wonju. Larsen had sent the other
members of his detachment on ahead with their equipment.
Before Larsen and Kessler left Kangnung, they helped the ROK
8th Division commander plan a route of withdrawal for his
division, south through P'yongch'ang and Tanyang to Pusan.
They stressed that he should stay in contact with the ROK 6th
Division on his left if possible and co-ordinate his withdrawal
with that unit.

The Fall of Seoul

Probably the first American in Seoul to learn of the invasion
was the KMAG radio operator, who received a message from
the Ongjin advisory detachment at about 0600 on 25 June.
Soon all the KMAG officers and men in Seoul were hurrying to
their posts. Initially, there was a decided air of scepticism among
the KMAG staff since border raids had been common for some
time. But when reports of the other attacks all along the Parallel came filtering in during the next few hours, the doubt faded.
The number and size of the offensives coupled with the fact that
the attacks were being made along the natural invasion routes

---

[8] Interv, Col Kessler.

into South Korea quickly ruled
out the possibility of mere
raids.[9]

Lt. Col. Carl H. Sturies was
in temporary command of the
advisory group.[10] Upon General
Roberts' departure from Korea
ten days earlier, the chief of
staff, Colonel Wright, had assumed command of KMAG
pending the arrival of Maj.
Gen. Frank A. Keating from
the United States. General
Keating had chosen to retire,
however, and the Department
of the Army had directed

COLONEL WRIGHT

Wright, who was on orders to attend the Industrial College of
the Armed Forces in the United States, to remain until a new
chief arrived. On this fateful weekend Wright unfortunately was
in Japan, bidding farewell to his family whom he expected soon
to follow to the United States.[11]

Once the members of the KMAG staff had accepted the fact
that the attacks probably constituted a major offensive, they
recommended to the Koreans that the defense plan drawn up
months before be put into effect. This, it will be remembered,
called for evacuating the Ongjin Peninsula, for the units west of
the Imjin River to withdraw to the south bank, and for the reserve divisions in the south to come north and counterattack on
order. The ROK Army Chief of Staff, Maj. Gen. Chae Byong
Duk, agreed, and his staff immediately set about alerting the
divisions.[12]

[9] (1) Interv, Schwarze with Schnabel, 13 Mar 51. (2) Ltr, Lt Col George R.
Sedberry, Jr., 22 Dec 53. (3) Ltr, Col Sturies, 9 Jan 54. (4) Ltr, Maj Ray B. May,
11 Feb 54. (5) Incl 2 to Ltr, Col Greenwood, 22 Feb 54. Exact times differ in the
various accounts and have been reconciled as much as possible.

[10] (1) GO 8, Hq KMAG, 20 Jun 50. (2) Ltr, Col Sedberry. (3) Ltr, Col Sturies.
(4) Ltr, Maj May. (5) Ltr, Col Greenwood.

[11] (1) Interv, Col Wright, 24 Nov 53. See also: Dept of State Msg 258 (sgd Webb)
to AMEMBASSY, Seoul, 18 Mar 50; Msg 731, Muccio to Secy of State, 22 May 50,
OCMH files.

[12] (1) Ltr, Col Sedberry. (2) Ltr, Maj May. (3) Incl 2 to Ltr, Col Greenwood.

Col. James S. Gallagher, senior advisor to the ROK 2d Division at Taejon, thus learned of the invasion at about 0800, when the 2d Division received orders to be ready to move north. KMAG headquarters telephoned about an hour later, with instructions for him and the members of his detachment to go north with the division. Since several of the advisors were in other towns of Ch'ungch'ong-namdo Province—at Ch'ongju, Yongju, and Anjung-ni—Gallagher notified them over the division's telephones and radios, and by early afternoon the entire division was in motion. The first trainload of ROK 2d Division troops from Taejon, including the division headquarters and elements of the ROK 5th Regiment, left with their American advisors for Seoul at 1430. The ROK 5th Division, farther south at Kwangju, received similar instructions early in the day and by nightfall was also on its way north with its advisors.[13]

The KMAG officers in Seoul remained with their Korean counterparts all day Sunday, watching an ominous picture develop on the situation maps. Advisors and Koreans alike were tense and excited. During the morning North Korean fighter planes strafed Seoul and Kimp'o Airfield, and the last doubts that the attacks along the 38th Parallel were part of a major offensive vanished.[14] Ambassador Muccio met with President Rhee during the day, and Rhee expressed great concern about the need for more arms and ammunition for his forces. The KMAG staff sent an urgent message to General MacArthur's headquarters, requesting that an emergency ten-day supply of ammunition to support 90 105-mm. howitzers, 700 60-mm. mortars, and 40,000 .30-caliber carbines be shipped to Pusan without delay. Ambassador Muccio also sent a message to Tokyo, in which he expressed his opinion that it would be catastrophic for the United States to permit the South Koreans to succumb for lack of ammunition.[15]

---

[13] Ltrs, Col Gallagher, 5 Oct 53 and 2 Nov 53. (2) Ltrs, Col Sedberry, Maj May, Col Greenwood.

[14] (1) Interv, Col Greenwood, 2 Feb 54. (2) Interv, Schwarze with Schnabel. (3) Ltr, Maj May. (4) Ltr, Col Sturies. (5) Incl 2 to Ltr, Col Greenwood.

[15] (1) Msg, USMILAT to CINCFE, 250425Z, 25 Jun 50. (2) Msg, USMILAT to CINCFE, 250530Z, 25 Jun 50. Both Msgs cited in Schnabel, Korean War, MS, ch. IV, p. 5.

Of particular concern to the members of the Advisory Group, now that the invasion had come, was the question of their mission. The terms of reference furnished a year earlier by the Department of the Army had not specified what KMAG's mission would be in the event of war.[16] Nor could Ambassador Muccio enlighten them on this point. Actually, there were three alternatives that immediately came to mind: they could take up arms and actively help the South Koreans repel the invaders; they could advise the ROK Army in combat operations; or they could leave Korea and abandon the republic to its fate. These alternatives involved questions of U.S. national policy and had to be decided on the highest levels of the United States Government.[17]

Still another possible course of action was suggested by Ambassador Muccio. He proposed that the entire American mission, civilian and military, gather at the Embassy and claim a status of diplomatic immunity if and when the North Korean Army captured Seoul. AMIK and KMAG officials succeeded in convincing Mr. Muccio that any of the other alternatives was preferable.[18]

In the absence of precise guidance from Washington, the Ambassador made preparations for evacuating American women and children to Japan. Early on 25 June he sent the U.S. naval attaché, Comdr. John P. Seifert, to Inch'on to make a survey of shipping. Seifert commandeered one of two vessels in the harbor, a Norwegian ship, the *Reinholt*. Although the *Reinholt* carried a cargo of fertilizer it was the cleaner vessel, and the crew began immediately to unload the cargo and clean up the ship. KMAG meanwhile sent officers and men to ASCOM City to set up a processing center as called for in the disaster plan. Arrangements were completed by midafternoon.[19]

As also prescribed by the disaster plan, American families in and around Seoul remained near their radios, waiting for news

[16] See DA Rad, WARX 90992, CSGPO to Chief, KMAG, 1 Jul 49.
[17] (1) Interv, Col Greenwood. (2) Ltr, Maj May. (3) Ltr, Col Sturies. (4) Incl 2 to Ltr, Col Greenwood.
[18] (1) Incl 2 to Ltr, Col Greenwood. (2) Ltr, Maj May.
[19] (1) Ltr, Maj May. (2) Interv, Col Greenwood. (3) Interv, Capt Schwarze, 20 Jan 54. (4) Capt. Walter Karig, USNR, Comdr. Malcolm W. Cagle, USN, and Lt. Comdr. Frank A. Manson, USN, "Battle Report," vol. VI, *The War in Korea* (New York: Rinehart and Co., Inc., 1952) pp. 25–27.

of a possible evacuation. Armed Forces Radio Station WVTP broadcasted bulletins every quarter hour during the day. Just after midnight Ambassador Muccio placed CRULLER in effect and notified the Departments of State and Defense. A WVTP radio bulletin directed all dependent women and children to be at the motor pool at Camp Sobinggo within three hours, whence they would be transported to Inch'on. The exodus of American families from Seoul to ASCOM City, and then to Inch'on, proceeded in an orderly manner, and by 1800 on Monday (26 June) all evacuees were aboard the *Reinholt* under the protection of circling U.S. Air Force planes from bases in Japan. The captain and crew of the *Reinholt* were magnificent during the hectic weekend, seemingly performing a miracle in preparing a ship normally accommodating twelve passengers to receive more than 700 women and children. Although most of the evacuees made the journey to Japan crammed into damp holds or sitting on deck, they traveled as comfortably as the ship's accommodations permitted.[20]

Colonel Wright returned from Japan early on Monday morning. He had learned of the invasion while attending church in Tokyo the day before, when a breathless messenger tiptoed down the aisle and informed him that he had "better get back to Korea." Upon arriving in Seoul, Colonel Wright hastened to his headquarters and learned that KMAG's dependent families were being loaded onto trucks and buses and taken to Inch'on.[21] As conditions grew worse north of Seoul, Wright decided to prepare for the movement of KMAG personnel south, with the idea that they could be evacuated by air or water from some point between Seoul and Pusan if necessary. The Department of the Army instructed MacArthur, who was responsible for KMAG evacuation, to select the course of action that offered the best chance of success.[22]

---

[20] (1) Interv, Col Wright, 24 Nov 53. (2) Interv, Capt Schwarze. (3) Major Activities, Opns Div, G–3, in History of Department of the Army Activities Relating to the Korean Conflict, 25 Jun 50–8 Sep 51, OCMH files. (4) See also Karig *et al., The War in Korea,* pp. 25–27.

[21] Interv, Col Wright, 24 Nov 53.

[22] See: (1) Msgs, ROB 002 and 003, Chief, KMAG, to DEPTAR, 26 Jun 50, OPS 091 Korea, sec. 1–C, case 14; (2) Msg, WAR 74140, DEPTAR to CINCFE, 26 Jun 50.

But, although the U.S. leaders in Washington were willing to permit the KMAG staff to evacuate Korea eventually if conditions deteriorated, the invasion had set in motion a train of events that dictated that KMAG remain as long as possible. The North Korean action had produced a reawakening of U.S. interest in Korea and a complete reversal of policy. At the request of the United States, the U.N. Security Council had convened at 1400, 25 June, in New York and had passed a resolution that branded the North Korean attack a breach of the peace and called for the immediate withdrawal of North Korean forces to the 38th Parallel.[23] The resolution requested all U.N. members to render every assistance to the United Nations in the execution of the resolution and to refrain from giving aid to the North Koreans. Since then the Joint Chiefs of Staff in Washington and Mac-Arthur in Tokyo had engaged in a number of teletype conferences to work out a U.S. course of action. MacArthur was informed that the Secretary of State wanted KMAG liaison officers to remain with their units as long as these were effective in combat. The Far East commander told the JCS that the ammunition that KMAG had requested on the first day was already being loaded on ships and planes at Yokohama and Tachikawa.[24]

Late on 26 June, Ambassador Muccio ordered nonessential members of the American mission to leave Korea and requested military aircraft from the Far East Command for their evacuation. Several hours later, following repeated recommendations by members of his staff, Colonel Wright decided to send to Japan all nonessential KMAG personnel, along with the group's personnel records and files. Still uncertain as to what was expected of the advisory group, Wright felt that little time remained for a decision on the matter, and also that a last-minute KMAG evacuation could be carried out more efficiently if the bulk of the group was gone. He therefore designated thirty-three key officers and enlisted men from his general staff and

[23] The Soviet delegate was boycotting the Security Council meetings at this time in protest against the continued seating of the delegate of the Republic of China instead of a representative of Communist China. Thus, he was not present and could not veto the resolution.

[24] Department of State, *United States Policy in the Korean Crisis* (Washington, 1950), pp. 1–2. See also Teleconference, TT 3418, between JCS, Secy Army and CINCFE, 26 Jun 50, cited in Schnabel, Korean War, ch. II, p. 11.

communications sections to remain with him, and sent the balance of the group by truck to an airstrip at Suwon. It was his intention that those who remained would stay with the Republic of Korea Army as long as any useful purpose could be served, and so long as no undue jeopardy was involved. In the event of imminent capture, they were to join the Ambassador's party and attempt to gain diplomatic immunity. Far East Air Force planes began arriving at Kimp'o and Suwon early on 27 June and shuttled back and forth during the day flying out AMIK personnel, missionaries, certain foreign nationals, and members of the military advisory group.[25]

Ambassador Muccio and his staff left Seoul for Suwon shortly after 0900 on 27 June, after notifying General MacArthur's headquarters that the Embassy radio station was about to be destroyed.[26] Later in the day, without consulting or notifying KMAG, the entire headquarters of the Republic of Korea Army moved south to Sihung, half way between Seoul and Suwon. The Americans had noticed considerable excitement among the members of the Korean staff but had had no real hint as to their purpose until they began leaving.[27] When the move became known, Colonel Wright gathered his own staff and started south to try and persuade the Koreans to return to Seoul. The ROK Army headquarters' flight left the ROK units engaged north of the Capital City without communications to headquarters and alarmed the civilian populace in Seoul.

Shortly after the KMAG convoy crossed the Han River, Colonel Wright received his first definite assurance that outside help was on the way. A message from General MacArthur came over the KMAG command radio (SCR–399) located in a 2½-ton truck in the column and informed Wright that the Joint Chiefs of Staff had directed MacArthur to assume operational control of all U.S. military activities in Korea, including

[25] (1) Interv, Col Wright. (2) Ltr, Maj May. (3) Incl 2 to Ltr, Col Greenwood. See also: Msg, Chief, KMAG, to CINCFE, MC–IN 79213, 27 Jun 50, copy in OPS File 091 Korea, case 14/5; Hist, AG Sec, KMAG, 10 Aug 50, KMAG File AG 314.7.

[26] (1) Interv, Maj Gen George I. Back, former Chief Signal Officer, GHQ FEC, 16 Dec 53. (2) Interv, Col William M. Thames, former member of GHQ FEC, Signal Sec, 16 Dec 53. (3) See also Incl 2 to Ltr, Col Greenwood.

[27] Interv, Col Wright.

KMAG. Furthermore, he was sending a team—later known as the General Headquarters Advance Command and Liaison Group (short title: GHQ, ADCOM)—under Brig. Gen. John H. Church to Korea.[28]

General MacArthur's promise of help was enough to convince the ROK Army chief of staff that he should return with his headquarters to Seoul. While at Sihung, Colonel Wright received another radio message from MacArthur, exhorting him to "be of good cheer" and stating that "momentous decisions" were pending.[29] Interpreting these two messages to mean that KMAG personnel should remain on duty in Korea, Wright dispatched an officer to the Suwon airstrip to recall the members of the advisory group who had not yet left for Japan. These, about thirty in number, returned to Seoul with Colonel Wright and the KMAG staff, and by 1800 that evening both the Republic of Korea Army headquarters and the U.S. Military Advisory Group were again established north of the Han River.[30]

Colonel Wright, having had no sleep since he left Japan, went to his quarters at Camp Sobinggo late on Tuesday night to rest. Sometime around 0200 on 28 June, Colonel Vieman (G–4 Advisor) awakened him and informed him that ROK divisions were withdrawing south through Seoul and that the Republic of Korea Army headquarters was again leaving the city. The ROK Army chief of staff, General Chae, had left about an hour earlier. Wright got up and started for the headquarters building, a few hundred yards away. En route, he saw the sky light up to the south and heard a tremendous explosion in the direction of the only Han River bridge over which vehicles and travelers on foot could still pass from Seoul to the south.[31]

Korean engineers under American supervision had wired the structure for demolition a day or two earlier. The bridge was a

[28] (1) Interv, Col Wright. (2) Msg, CINCFE to Chief, KMAG, ZX 49396, 27 Jun 50, G–3 091 Korea, sec. II, case 26.
[29] Although several sources (Wright, Greenwood, Sedberry, and May) mention this second message, the writer has not found a copy in the files available to him.
[30] (1) Interv, Col Wright. (2) Ltr, Maj May. (3) Interv, Schwarze with Schnabel. (4) Ltr, Lt Col Sedberry. (5) Incl 2 to Ltr, Col Greenwood. (6) See also Msg, CINCFE to DA, CX 56847, 27 Jun 50, OPS 091 Korea, case 14/9.
[31] (1) Interv, Col Wright. (2) Interv, Col Lewis D. Vieman with Col Appleman, 16 Jun 54. (3) MS prepared by Lt Col Lewis D. Vieman, 15 Feb 51, in OCMH files. (4) See also Ltr, Col Sedberry.

large, four-span affair, and the engineers had packed great quantities of explosives around the concrete abutments. The bridge was to be blown only after the capital had fallen to the enemy and after the ROK soldiers and friendly civilians north of the river had crossed it to safety. When Colonel Wright reached the ROK Army headquarters building, he found the Koreans dismayed and in various stages of departure. The bridge had been exploded from the south bank soon after General Chae's departure, and when the explosion had occurred more than a thousand ROK soldiers and civilians had been on that part of the span that was over water. From five to eight hundred were killed outright or drowned. Three American newspaper correspondents were wounded by the blast. Vehicles had been crossing in several lanes, bumper to bumper, and most of these were destroyed.[32]

The demolition of the bridge cost not only the lives and equipment destroyed by the blast, but also dealt a heavy blow to the ROK Army units left on the north bank of the river. With the major escape route cut off, they and their equipment were marooned. Disintegration of morale among soldiers and civilians alike in the Seoul area was rapid, and panic and confusion followed.[33]

Realizing that the end was near, Colonel Wright at 0300 ordered the remainder of the advisory group to leave Seoul. Stray rounds of enemy artillery fire were landing in the Sobinggo area, and small arms and automatic weapons fire was clearly audible in the distance. Colonel Vieman had formed a convoy of approximately fifty KMAG vehicles loaded with gasoline, food, and limited amounts of personal clothing. After burning certain classified files, the Americans climbed aboard jeeps and trucks, and the KMAG convoy moved off in the darkness toward Seoul's East Gate.

---

[32] (1) Intervs, Wright and Greenwood, and Schwarze with Schnabel. (2) Ltrs, Col Scott, Lt Col Sedberry, Maj May. (3) Vieman MS. (4) Interv, Maj Gen Chung Chung Kuk, 24 Oct 53. Many KMAG personnel who were present in Seoul at the time of the explosion are convinced that Chae personally ordered the bridge blown after he had crossed. There was also a possibility that the Vice Minister of Defense had given the order. A ROK Army court-martial later tried and executed the Army chief engineer as being the responsible officer. For a discussion of the affair, see Appleman, *South to the Naktong, North to the Yalu*, ch. III.

[33] (1) Interv, Schwarze with Schnabel. (2) Interv, Col Wright *et al.*

Another bridge crossed the Han River about eight miles east of the city. The KMAG group hoped to pass over the structure to the south bank. On the way to that point, however, ROK soldiers informed the Americans that the bridge was gone, so the column turned around and returned to the Sobinggo area. A party of KMAG officers and men then went to the main blown bridge to determine if it could be crossed by foot, and also to see if ferries, which normally operated some distance upstream, were in operation. The results of the reconnaissance were disappointing. At this point, Col. Lee Chi Up of the ROK Army appeared and stated that he could get the Americans across the river. The convoy slowly edged its way through milling throngs of terrified Koreans to the banks of a dike along the river east of the ferries. Boats of all description, rafts, logs, and swimming humanity crowded the stream. Colonel Lee, by putting a bullet through the shirt of a boatman, persuaded a large raft to come in and take the Americans aboard. Many other Koreans were trying to obtain passage by the same expedient, which made the crossing site a dangerous locale.[34]

Although it was clearly impossible to save all of his vehicles, Colonel Wright was determined to save the radio truck. He therefore kept with him two officers and three noncommissioned officers, and sent the rest of the group across to the south bank. The six who remained procured another large raft and, after considerable difficulty, managed to get the cumbersome vehicle down the steep bank of the dike and onto the raft. Then they crossed themselves. By this time it was getting light and North Korean artillery fire was falling on the south bank.[35]

While Wright and his group traveled over back roads to Suwon in the radio truck, the main body of KMAG advisors from Seoul pushed on cross country on foot. Colonel Lee, who had accompanied this group, commandeered a ROK Army jeep and drove on ahead to secure transportation for the remainder of the party.[36]

---

[34] (1) Interv, Col Wright. (2) Interv, Schwarze with Schnabel. (3) Vieman MS. (4) Ltr, Maj May, 23 Apr 54.

[35] Interv and Ltrs, Wright, Schwarze, Vieman, May.

[36] (1) Interv, Col Wright. (2) Ltr, Maj May, 23 Apr 54. (3) Interv, Schwarze with Schnabel. (4) Vieman MS. (5) Marguerite Higgins, *War in Korea,* (New York: Doubleday & Co., Inc., 1951), pp. 28–29. Colonel Wright states that Miss Higgins' account of events during this period seems to be essentially correct.

As they trekked south, the first indications of the help promised
by MacArthur appeared overhead. U.S. Air Force planes roared
by and strafed and bombed Seoul.

The commitment of U.S. aid had swiftly followed the passing
of the second Security Council resolution on 27 June. When the
North Koreans paid no attention to the U.N. demand that they
withdraw to the 38th Parallel, the Security Council recommended that all U.N. members furnish such assistance to the
Republic of Korea as was necessary to repel the North Korean
attack and to restore international peace and security in the area.
President Truman had swiftly ordered MacArthur to use U.S.
air and sea forces to give the ROK forces cover and support and
had instructed the Seventh Fleet to neutralize Formosa.[37] The air
support could not save Seoul at this late juncture, for the North
Koreans were already on the outskirts. The remnants of the ROK
forces fought well under the circumstances and delayed the capture of the city until 28 June, when they were forced to abandon
the defense.

Behind the Lines

While the North Korean forces pushed forward on all fronts,
the KMAG advisors farther to the south sought to help organize
the rear areas for the defense of the Republic of Korea. On 25
June the senior advisor to the ROK 3d Division, Lt. Col. Rollins
S. Emmerich, was in Chingju with the 3d Division commander,
Col. Yu Sung Yul, attending a conference on counterguerrilla
operations. On their way back to Taegu, Korean policemen
stopped their vehicles, shouting excitedly that the division commander was to phone Taegu immediately.[38] While Colonel Yu
talked with his headquarters, interpreters informed Colonel Emmerich that war had come to Korea. The convoy reached Taegu
at about 1800, and Emmerich learned that the ROK 3d Division's 22d Regiment, engineer combat battalion, and antitank

---

[37] U.S. Senate, 83d Congress, 1st Session, *The United States and the Korean Problem: Documents, 1943–1953,* (Washington, 1953), pp. 36–37.

[38] Unless otherwise indicated, this account of events in Taegu and Pusan is based
on a document entitled Early History of the Korean War 1950, prepared by Col.
Rollins S. Emmerich for OCMH. Colonel Emmerich writes that Maj. Percy Austin
and Maj. Harold Slater, former members of KMAG, assisted him in piecing together
the story. Hereafter this document will be cited as Emmerich MS.

KMAG GROUP LEAVING SEOUL

company had been ordered to Seoul by General Chae and had
long since departed. Three KMAG officers had gone with them.

Great uncertainty mingled with excitement that night in
Taegu. Communications with the north were poor, and no one
knew how far into South Korea the Communists had penetrated. Most reports came through ROK National Police channels and were vague and contradictory. Wild rumors circulated
about the city. Since the Taegu area was a center of guerrilla
activity, there were widespread fears of an uprising by under-
ground elements or of a guerrilla attack on the town. The
provincial governor, the ROK 3d Division staff, Colonel Emmerich, the local chief of police, his American advisor, Maj.
Kirby Guillory, and the mayor of Taegu met several times
during the evening in an effort to devise a plan of defense in
case either event should occur.

Late on Sunday night KMAG headquarters radioed word
that American women and children were to be evacuated to
Japan, and all but two American families in Taegu left immediately for Pusan accompanied by ROK Army military police. The two remaining families waited until the following

morning when, also escorted by military police, they boarded
a heavily loaded freight train going to the south. By this time
masses of Koreans were on the move toward Pusan, and trains
and roads were crowded. After their families had departed, the
advisors at Taegu waited uncertainly, not knowing what was
expected of them. Police reports from Suwon indicated that
the situation north of Seoul was grave, with some ROK units
in full retreat.

Early on 27 June Ambassador Muccio radioed that the 3d
Division advisors were to leave their counterparts and report
to Pusan. The advisors formed a convoy of eleven military vehicles and one civilian car, and Emmerich gave instructions
concerning what each person would do in the event of a guerrilla attack or in case the column ran into a roadblock. He
also issued Special Services shotguns to supplement the group's
individual arms. As was the case in Seoul a little more than
twelve hours later, when the KMAG headquarters group wended
its way through streets congested with frightened people, the
members of the Taegu detachment found it difficult to leave
the city. Anxious Koreans begged to go with the Americans,
and some tried to climb aboard their vehicles. Much of the
time it was possible to move only with the help of the Korean police, who escorted the column through the narrow streets.
Nor did passage improve during the remainder of the trip to
Pusan; late in the evening a heavy rain began to fall, and roads
became muddy and treacherous.

The column reached Pusan the following morning, after
abandoning a jeep and trailer and one three-quarter-ton truck.
In the city the group made for Hialeah, a compound of seventy-
five houses normally occupied by members of the American
mission and their families. As the convoy approached the compound, Colonel Emmerich and his group saw hundreds of Koreans milling about the high wire enclosure, many of whom
had American household furnishings in their possession. A commissary building inside had been broken open, and Koreans
were throwing canned food over the fence. Others were push-
ing private cars, jeeps, trucks, and ambulances out through

the gate of the compound, loaded with furniture and personal belongings.

Emmerich's group dispersed the Koreans by firing weapons over their heads and went into the enclosure to see if any Americans remained inside. At the Club Flamingo they found Mr. Thomas Reiner and several other members of the local ECA office, huddled around a tiny ham radio. Reiner was in touch with GHQ in Tokyo and was transmitting such information as he possessed. Emmerich's party also found Capt. Gerald D. Putnam, advisor to the ROK 23d Regiment, in his quarters. Putnam had processed evacuees aboard two vessels in Pusan Harbor, and had not slept since the preceding Saturday night. From him Colonel Emmerich learned that dependents from Pusan, Taejon,[39] and Taegu had boarded an American ship, the *Pioneer Dale,* the day before and had sailed for Japan. Another American vessel, the *Letitia Lykes,* loaded with AMIK personnel and KMAG advisors from scattered points in southern Korea, was still in port.

Emmerich also learned that he could make contact with Tokyo by telephone from Reiner's ECA office. Since there had been no further word from Seoul regarding evacuation, and none at all from Japan, he decided to call General Headquarters, Far East Command, and ask for instructions. For security he first gathered the members of his party and took them to Reiner's office on the third floor of a downtown store building and had them set up sleeping quarters there. Then he called Tokyo and talked with the GHQ Chief Signal Officer, Brig. Gen. George I. Back.

If Colonel Emmerich in Pusan knew little of the situation in Korea, General Headquarters in Tokyo knew less. General Back's first questions concerned what Emmerich knew and whether information was reaching Pusan from the battle front. At first both officers tried to preserve some sort of signal security by garbling their conversation with similies; however, in view of the emergency and of the importance of time, they soon dispensed with unnecessary wordage. General Back told Emmerich to stand by for instructions.[40]

[39] See Ltr, Col Gallagher, 5 Oct 53.
[40] (1) Interv, Maj Gen George I. Back, 16 Dec 53. (2) Emmerich MS, pp. 12–13.

With the fate of KMAG headquarters in Seoul unknown, Colonel Emmerich next decided, as the senior officer in Pusan, to organize a headquarters with the KMAG personnel available to him. Early on 28 June he published a general order establishing the Provisional Korean Military Advisory Group Headquarters, Pusan, Korea. A following special order designated himself as commanding officer and appointed a staff of seven KMAG officers and four (volunteer) ECA civilian employees to whom he assigned tasks of a logistical nature. After activating the headquarters, Emmerich sent Captain Putnam out to the *Letitia Lykes* to order ashore those KMAG personnel who were aboard.

The long distance telephone line between Pusan and Japan was in constant use during the following few days. Maj. Gen. Charles A. Willoughby's G–2 office in Tokyo called with requests for information, which Colonel Emmerich could fill only by repeating vague reports submitted by the Korean National Police. The advisors in Pusan phoned weather reports twice daily to the U.S. Air Force Base at Itazuke. There were calls to and from General Back, and the U.S. naval headquarters of Vice Adm. C. Turner Joy and Rear Adm. Albert K. Morehouse in Tokyo. Meanwhile, the advisors to the ROK 6th and 8th Divisions arrived from Wonju, after traveling southward day and night by jeep.[41]

The Provisional KMAG headquarters grew quickly. By 29 June Colonel Emmerich was in command of 22 officers, 34 enlisted men, 6 ECA volunteers, and 2 missionaries (also volunteers). On that day he sent three officers and three enlisted men to Taejon, two officers to rejoin the ROK 3d Division at Taegu, and a few communications personnel to the Korean Coast Guard base at Chinhae. He also appointed an administrative officer and detachment commander and ordered housing, messing, and motor pool facilities organized at the American compound (Hialeah) in Pusan.

------

[41] (1) Interv, Col Kessler. (2) Emmerich MS, p. 16.

Efforts To Aid Stabilization

General Church and his team left Tokyo early on 27 June with orders to proceed to Seoul. Initially, this group was simply a survey and liaison section of some fifteen officers, who were supposed to determine the minimum amounts and types of aid required by the ROK forces to hold the Seoul-Kimp'o-Inch'on area. They were also advised that the possible use of U.S. ground troops should be taken into consideration, although no decision had been made as yet on that score. En route to Korea, General Church was told to land at Suwon instead, where his group would be the General Headquarters Advance Command and Liaison Group. Church was welcomed at Suwon by Ambassador Muccio and set up a command post in the buildings of an agricultural college west of the town. The only KMAG personnel then in Suwon were the members of a radio team attached to the Ambassador. General Church established radio contact with Tokyo and spent the night making plans with his staff for stabilizing the situation and reorganizing the Republic of Korea Army.[42]

The Chief of Staff of the ROK Army and his staff appeared in Suwon early on 28 June and set up headquarters in the building with the GHQ, ADCOM, command post. Members of the U.S. Military Advisory Group arrived in groups during the day, and by dusk all who had fled Seoul early that morning had been accounted for. Many had not slept for several nights and were exhausted.[43]

[42] (1) Interv, Lt Col Winfred A. Ross (Signal Officer, GHQ ADCOM), 16 Dec 53. (2) Informal notes entitled History of ADCOM, by Lt Col Olinto Mark Barsanti (G–1 GHQ ADCOM), attached as Incl to Ltr, Hq FEC to CG USAFFE, Attn: Mil Hist Sec, 20 Mar 53, sub: Hist of ADCOM, OCMH files. (3) Opns Instructions to Gen Church, 26 Jun 50, from G–2 Sec GHQ FEC, OCMH files. (4) Directive from Brig Gen Edwin K. Wright to Gen Church, received by phone at Itazuke, Japan, 1425, 27 Jun 50, OCMH files.
[43] (1) Interv, Col Sterling Wright. (2) Interv, Capt Schwarze with Maj Schnabel. (3) Interv, Maj Frank W. Lukas, 21 Apr 54. (4) Interv, Capt Lloyd C. Schuknecht, Jr., former GHQ ADCOM Crypto Officer, 18 Dec 53. (5) Informal notes, Lt Col Barsanti, cited in preceding note. Lt. Col. Ross recalls a message delivered to him at Suwon by an enlisted KMAG radio operator. The message consisted of several wavy lines scrawled across a message blank; in his extreme fatigue the soldier had thought that he was writing words and sentences.

General MacArthur visited Suwon on 29 June and went north to inspect the battle area along the Han River. Before his return to Japan he announced to the ADCOM group that he intended to recommend to the Joint Chiefs of Staff that he be given permission to commit U.S. ground forces in Korea. His request reached the President the following day and was quickly approved.[44]

Before the first U.S. ground troops reached Korea, the Americans pulled out of Suwon. While General Church and Colonel Wright were out of town on other missions, misleading reports of an approaching enemy column posed the possibility of an attack on the night of 30 June. What later turned out to be a false alarm caused the U.S. staff to pack up hurriedly and travel through eighty miles of driving rain to Taejon. This time it was the Americans who left the ROK Army headquarters behind and decamped hastily. At Taejon KMAG and ADCOM set up a new headquarters on 1 July, and Wright sent five of his advisors back to Suwon to encourage the Koreans and to send back information.[45]

By the end of June, the North Koreans were in possession of all territory north of the Han River and had shattered most of the ROK forces. Almost half of the Army—44,000 out of 98,000—had been killed or captured or were missing, and only two divisions, the 6th and 8th, had been able to retreat with their equipment and weapons intact. Many of the 54,000 troops that remained had lost or discarded even their personal weapons and equipment.[46] To help collect stragglers and reorganize the disrupted units as they moved southward, Colonel Wright sent advisors to key points along the main routes of retreat. He sent other members of his staff north on patrol duty to collect

---

[44] (1) Interv, Col Sterling Wright. (2) GHQ SCAP, FEC, UNC Command Report, 1 January–31 October 1950, G–3 Sec, p. 17. (3) Msg, JCS 84718, JCS to CINCFE, 30 Jun 50.

[45] (1) Interv, Col Ross. (2) Informal notes, Col Barsanti. (3) Interv, Capt Schuknecht. (4) Interv, Col Greenwood. (5) Ltr, Lt Col Peter W. Scott to unidentified friend, written sometime in July 1950, sent by Scott to Appleman. (6) Ltr, Lt Col Peter W. Scott, 26 Mar 54. For an account of the circumstances surrounding the American's flight from Suwon, see Appleman, *South to the Naktong, North to the Yalu*, ch. V.

[46] Appleman, *South to the Naktong, North to the Yalu*, ch. III.

accurate information on the whereabouts of the North Korean forces.[47]

The situation in Korea on 1 July, when the first elements of the U.S. 24th Infantry Division arrived by air in Pusan, was not reassuring. The enemy had begun to cross the Han despite the bitter resistance by the remnants of the ROK 1st and 7th Divisions. The ROK 6th and 8th Divisions were pulling back in the east in good order, it was true, but the 2d, 5th, and Capital Divisions were scattered and disorganized.[48]

The commanding general of the U.S. 24th Division, Maj. Gen. William F. Dean, came to Korea two days later. On 4 July, at General MacArthur's direction, General Dean assumed command of all U.S. Army Forces in Korea and established a headquarters (USAFIK) at Taejon. In so doing he assumed operational control of the GHQ Advance Command Group and also of KMAG. His first special order appointed General Church as his deputy and twenty officers from ADCOM and KMAG as members of his general and special staffs. Of the latter, a total of nine, including the adjutant general, surgeon, judge advocate, inspector general, special services officer, finance and disbursing officers, provost marshal, and headquarters commandant were KMAG officers. General MacArthur on 4 July also ordered a base command to be commanded by Brig. Gen. Crump Garvin, established at Pusan.[49]

On 7 July the U.N. Security Council asked the United States to establish a unified command for all the forces fighting against the North Koreans. Many U.N. members had made offers of contributions of forces up to this time and there was need for an over-all commander. President Truman quickly accepted and on the following day authorized MacArthur to set up a United Nations Command (UNC).[50]

---

[47] (1) Interv, Col Greenwood. (2) Interv, Capt Schwarze. (3) Interv, Maj Lukas. (4) Ltr, Maj May, 21 Apr. 54. (5) See also Memo, Chief, KMAG, to all Korean Army Advisors, 8 Jul 50, KMAG File AG 210.3 (101).

[48] Appleman, *South to the Naktong, North to the Yalu,* ch. V.

[49] See: (1) Msg, CINCFE to DEPTAR, C56942, 30 Jun 50; (2) GO 11, GHQ FEC, 4 Jul 50; (3) GO 1, Hq USAFIK, APO 301, 4 Jul 50; (4) SO 1, Hq USAFIK, APO 301, 4 Jul 50; (5) Informal notes, Col Barsanti; (6) Hist, AG Sec, KMAG; (7) GHQ SCAP, FEC, UNC, Command Rpt, G–3 Sec, 1 Jan–31 Oct 50, p. 21.

[50] New York *Times,* July 8, 9, 1950.

Activity increased at Pusan, where Colonel Emmerich and his small detachment worked day and night preparing for the arrival of American troops and equipment. After arranging with Korean authorities to have the Pusan airstrip repaired and strengthened, they conscripted laborers for repairing roads and bridges and unloading ships at the port. When the first U.S. units arrived, they furnished the commanders with information about conditions and geography in Korea and helped them obtain transportation northward for their troops. On 2 July the KMAG officers and men who had been evacuated from Suwon and Pusan returned from Japan on an ammunition ship, the *Sergeant Keathley*. This group had flown to Itazuke and had remained with the 24th Division until General Headquarters, Far East Command, ordered them to return to Korea. Upon their arrival in Pusan, Colonel Emmerich sent most of them on to Taejon by train.[51]

Colonel Wright radioed Emmerich during this period and requested him to gather and send forward as many vehicles as possible from Pusan. Nearly all of KMAG's vehicles had been abandoned in Seoul, and transportation was now a serious problem for the advisory group. Emmerich's staff succeeded in collecting a total of forty-eight trucks, jeeps, ambulances, and civilian cars, which he sent north on flatcars guarded by seven officers and three enlisted men from his detachment.[52]

Among the KMAG personnel who returned from Japan were the three advisors who had gone north from Taegu with the ROK 22d Regiment on 25 June. Colonel Emmerich sent them directly to Taegu to join the two advisors already with the ROK 3d Division. He also sent two KMAG officers and two enlisted men up to the east coast road to Yonghae, where elements of the ROK 3d Division were in contact with North Korean forces. On 4 July Emmerich went to Taegu himself, where he decided to establish another small headquarters to assist American units as they came into that area. With a base command established

---

[51] (1) Emmerich MS, pp. 16–25. (2) Hist, AG Sec, KMAG. (3) See also GHQ SCAP, FEC, UNC, Command Rpt, an. II (G–1 Log), sec. III, 2 Jul 50, items 1, 101, 102.
[52] Emmerich MS, pp. 20–21. See also Interv, Col Kessler, 24 Feb 54.

at Pusan, Emmerich felt that there was no longer any need for his presence at the port.[53]

North Korean forces on 5 July thrust aside two reinforced companies of U.S. infantry sent to meet them at Osan and pressed southward. As U.S. 24th Division troops took up positions north of Taejon, the remnants of the ROK Army began moving into the mountainous country to the east where it was expected that there would be little enemy armor. Two KMAG field grade officers left Taejon on 11 July for Kumch'on, to help organize a forward command post for the ROK Army, and about one-half of all KMAG headquarters personnel in Taejon went on to Taegu to establish a main headquarters there. The KMAG message center at Taejon closed out on 14 July.[54]

The U.S. 25th Division began arriving in Korea on 9 July and commenced a series of delaying actions near Hamch'ang, north of Kumch'on. The U.S. 1st Cavalry Division followed nine days later and engaged the enemy south and east of Taejon, which fell on 20 July. The battered Republic of Korea divisions moved slowly to the east flank of the evolving United Nations line, fighting as well as could be expected under the circumstances. In the west, North Korean units continued south to Kwangju and then turned east for a final push toward Pusan, while the United States and ROK forces withdrew south and east to form what was to be known as the Pusan Perimeter. In the meantime, Lt. Gen. Walton H. Walker arrived from Japan and established the headquarters of the Eighth United States Army in Korea (EUSAK), on 13 July at Taegu. He assumed command of all USAFIK elements, including KMAG, and of all logistical installations and communications facilities, except certain General Headquarters personnel who returned to Japan.[55]

---

[53] (1) Emmerich MS, pp. 25, 31–32. (2) See also Schnabel, Korean War, ch. IV, pp. 10, 23.

[54] (1) Hist, AG Sec, KMAG. (2) See also: KMAG Fwd G–3 Jnl, 14 Jul 50, KMAG File AG 370.2; handwritten note to Maj Greenwood, sgd Wright, in KMAG File AG 312. (Maj Greenwood noted that he received the message at 1330 [14 Jul 50].)

[55] Msg, CX 20003 ADVR, CG EUSAK to CG USAFIK, info Chief, KMAG, 13 Jul 50. See also GHQ FEC Annual Hist Rpt, G–1 Sec, an. II, sec. IV, 14 Jul 50, item 107.

GENERAL FARRELL

The Eighth Army commander assigned Brig. Gen. Francis W. Farrell to the advisory group on 25 July. General Farrell had recently arrived from the United States and had been scheduled to command the artillery of a U.S. division. Sudden command changes resulting from the disappearance in action of General Dean on 20 July had left Farrell unassigned, and five days later he assumed command as chief of KMAG. Colonel Wright, who had been with the group since August 1948, left on 4 August to attend the Industrial College of the Armed Forces in the United States as originally scheduled.[56]

As United States and ROK forces continued withdrawing to the south and east, the ROK Army's forward command post moved with its advisors from Kumch'on to Uisong on 25 July and to Sinnyong on 3 August. Three days later the Koreans and Americans pulled back to Taegu, where the KMAG main headquarters was set up with the ROK Army Headquarters. On this day officers and men of the advisory group established a KMAG rear headquarters at Pusan, in preparation for further withdrawals.[57]

Thus, the end of the first six weeks of war found the U.S. and ROK forces compressed into the Pusan Perimeter and still fighting desperately to stabilize the situation. The arrival of U.S. reinforcements and indications that the North Korean forces had just about reached the end of their string seemed to promise a breathing spell ahead. The enemy was operating at the end of

[56] (1) Interv, Maj Gen F. W. Farrell, CG 82d Airborne Div, Fort Bragg, N.C., 29 Dec 53. (2) Interv, Col Wright, 24 Nov 53. (3) See also 1st Ind to Ltr, CG EUSAK, sub: Assignment of General Officers, 18 May 51, KMAG File AG 210.

[57] KMAG Fwd G–3 Jnl, 25 Jul 50 and 3 Aug 50, KMAG File AG 370.2. (2) See also KMAG Rear G–3 Jnl, 5 Aug 50 and 6 Aug 50, KMAG file AG 370.2.

long supply lines exposed to U.S. air attack and had taken considerable casualties in men and equipment in their all-out drive. In their expectations that the United States would not intervene or would intervene too late, they had guessed wrong. Time, which at first had appeared to be in their favor, was now beginning to switch to the advantage of the new United Nations Command.

CHAPTER VII
The Road Back

During the retreat toward Pusan, the KMAG advisors had been forced on many occasions to drop their advisory roles and become operational. Faced with a desperate situation, they insisted that their suggestions be followed, and in the field they virtually commanded ROK Army formations. When it was necessary to act forcefully, they threatened and bullied the ROK officers into compliance. The methods were sometimes harsh but frequently the only means of slowing the rout and making the ROK forces take up defensive positions along the way south. Had the KMAG advisors not employed such measures in the time of crisis, the U.S. aid from Japan and the United States might well have arrived too late to have saved South Korea.[1]

As the front stabilized along the Pusan Perimeter and U.S. and U.N. aid began to arrive, KMAG resumed its advisory role and started anew to reconstitute the ROK forces. During the period between August and November 1950, the ROK Army had an opportunity to reorganize and rebuild its strength.

The Pusan Perimeter defense lines held off the North Korean attacks until mid-September, when MacArthur launched an amphibious assault at Inch'on. The success of this maneuver was followed by an Eighth Army breakout of the Pusan Perimeter and a dramatic turning of the tide of military fortune.

Faced by the possibility of encirclement by the United Nations Command forces, the North Koreans began a general withdrawal. Resistance became scattered and desultory as the UNC troops drove back toward the 38th Parallel. In early October the U.S. decision to cross the parallel and unify Korea won tacit United Nations approval, and MacArthur's forces swept north to the Yalu.[2]

---

[1] (1) Intervs, Col Greenwood, Capt Schwarze, Maj Lukas. (2) Ltr, Maj May, 23 Apr 54. (3) See also Blumenson *et al.*, Special Problems, ch. I.

[2] See Appleman, *South to the Naktong, North to the Yalu,* for the details of these operations.

The Task of Reconstruction

The hard blows that the North Koreans had dealt the ROK forces in the early weeks of the war had shattered some units completely and disorganized others. Only a few, such as the ROK 6th and 8th Divisions, had come through relatively unscathed. The loss of weapons and equipment was in some ways even more serious, for manpower could be replaced without difficulty. To complicate the situation further, most of the ROK Army records had been lost during the retreat.

Before the work on reconstitution could begin, it was necessary to assess what was left of the old ROK Army and to discover what would be needed to do the job adequately. Estimates in July placed ROK strength at between forty and sixty thousand troops, mostly infantry spread among the ROK 1st, 3d, 6th, 8th, and Capital Divisions, and some miscellaneous service units. Taken all together, there were enough men for about three or four divisions, with limited artillery, engineer, and signal support.[3]

Logistically, the ROK Army was in dire straits. An estimated 70 percent of its supplies and equipment, together with all technical services installations in and around Seoul, had been captured or destroyed. Its supply system was practically nonexistent, and the Koreans had done little to improvise measures in order to bring up the few stocks remaining at their disposal. A survey of weapons, including those in the hands of ROK troops, a small quantity that had been rushed to Korea from Japan shortly after the invasion, and others scheduled for later delivery, showed an estimated 18,000 rifles (M1), 22,000 carbines, 270 mortars (81-mm.), 800 rocket launchers (2.36-inch), 180 heavy machine guns, 39 57-mm. antitank guns, 52 105-mm. howitzers, and 8 155-mm. howitzers available to the Koreans as of 4 July 1950.[4]

The re-equipment of ROK forces actually had begun as early as 26 June 1950, when Colonel Wright transmitted to Tokyo a

[3] (1) Staff Study on Re-equipping and Support of the ROK Army's Ground Forces, incl to Ltr, FEC to EUSAK, 20 July 50, sub: ROK Ground Forces, KMAG AG 400. (2) Blumenson et al., Special Problems, ch. I. (3) Ltr, Adv AG to Deputy Chief, KMAG, 11 Aug 50, sub: History Korean Army AG Section, KMAG 314.7.
[4] (1) Blumenson et al., Special Problems, ch. I, pp. 9, 11, 13–14. (2) Schnabel, Korean War, ch. IV, p. 8. Presumably the 155-mm. howitzers arrived from Japan very early in the month.

detailed list of the types of supplies required by the Koreans. He had requested that the listed items be shipped as soon as possible to Pusan, with signal corps radio tubes and antitank mines rushed by air. Some of this equipment arrived before the airfield at Suwon closed down, and the balance reached Pusan by ship within a few weeks. On 6 July General Church requested that the Far East Command establish an automatic supply for ROK forces similar to that established a few days earlier for U.S. forces in Korea. However, the Koreans would not need recoilless weapons and would operate with one-third the normal motor transportation and one-third of the signal equipment. The ROK forces would not require an automatic supply of rations and clothing, he noted.[5]

As the Far East Command had not expected a war of major proportions, much less the destruction of a good part of the Republic of Korea Army, there were then few military stocks in Japan that could be turned over to the Koreans. Moreover, priority for resupply naturally fell to U.S. units, and with these sustaining heavy losses during the retreat of the early part of the conflict, a large-scale re-equipment of ROK forces had to be delayed. And since railroad facilities and roads in South Korea were jammed with U.S. troops and supplies, it was extremely difficult for KMAG to distribute even the limited amounts of supplies and equipment turned over to the Koreans. At Pusan a KMAG officer was assigned with instructions to see that supplies and equipment intended for the Korean Army were unloaded and forwarded "expeditiously," and that they retained their "integrity and identity." [6]

As if all this were not enough, it became clear very early that the Korean Army G–4 Section was unable to cope with complicated logistical problems. These devolved increasingly upon the advisory group for solution, and KMAG advisors had to assume

[5] (1) Msg, ROB 084, Chief KMAG to CINCFE, 26 Jun 50. (2) Msg, ROB 013, KMAG to CINCFE, 2 Jul 50. (3) Msg, ROB 014, KMAG to CINCFE, 2 Jul 50. (4) Msg, ROB 118, ADCOM to CG Eighth Army, 6 Jul 50. These msgs are cited in Schnabel, Korean War, ch. IV, pp. 4–8. (5) See also Msg, 929, US Ambassador Korea, sgd Muccio, to State Dept, 25 Jun 50.
[6] (1)Ltr, G–4 Adv (sgd Vieman) to Maj Brannon, KMAG, CO Pusan Base Command, 16 Jul 50, copy attached to KMAG Daily Jnl, entry for 16 Jul 50, KMAG AG 370. (2) Blumenson et al., Special Problems, ch. I, pp. 13–15.

responsibility for planning, requisitioning, allocating, storing, shipping, and related functions. In solving supply problems the KMAG officers were forced to exercise the utmost ingenuity. Initially, they had almost literally to "beg, borrow, and steal" from Eighth Army units, and whether or not ROK units received the supplies and equipment thus procured depended upon the advisors' talents for improvising transportation.[7]

The advisory group began reorganizing the ROK Army by recommending that the Koreans group the surviving divisions under two corps headquarters. In a country where communications were limited, such a move would permit more local control and in general facilitate reorganization. The Koreans agreed to this move and activated Headquarters, ROK I Corps, at Ch'ongju about 8 July 1950, and Headquarters, ROK II Corps, at Hamch'ang six days later. About this time the ROK Government replaced General Chae with Maj. Gen. Chung Il Kwong as the ROK Army Chief of Staff. ROK I Corps assumed immediate control of the Capital and 1st Divisions; ROK II Corps, when activated, assumed control of the 3d, 6th, and 8th Divisions. KMAG headquarters assigned a few advisors to each corps headquarters, whose Korean commanders and staffs began learning corps operations and administration the hard way under combat conditions.[8]

With the two corps in operation, the advisory group sought during the next month to bring the five remaining ROK divisions up to strength. Some of the original eight divisions had not been completely formed before the war. For example, the ROK 3d and 8th Divisions consisted of two regiments apiece, and the Capital Division had been largely a "paper" division. The problem was not one of manpower, for many ROK troops had drifted south after their own units were destroyed and had been inte-

---

[7] Blumenson *et al.*, Special Problems, ch. I, 10–11, 13–15.

[8] (1) Interv, Col Kessler. (2) Interv, Maj James H. Hausman, 24 Mar 54. (3) Ltr, Maj May, 23 Apr 54. (4) G–3 Opns Rpt, GHQ FEC, 16 Jul 50, item 22. Two KMAG documents list the ROK 2d Division as being under ROK I Corps in July 1950. All other evidence shows that this division was rendered combat ineffective during the first week of the war and that a new ROK 2d Division was formed in November 1950. (5) See: Ltr to Col McPhail, 8 Jul 50, sub: Ltr of Instructions, KMAG AG 210.3; Ltr, Adv G–1 to Asst CofS, G–1, EUSAK, 18 Jul 50, sub: Duty Assignments, Officers of KMAG, KMAG AG 210.3 (100).

grated into other units. Moreover, when ROK commanders needed replacements, they simply sent "recruiting" parties to nearby towns and villages and drafted young men on the spot. Thus, in July and August KMAG helped the Koreans form additional regiments and other types of units.

The formation of the ROK 26th Regiment in August was typical of the haste and expediency surrounding KMAG's operations at the time. Early in August the KMAG G–3 Advisor called Capt. Frank W. Lukas in from the field and ordered him to activate a new regiment for the ROK 3d Division. Lukas obtained two interpreters from ROK Army headquarters and got in touch with the appropriate ROK Army staff officers in Taegu. These, with the aid of the police and other city officials, drafted youths on the streets of the town, and within a day or two they had nearly 1,000 recruits. As men were drafted, Lukas and his Korean officers formed squads, platoons, companies, and, finally, two battalions. The most intelligent-appearing recruits were designated NCO's and platoon leaders, while the officers who had helped to recruit them became company, battalion, and regimental commanders and staffs. When the two battalions were organized, the KMAG G–4 somehow obtained enough rifles for them. Lukas then took his regiment outside the city and allowed each man to fire nine rounds of ammunition. Shortly thereafter the regiment, clad in an assortment of civilian clothes, school uniforms, and odds and ends of U.S. Army uniforms, boarded a train at Taegu and traveled east to a sector near P'ohang-dong, where, in less than a week after its activation had been ordered, it entered combat. The ROK 26th Regiment received no formal training until April 1951.[9]

General MacArthur, meanwhile, on the strength of a study made by members of his staff on 17 July 1950, concluded that the maximum ground effort of which the Republic of Korea Army was capable in the immediate future was limited to four infantry divisions, including the support required to make them effective in battle. He told the Department of the Army on 31 July that he planned to re-equip the ROK Army on this basis, though without certain heavy equipment. Some items had al-

---

[9] Based on Interv, Maj Frank W. Lukas, 21 Apr 54.

RECRUITS FOR THE ROK ARMY ON WAY TO A TRAINING CENTER

ready been furnished the Koreans, he said, and he was screening his stocks in Japan to determine what other equipment could be spared; some items would be requisitioned from the United States.[10]

Both Ambassador Muccio and General Walker disagreed with MacArthur's staff estimate. On 1 August Muccio offered his view to the Secretary of State, arguing that the United States should arm as many able-bodied South Koreans as possible without regard to the prewar limitation. He and Walker, he went on, felt that the South Koreans should make the largest possible contribution of manpower to help defeat the North Koreans and to save American lives. Moreover, Muccio continued, it was probable that enemy guerrillas would continue to fight in mountain areas after the end of major operations in Korea, and ROK troops

---

[10] (1) Staff Study on Re-equipping and Support of the ROK Army's Ground Forces, cited n. 3(1), above. (2) Msg, CX 59051, CINCFE to DEPTAR, 31 Jul 50. (3) See also: Memo, Maj Gen Robinson E. Duff, Dep CofS, G–3, for Gen Bolté 1 May 51, sub: Composition of ROK Armed Forces, KMAG FE&Pac Br, G–3, folder 2, tab H; Ltr, Chief KMAG (sgd Wright) to CG EUSAK, sub: Requirements for Re-equipping of Korean Army 21 Jul 50, KMAG AG 475.

should be used to the greatest extent possible for their suppression.[11]

How great an influence Muccio's and Walker's opinions exerted upon MacArthur's *volte-face* one week later is unknown, but he did reverse his earlier decision. On 9 August he authorized General Walker to increase "at once" the strength of the ROK Army to any level he deemed advisable and practicable. Following conferences between members of his staff and KMAG representatives, the Eighth Army commander submitted a plan for activating five new ROK divisions along with corps and army units needed to support a ten-division Republic of Korea Army. His schedule called for activating one division by 10 September, and one additional division by the 10th of each month following until five divisions had been formed. Technical services units would be activated in phase with the divisions as the availability of equipment permitted. MacArthur concurred with this plan and asked the Department of the Army whether it could furnish the necessary equipment for such a program from zone of interior stocks. The Department of the Army replied on 2 September that minimum initial equipment (except specified items of heavy engineer, signal, and ordnance equipment) could be supplied for new ROK divisions beginning 10 November 1950 and directed MacArthur to submit requisitions for the equipment needed.[12]

The KMAG staff hastily drew up Tables of Organization and Equipment, based on the U.S. infantry division of 1942 with the majority of heavy armament omitted. General MacArthur sent additional equipment from his own stocks and gave the Koreans some nonstandard items procured locally. Within six weeks he was able to report to Washington that three new ROK divisions, the 7th, 11th, and 5th, had been activated and partially equipped, and that the activation of two more, the 9th and 2d, was "being implemented." This had been done, he said, without jeopardizing the resupply of his forces engaged in combat. He requested

---

[11] Msg, State 98, USAMB Korea to Secy State, 1 Aug 50.

[12] (1) Msg, CX 59709, CINCFE to COMGENARMYEIGHT (Adv), Info DA, 9 Aug 50. (2) WD (EUSAK), G–4 Rpt, 19 Aug 50. (3) Msg, CX 60760, CINCFE to DEPTAR, 21 Aug 50. (4) Msg, WAR 90530, DA to CINCFE, 2 Sep 50. See also: Memo, Duff for Bolté cited n. 10, above; OPS Memo for Rcd, sub: Supply of ROK Divs, G–3 File 091 Korea, case 198; MS, Development of ROKA Following the Outbreak of War, undated, in KMAG, FE&Pac Br, G–3, folder 1, index 28.

that the equipment promised for the support of these five new divisions be shipped as soon as possible.[13]

The manner in which the ROK 2d Division was formed was reminiscent of the ROK 26th Regiment's activation many weeks earlier. Early in November General Farrell called Maj. Thomas B. Ross, Assistant G–3 Advisor, to his office and asked him how long it would take him to form another division for the ROK Army. Ross replied that several weeks should be sufficient, whereupon the chief of KMAG laughed and informed the young officer that he expected the division to be formed by the following day.[14] There were at that time three Korean personnel centers in the vicinity of Seoul where recruits were gathered before being processed. Major Ross visited each of these centers in turn and requested the Koreans in charge to line up recruits in groups of about two hundred. He designated each group as a company, formed companies into battalions, and designated each center as a regiment. For company officers and noncommissioned officers he, like Major Lukas, selected the most intelligent looking men in each group, and then obtained officers from ROK Army headquarters for the division's battalion, regimental, and division commanders and staffs. KMAG headquarters scraped together a detachment of advisors and assigned it to the division and, a few days after General Farrell's talk with Ross, the ROK 2d Division left on its first mission.

In early November the Eighth Army's combat divisions were in the vicinity of Kunu-ri, in North Korea; the U.S. X Corps was north and east of Hungnam. Between these main forces and the 38th Parallel, on the eastern half of the peninsula, were large groups of guerrillas. The ROK 2d Division's mission was to go north through Ch'unch'on and Hwach'on and engage and destroy these guerrilla forces. As each ROK soldier boarded a

---

[13] (1) Msg, CX 67400, CINCFE to DEPTAR, 25 Oct 50. (2) Memo for CofS, GHQ FEC, from G–3 Sec, E.K.W. [Wright], 8 Nov 51. (3) Incl 1 to Memo for Rcd, G–3 (sgd Ross) to Chief, KMAG, sub: Liaison Visit to GHQ FEC, undated, KMAG AG 337. (4) Memo, Duff for Bolté, cited n. 10 above. (5) OPS Memo for Rcd, cited n. 12, above. (6) WD (EUSAK), G–4 Rpt, 19 Aug. 50. (7) DF, Chief, KMAG to G–3 EUSAK, 18 Jan 51, sub: 4.2-inch Mortars, Korean Army, KMAG AG 470. Actual numerical designations were extracted from EUSAK War Diaries, Oct, Nov, Dec 50, and Memo for CofS, GHQ FEC, sgd Wright (G–3), 15 Sep 50, OCMH files.

[14] Based on Interv, Col Ross, 15 Dec 53.

truck at his respective center, he received an M1 rifle. Some received automatic rifles or light machine guns and on the trip north the division devoted about one-quarter of each day to training. The ROK 2d Division eventually became an effective combat unit in spite of the haphazardness surrounding its formation.

Replacements and Training

The provision of manpower and equipment for the ROK units was but one facet of the rebuilding task that had to be done in the summer and fall of 1950. The problem of obtaining men was in itself simple to overcome, but time could not be so easily won, as long as the heavy pressure of battle continued. All too frequently the new replacements were thrown into combat after but a few days of training. Others were impressed as laborers to carry supplies and equipment and received no formal training at all. What was needed was a system of collecting replacements centrally and, more important, of training them properly before assigning them to units.[15]

Before the outbreak of war, the training of recruits had been handled on a unit basis. Each division had enlisted and trained its own men, and when hostilities came the ROK Army still had no effective replacement training system in operation. The requirements of war soon demonstrated the need for a central system, and the first replacement training center (RTC) was established at Taegu in mid-July under the supervision of three KMAG officers and five NCO's. In August a second training center opened northwest of Pusan at Kumhae with one KMAG advisor on hand. Each of the RTC's turned out 150 trainees a day for the five ROK divisions then organized. At first KMAG planned to have the recruits go through a ten-day cycle of training, with emphasis on such essentials as rifle marksmanship, but even this short period had to be reduced at times because of the urgent need for replacements in the line. The training of recruits was further limited by the usual dearth of facilities and

---

[15] (1) Interv, Maj Lukas. (2) Ltr, Maj May, 23 Apr 54. (3) Emmerich MS, pp. 18, 48, 76. (4) Blumenson et al., Special Problems, ch. I, p. 12.

equipment. The huge losses of weapons during the first week of the war had created acute shortages of rifles and machine guns, and none could be spared from the combat units to train the replacements. Under these conditions old Japanese rifles, unserviceable weapons, and even captured enemy guns were used to give the trainees an opportunity to fire a few practice rounds before facing the enemy.[16]

A third training center was organized during August at Kup'o-ri, also near Pusan, a fourth by the end of the month at Samnangjin, northwest of Pusan, and a fifth by 8 September on the island of Cheju-do. By this time, 1,000 replacements were flowing each day from the RTC at Taegu, the centers at Kumhae and Kup'o-ri were turning out 500 daily each, and the center at Samnangjin was able to furnish a daily quota of 200. The training center on Cheju-do produced 750 each day. KMAG officers and NCO's supervised each of the RTC's on the mainland.[17]

Behind the swift expansion of the ROK centers in July and August lay the needs of both the ROK and the Eighth Armies during this period. General MacArthur was preparing for the amphibious operation at Inch'on in September and diverting U.S. replacements into the U.S. 7th Infantry Division in Japan. In the meantime the hard-pressed American divisions in Korea fell understrength. On 9 August MacArthur directed General Walker, the Eighth Army commander, to fill up each U.S. company and battery with 100 ROK soldiers. Thus, of the 2,950 ROK replacements produced daily at the RTC's, 500 were diverted each day into U.S. units in August while the remainder were sent to the ROK divisions. The ROK replace-

[16] (1) Blumenson et al., Special Problems, ch. I, p. 12. (2) War Diary (EUSAK), G-1 Rpt, 1 Sep 50. (3) Operations Research Office, Report ORO-R-4 (FEC), Utilization of Indigenous Manpower in Korea (Baltimore, Johns Hopkins University, 1951). Because information about the ROK-KMAG replacement training system through January 1951 is fragmentary and conflicting, this section is a compilation of data from the sources cited, reconciled as much as possible with other sources.
[17] Memo for Col Conley (sgd Mize), 8 Sep 50, sub: Korean Training Centers, War Diary (EUSAK), G-1 Rpt, 8 Sep 50. This memo does not list the officers in charge as KMAG personnel, but a KMAG roster dated 19 July 1950 identifies them as members of the U.S. Military Advisory Group.

ments sent to American units were designated the Korean Augmentation to the U.S. Army, or KATUSA.[18]

By fall the ROK Army's replacement system was well established, at least for immediate needs, with recruits receiving up to sixteen days training. RTC No. 1, at Taegu, was the largest of the five in operation, where recruits received not only instruction in the use of basic weapons, but also were trained in elementary tactics. Because by then it was possible to assign replacements with more discrimination, the Taegu RTC was organized into specialized battalions: four rifle, two carbine, one automatic rifle (BAR), one machine gun, one mortar, and one "rocket" (presumably rocket launcher). Recruits in each of these battalions were taught to use that particular weapon and were instructed in its tactical employment. Early in December 1950 the recruit training period was extended to twenty-one days, under the same battalion organization, and remained thus until the end of January 1951, when all RTC's were consolidated on Cheju-do.[19]

Closely allied to the problem of replacements was the training of Korean officers. Many had been killed, wounded, or captured during the initial actions, and the ROK Army needed new officers badly. The North Korean Army had overrun the ROK Army's schools shortly after 25 June, and the bulk of the instruction and training materials had been lost or destroyed. This meant that new schools would have to be organized, at different locations, and new programs of instruction developed. Although both KMAG and the ROK Army were concentrating on fighting the war and were in no position to divert personnel or other resources to establishing a school system as elaborate as that developed before the invasion, the experience gained in setting up and operating schools in 1949

[18] (1) War Diary (EUSAK), G–1 Rpt, 16 Aug 50. (2) Circular 21, CG EUSAK, in WD (EUSAK), G–1 Rpt, 22 Aug 50. (3) Memo to CG (EUSAK), 1 Sep 50, sub: Korean Augmentation, WD (EUSAK), G–1 Rpt, 1 Sep 50. For a description of the RTC at Kup'o-ri, which supplied KATUSA replacements, see Memo for Rcd, sub: Inspection Korean Replacement Center, Kup'o-ri, WD (EUSAK), G–3 Rpt, 9 Sep 50.
[19] Office of the Army Attaché, Seoul, Rpt R–24–52, 25 Jun 52, G–2 Doc Lib, DA, ID 871092.

and 1950 permitted a resumption of schooling much earlier than might otherwise have been the case.[20]

The first school to reopen was actually a combined school. Infantry, artillery, engineer, ordnance, and signal instruction for officer candidates was set up at Tongnae, a few miles north of Pusan, under the supervision of Maj. John B. Clark, who had organized the ROK Infantry School in 1948. The new school was called the Korean Army Ground General School and began its operations with an officers candidate course for 200 students on 28 August. The six weeks of instruction contained four weeks of general training and two weeks of specialized branch training. At the same time the school began two-week courses for 200 ROK noncommissioned officers, along with a special two-week course for lieutenants of the ROK National Defense Corps (somewhat comparable to the National Guard of the United States). The total number of KMAG personnel assigned to the Ground General School in late 1950 was eight officers and four noncommissioned officers. This emergency schooling program continued until January 1951, when both the ROK Army's school and replacement training systems were revised.[21]

The Advisor in Combat

While the reconstruction process was going on, U.S. military advisors also had to cope with the critical problem of keeping the ROK tactical units in the war. The bulk of the KMAG effort during the early part of the conflict had to be devoted to combat operations to insure that the ROK forces manned and fought their positions. Since the enemy had better equipment and training, the advisors had to work hard to stiffen the ROK capability and desire to resist.

The problems that the advisors had faced in peacetime were now compounded by war. Since the ROK units were usually stationed in the more mountainous areas along the

[20] Blumenson et al., Special Problems, ch. I, pp. 16–18. (2) Office of the Army Attaché, Seoul, Rpt R–24–52, 25 Jun 52, G–2 Doc Lib, DA. (3) ORO Rpt, ORO–R–4 (FEC), Utilization of Indigenous Manpower in Korea, pp. 25–40.
[21] See ch. VIII, below.

front where communications were difficult, most of the advisors had to operate independently of KMAG and Eighth Army headquarters and had to rely heavily upon their own judgment and resourcefulness. Although they normally advised on levels from one to three times higher than those commensurate with their rank and experience, responsibility for the success or failure of a Korean unit seemed to be theirs alone. Isolated as they often were by distances, poor roads, and long periods of bad weather, KMAG had no sure means of supplying them with rations and other necessities; therefore they ate Korean food for protracted periods and borrowed clothing, gasoline, and tentage where they could. Since their numbers were small, they sometimes maintained around-the-clock schedules for days on end, unable to get even a few hours of unbroken sleep.[22]

The South Korean lack of military know-how, the inadequate training of their leaders and men, the shortages in heavy weapons and other items such as signal equipment were residual problems that the KMAG advisors had wrestled with before the war. These were familiar obstacles that had to be overcome by the advisor on an individual basis as they arose. Now there was a new urgency, since life and death for the men involved and disaster and defeat for the United Nations Command were at stake.

The language barrier, too, it developed, could be a hinge upon which an operation turned. While experienced advisors had probably worked out a *modus operandi* of sorts during their earlier service, new advisors had to depend entirely upon the interpreters furnished by ROK Army headquarters [23] or their counterparts' knowledge of English. Partly for this reason, parallel lines of communication had to be set up on lower levels at a time when KMAG could ill afford to spare signal personnel from other duties. ROK Army signal communications were "unreliable, slow, and dangerously insecure," [24] and a double net-

---

[22] (1) Intervs, Col Greenwood, Col Kessler, Maj Lukas, Capt Schwarze. (2) Ltr, Maj May, 23 Apr 54. See also Blumenson *et al., Special Problems,* ch. I, p. 30.

[23] (1) Interv, Lt Col Thomas E. Bennett, 20 Feb 52. (2) Interv, Lt Col Carl E. Green, 21 Apr 54. (3) Interv, Maj Lukas, 21 Apr 54.

[24] Ltr, Gen Farrell to CG, EUSAK, 10 Aug 50, sub: Emergency Personnel Requisition, KMAG AG 210.3 (106).

work was necessary if messages from the ROK Army–KMAG headquarters level were to reach their destinations and be understood by both the advisors and their counterparts.[25]

In addition, the ROK Army generally lacked the wherewithal to fight the war. This brought about such situations as later described by Maj. Ray B. May, who joined the ROK 1st Division on 15 July 1950. Wrote this officer: ". . . we had a total of fourteen 105-mm. howitzers, no 4.2″ mortars, recoilless rifles or tanks. We were trying to hold a 22 km. front, mostly with rifles." The fact that some ROK divisions were required to man approximately the same frontages as U.S. divisions, though with comparatively little artillery and armor support and in rougher country, also helped to explain the Koreans' inability to hold their sectors.[26]

Some problems were relatively new. Before hostilities began, a Korean soldier could be trained over a period of time after he joined his unit. Now, when time was at a premium and the need for trained men was greatest, the replacements sent to the front were raw recruits. Receiving only ten days of quick instruction and seldom firing more than one clip of rifle ammunition, they could not be expected to perform like trained combat soldiers. The lack of training also contributed to their difficulty in holding on to the terrain they were defending and caused them to suffer heavier casualties than their more experienced compatriots. As often happens under such circumstances, the behavior of the unit depended heavily upon the caliber of the commander; if he were competent and a good leader, his command reflected it and vice versa.[27]

While the quality of the ROK replacements was not likely to grow better until the tactical situation at the front stabilized or improved enough to permit the RTC's to produce better-trained soldiers, the advisor could help at the local level. One KMAG officer, realizing that the ROK 6th Division's replace-

---

[25] Blumenson et al., Special Problems, ch. I, pp. 22–23. See Communications Procedures in Allied Operations, prepared by the Signal School, Fort Monmouth, N.J., pp. 36–42, OCMH files.

[26] Ltr, Maj May, 23 Apr 54.

[27] (1) Ltr, Maj May. (2) Interv, Col Sorensen, 17 Dec 52. (3) Blumenson et al., Special Problems, ch. I, p. 12.

ments were going into battle without knowing anything about their weapons or what was expected of them, initiated a short course of instruction at the division level in weapons and basic tactics. By demonstrating, drawing sketches on the ground, and using sign language, he showed new men how to line up their front and rear sights, how to adjust for windage, and how to fire correctly. Similarly, he demonstrated a few principles of fire and movement—how to advance by rushes, how to cover the advance of other soldiers, and how to assault a position. This brief schooling, he discovered, made a tremendous difference in the division's efficiency.[28]

The individual response of the KMAG advisors to the challenge presented by the retreat and disorganization of the ROK Army during the initial phase of the war was a tribute to the caliber of the group. Working feverishly against time and operating on a shoestring under battle conditions, they managed to hold the ROK units together and begin the task of reconstitution. In view of the difficulties under which the advisors worked, the performance of the ROK forces during the advance to the Yalu in September and October was a testimonial to the sterling effort that the KMAG advisors had made during the summer of 1950.

---

[28] Interv, Col Sorensen.

CHAPTER VIII

The Task Ahead

In October 1950 the end of the war seemed to be in sight, for the United Nations Command encountered no serious opposition from the North Korean forces in the drive toward the Manchurian frontier. The Chinese prisoners of war that were captured in the fighting gave warning of wholesale Chinese Communist intervention in the conflict, as did the politicians at Peiping, but these were ignored. In November as the U.N. Command tried to reach the Yalu, the large body of Chinese troops that had crossed into North Korea struck hard and soon had the U.N. Command forces in full retreat back to the 38th Parallel and beyond. What MacArthur termed a *new war* had begun with a stronger foe and perhaps was being fought for higher stakes.

The Growth of KMAG

It was inevitable that KMAG should be affected by the quick shifting of the fortunes of war in the last half of 1950, and it was also inevitable that its official status should change as the character of the war altered. General Walker's Eighth Army had assumed operational control of the advisory group on 13 July 1950, but KMAG was not actually assigned until 14 September. Moreover, KMAG did not become an assigned part of the Far East Command until 29 August, when, at MacArthur's request, the Department of the Army released KMAG in order to facilitate its administration during the emergency. At that time KMAG lost its status as a Department of the Army administrative unit and became an Army unit. This change was not officially made in Eighth Army orders until 10 January 1951.[1]

Formally or not, KMAG became an integral part of the Eighth Army when General Walker assumed command in Korea. The

---

[1] (1) Msg, CX 62333, CINCFE to EUSAK, 7 Sep 50. (2) Msg, WAR 90144, WAR to CINCFE, 29 Aug 50. (3) GO 212, Hq EUSAK, 24 Dec 50, as amended by GO 17, 10 Jan 51. See also: Ltr, Chief, Manpower Control Div, to TAG, 28 Aug 50, sub: Transfer of KMAG, DAAA G–1 334; Ltr, Chief, KMAG, to CINCFE, 28 Dec 50, with Incls, sub: Redesignation of Unit, Eighth Army File, AG 322; Msg, CX 51551, CINCFE to EUSAK *et al.*, 19 Dec 50, Eighth Army File, AG 322.

group's job as such—in addition to its primary mission of assisting the ROK Army—was to maintain liaison between Eighth Army headquarters and the Koreans, thereby keeping General Walker informed about the ROK Army's activities and capabilities and insuring that his directives were carried out.[2]

KMAG shared headquarters with the ROK Army in Taegu and maintained contact with Eighth Army headquarters through liaison officers. For the logistical support of the group, KMAG drew supplies directly from Eighth Army agencies.[3]

Soon after General Walker assumed control of KMAG, the Eighth Army sought to reduce materially the size of KMAG headquarters and incorporate the advisory group as a fifth EUSAK general staff section (G–5). General Farrell protested this move on 25 July, pointing out that the group had operational as well as supervisory responsibilities. KMAG advisors, scattered in the field, often had to be supported logistically by unorthodox methods, and on occasion advisors had to take virtual command of ROK Army units and tactical situations. For these reasons, it appeared to KMAG's chief that the advisory group needed a substantial headquarters to support its field personnel. Furthermore, Farrell noted, since it could be assumed that KMAG's mission would continue after the war in Korea had ended, the group would have to "start out from scratch" at a later date if it were reorganized radically to conform with a temporary situation.[4]

Although recommending that KMAG remain in essentially its original form, with its staff and advisory functions, the chief of

---

[2] General Walker assumed command of all ROK ground forces on 17 July 1950, as directed by General MacArthur at the request of Syngman Rhee. See: (1) WD (EUSAK), Summary, entry for 17 Jul 50, p. 8; (2) Command Rpt, GHQ SCAP, FEC, UNC, 1 Jan–31 Oct 50, G–3 Rpt, pt. I, p. 26, par. 56.

[3] Memo, Gen Duff, Actg ACofS, G–3, DA, for Lt Gen Alfred M. Gruenther (Deputy CofS, P&CO), 27 Oct 50, sub: Status of Korea Military Advisory Group (KMAG), G–3 091 Korea, case 216. (2) Advisor's Handbook, KMAG, 1 Mar 51, copy in KMAG File, FE&Pac Br, G–3, folder 20. (3) Information Folder, ROKA and KMAG, 1 May 53, KMAG File, FE&Pac Br, G–3, folder 6A, sec. I, tab E. (4) Blumenson et al., Special Problems, ch. 1, pp. 15–16, 30. (5) SOP for Internal Supply, 20 Dec 50, in Advisor's Handbook, 1 Mar 51, app. 1. In OCMH files, a KMAG roster dated 19 July 1950 lists a total of ten KMAG liaison officers attached to EUSAK headquarters.

[4] (1) Ltr, Chief, KMAG, to Deputy CofS EUSAK, 25 Jul 50, sub: Reduction of KMAG Staff, KMAG File AG 322. (2) See also KMAG Staff Memo 41, 30 Jul 50, KMAG File AG 314.7.

KMAG G–2 Advisor Briefs ROK Engineer Platoon *about to set out on reconnaissance patrol.*

KMAG admitted that the group could operate efficiently with fewer administrative personnel. If Eighth Army would assume responsibility for KMAG's personnel administration, finance activities, inspector general and special services functions, general supply (leaving KMAG one supply officer), and general courts-martial authority, the personnel ordinarily concerned with those activities could be reassigned or dropped by the advisory group. Such a shift should be gradual, he warned, inasmuch as further developments in the tactical situation would clarify KMAG's responsibilities and methods of operating. Upon approval by Eighth Army of these proposals, the advisory group would prepare and submit a complete, revised Table of Distribution.

General Farrell urged General MacArthur on 28 July 1950 to relieve KMAG of the responsibility for advising the Korean Coast Guard. Along with increasing American participation in the Korean conflict, U.S. naval personnel had so taken over the advisory functions formerly discharged by Department of the Army civilians under KMAG that the duties of the latter had all but ceased to exist. General Walker concurred, and on 4 August 1950 General MacArthur transferred the Coast Guard advisory responsibility to the U.S. Commander of Naval Forces, Far East (COMNAVFE).[5]

The Eighth Army approved General Farrell's recommendations concerning KMAG's organization on 28 July,[6] and on 16 August he submitted a Table of Distribution calling for 559 officers and men with advisors down to the regimental level in the ROK Army. In justifying this T/D Farrell noted that combat operations, the ROK Army's reorganization, and the necessity for maintaining a twenty-four hour coverage in staff sections, together with a pressing need for a reliable internal communications system, had suggested additional modifications in the KMAG structure. Although it had been possible to bring about a reasonable state of efficiency in most advisory sections by using former administrative KMAG personnel and also by curtailing advice to the Koreans in certain fields, there were still organizational weaknesses that the proposed Table of Distribution would rectify.[7]

The principal deficiencies were in the Field Artillery, Ordnance, and Signal Sections; all required additional personnel. Two officers and one enlisted man, carried in the G–3 Advisory Section, had been enough to take care of the ROK Army's artillery requirements in peacetime. The revised Table of Distribution called for 18 officers and 18 enlisted men, on the basis of 2 officers and 2 enlisted men for each ROK division artillery battalion (when formed) and for the ROK Army Headquarters Artillery Section. The Ordnance Section's original allotment of

---

[5] (1) Ltr, Chief, KMAG, to CINCFE (through CG EUSAK), 28 Jul 50 sub: Korean Coast Guard, KMAG File AG 091.7. (2) Ltr, Comdr Speight, USCG (Ret) to Chief KMAG, 21 Jul 50, sub: Present Assignment, Report on, KMAG File AG 091.7. (3) Msg, CX 59229, CINCFE to WAR, COMNAVFE, EUSAK, Info AMIK, 4 Aug 50. See also Ltr, Comdr Speight, USCG, sub: Submission of Information Concerning U.S. Advisory Group to Republic of Korea Coast Guard, 16 Sep 53.

[6] 1st Ind to Ltr, Chief, KMAG, to Dep CofS, EUSAK, 25 Jul 50, sub: Reduction of KMAG Staff, KMAG File AG 322.

[7] Ltr, Chief, KMAG, to CG EUSAK, 16 Aug 50, sub: Justification of Revised T/D, KMAG File AG 322.

7 officers and 20 enlisted men had been adequate when the ROK Army's ordnance supply and maintenance installations were concentrated in the vicinity of ASCOM City. Now that ordnance activities were greatly expanded and dispersed, many more ordnance advisors were needed. KMAG's need for additional signal specialists was greatest of all. Since operationally the advisory group was concerned with ROK forces approximately the size of a United States corps, it was of the utmost importance that an adequate communications system be an integral part of the KMAG organization. The quota of 8 officers and 66 enlisted men authorized under the prewar table of distribution was completely inadequate to meet the conditions under which the advisory group was operating and could expect to operate in the foreseeable future. ROK Army signal troops, moreover, had little chance of improving while the few signal advisory personnel at KMAG's disposal had to be used to maintain and operate its own communications system. The revised T/D called for a signal section of 16 officers and 177 enlisted men, which General Farrell considered to be the minimum number required for maintaining both the control and information facilities needed by the advisory group.

As KMAG's responsibilities increased during July and August, it became clear that the U.S. Military Advisory Group would operate more efficiently as a major subordinate command of Eighth Army than as a combined EUSAK staff section and operating agency. Not only was control and the logistical support of field advisors increasingly difficult because of rugged terrain, inadequate communications facilities, and great distances between ROK units, but experience also showed that the ROK Army needed many more U.S. advisors. At the suggestion of the EUSAK G–3 Section, therefore, KMAG drew up another Table of Distribution. The newest T/D restored the administrative functions assumed by Eighth Army headquarters, provided advisors down to the battalion level and more advisors to most other advisory sections, and called for a total of 835 officers and men.[8]

---

[8] (1) Informal Check Sheet, attached to Ltr, Chief, KMAG, to CG EUSAK, 16 Aug 50, sub: Justification of Revised T/D, EUSAK File AG 320.3. (2) Ltr of Transmittal, Chief, KMAG, to CG EUSAK, 18 Sep 50, KMAG File AG 312. (3) Ltr, CG EUSAK to CINCFE, 26 Sep 50, sub: Tables of Distribution for Korean Military Adivsory Group, EUSAK File AG 322.

The Eighth Army commander approved this table on 26 September. Two weeks later General MacArthur's adjutant general, Brig. Gen. Kenneth B. Bush, notified General Walker that the Commander in Chief "appreciates the requirement during current hostilities for an appreciable augmentation" of KMAG, but that he considered it inadvisable "at this time" to propose to the Department of the Army a permanent increase in the size of the advisory group. There was no objection, Bush noted, to the authorization of a temporary overstrength for KMAG to the extent deemed necessary and from sources available to General Walker.[9]

General MacArthur's refusal to endorse a permanent increase in KMAG's strength undoubtedly sprang from the anticipation in September that an early end to the war in Korea was in sight. KMAG's existence, it will be recalled, had been approved by President Truman in March 1949. At that time he had set forth specifically the size of the Korean security forces to be supported by the United States and listed the broad functions of KMAG. Although the conditions prompting the President's action had been overtaken by war, the Department of State in 1950 was known to feel that there should be no change in KMAG's make-up until certain policy decisions regarding the postwar relationship between the United States and the Republic of Korea had been made. For example, the degree of responsibility for Korea retained by the United Nations could affect such decisions.[10]

But as an operational element of Eighth Army, with greatly increased responsibilities, the U.S. Military Advisory Group had to expand beyond its inadequate Table of Distribution. Designed originally to advise 6 Korean divisions in peacetime, KMAG could not possibly do justice to 10 ROK divisions and 3 ROK corps headquarters under combat conditions.[11] General

---

[9] (1) Ltr, CG EUSAK to CINCFE, 26 Sep 50, sub: Tables of Distribution for Korean Military Advisory Group, with 1st, 2d, and 3d Inds, EUSAK File AG 322. (2) See also Ltr, Chief, KMAG, to CG EUSAK, 11 Jan 49, sub: Monthly Personnel Strength Rpt, KMAG File AG 210.

[10] (1) See Memo, Duff for Gruenther, 27 Oct 50, sub: Status of Korea Military Advisory Group. (2) See also JCS 1776/146.

[11] The ROK III Corps was activated in October 1950. See WD (EUSAK), Oct 50, sec. I, p. 29.

TABLE 2—KMAG STRENGTH, JULY 1950 THROUGH SEPTEMBER 1951[a]

Reporting date	Officers	Warrant officers	Enlisted men	Total
31 July 1950_____	[b] 175	5	290	470
31 August 1950_____	175	4	256	435
30 September 1950_____	199	3	245	447
31 October 1950_____	274	3	232	509
30 November 1950_____	337	3	292	632
31 December 1950_____	356	4	386	746
31 January 1951_____	356	3	385	744
28 February 1951_____	401	3	400	804
31 March 1951_____	407	3	454	864
30 April 1951_____	427	3	493	923
31 May 1951_____	416	5	563	984
30 June 1951_____	411	5	504	920
31 July 1951_____	397	5	540	942
31 August 1951_____	408	15	632	1,055
30 September 1951_____	454	14	840	1,308

[a] Carried as 8668th AAU, Jul–Dec 50.
Carried as 8202d AAU, Jan–Sep 51.
[b] Includes one nurse.

Source: From Strength in Troop Program Sequence by Organization and Type of Personnel (CSCAP–13) Statistical and Accounting Branch, Adjutant General's Office, Department of the Army.

Walker authorized the advisory group to operate temporarily overstrength as suggested by General Bush, and KMAG's strength rose from 447 at the end of September 1950 to 509 by 31 October, and then sharply to 746 by the end of the year.[12] (*Table 2*) In form, KMAG remained essentially the same, though expanded in all quarters, and with the same basic weaknesses.[13] For example, some ROK battalions had to do without advisors in order that ROK corps headquarters might have advisory supervision.

On 15 October, following the collapse of the North Korean Army, President Truman and General MacArthur met on Wake

[12] Strength figures extracted from Strength in Troop Program Sequence by Organization and Type of Personnel (CSCAP–13), entries for dates cited, Statistical and Accounting Branch, AGO, DA. Colonel Greenwood writes that the overstrength authorization was unlimited. Ltr, 14 May 54.

[13] It has been virtually impossible to reconstruct KMAG's organization as it actually was at any specific time before March 1951. Conditions in the summer and fall of 1950 made it difficult for the KMAG staff to incorporate plans, policies, and procedures into memorandums, circulars, and other records. Much of the administrative work affecting KMAG's organization was carried out informally by telephone or in personal conversations.

Island to discuss important questions brought up by the prospective end of major hostilities in Korea. Not the least of these questions concerned KMAG, and its place in the postwar period. During the conference General MacArthur stated that the advisory group "should be continued indefinitely," an opinion probably based less on an appreciation of the group's accomplishments (which he praised highly) than on a recognition that Korean forces would need continued guidance in the future. He also told Mr. Truman that Korea "should have about ten divisions" after the war, and followed this on 24 October with specific recommendations that Korean postwar forces consist of ten infantry divisions and supporting units with a total strength of 250,000 men.[14]

KMAG's future was also the concern of Maj. Gen. Robinson E. Duff, Acting Assistant Chief of Staff, G–3, in Washington. On 27 October 1950 he informed Lt. Gen. Alfred M. Gruenther, Deputy Chief of Staff for Plans and Combat Operations, that KMAG should be continued in the postwar period. Moreover, after thoroughly reviewing the conditions under which the advisory group had been formed, and those under which it operated in late 1950, General Duff noted that G–3 had "perceived the possible necessity for revising KMAG's structure and mission" and had accordingly included "appropriate questions" to be taken up by a party of Department of the Army representatives then en route to the Far East on an inspection tour.[15]

The KMAG staff, disappointed by unsuccessful attempts to have a more appropriate Table of Distribution approved, prepared to submit its case to General MacArthur. Among other complaints, the advisory group held that a mere temporary authorization to operate overstrength, while providing a basis for requisitioning advisors to meet the rapidly changing size and

---

[14] (1) *Substance of Statements Made at Wake Island Conferences on October 15, 1950*, compiled by General of the Army Omar N. Bradley from notes kept by the conferees from Washington (Washington, 1951). (2) Msg, CX 67296, CINCFE to DEPTAR, 24 Oct 50. (3) G–3 Memo for CofS USA, 30 Oct 50, sub: Postwar Korean Military Establishment (JCS 1776/146), G–3 File 091 Korea, case 216. See also below, page 169.

[15] Memo, Duff for Gruenther, 27 Oct 50, sub: Status of KMAG. A perusal of G–3 File 333 Pacific (1950), which contains reports submitted by inspection parties to FEC during that period, does not reveal the nature of G–3's questions or whether they were ever asked or answered.

composition of the ROK Army, had the effect of blocking promotions within KMAG. Many advisors were junior company and field grade officers who had done a splendid job during some of the most difficult periods of the war; the realization that their chances of being promoted were virtually nil, together with the knowledge that many of their contemporaries with U.S. units were enjoying one- and two-grade promotions, was having a serious effect upon morale.[16]

The intervention by the Chinese Communists in November 1950 caused the advisory group to review even more fully the problem of its organization. If, as seemed likely, major operations were to continue indefinitely in Korea, KMAG could not go on as it had been, frantically juggling personnel in order to provide the minimum essential advisory supervision for the ROK Army. During the winter the KMAG staff therefore prepared yet another Table of Distribution, one based on ten ROK divisions and two corps headquarters, authorizing a total of 1,013 personnel. This T/D, if approved, would bring KMAG's strength up to a reasonable figure and, it was hoped, rectify once and for all the weaknesses of the old organization. At full strength the group would be able to furnish advisors to all ROK Army tactical and technical units, without a doubling up of advisory jobs. It would be possible to assign advisors to all ROK Army schools and training installations in sufficient quantities without diverting personnel from other advisory duties. Communications within the group would be more efficient, and signal advisors would be able to devote themselves exclusively to the improvement of ROK Army signal personnel. In addition, the new T/D would make possible better administrative and logistical support to KMAG personnel.[17]

This Table of Distribution went forward (probably in January or February 1951), was approved by the Far East Command on 16 March 1951, and became effective on 20 March

---

[16] (1) Ltr, Col Greenwood, 14 May 54. (2) Interv, Col Ross, 15 Dec 53. (3) See also Memo to Senior Corps and Div Advisors, 29 Sep 50, KMAG File AG 210.

[17] (1) Ltr, Col Greenwood, 14 May 54. (2) Ltr, Chief, KMAG, to CG EUSAK, 16 Aug 50, sub: Justification of Revised T/D, EUSAK File 320.3. (3) Ltr, Gen Farrell to CG EUSAK, 10 Aug 50, sub: Emergency Personnel Requisition, KMAG File 210.3 (106). (4) Ltr, CG EUSAK to CINCFE, 26 Sep 50, sub: Tables of Distribution for Korean Military Advisory Group, EUSAK File AG 322.

1951.[18] (*Chart 2*) Still, the mere approval of a Table of Distribution did not guarantee that the personnel authorized under it would be available at once. As had been the case in 1949, following the establishment of the advisory group, KMAG was unable to meet its new strength ceiling for several months. From a total strength of approximately 850, reported shortly after its reorganization became effective, the group expanded slowly until it reached a total strength of 1,055 on 31 August 1951. (*See Table 2*)

Improving the ROK Army

In approving the ten-division ROK Army organization proposed by General Walker in August 1950, both General MacArthur and the Department of the Army assumed that President Truman's directive of 27 June empowering them to go to the aid of the Republic of Korea gave them sufficient authority to exceed the 65,000-man limitation on U.S. support of Korean forces established in 1949. There had been no Congressional approval of their program, nor had specific written authority by the President ever been received at the Pentagon. At an Army Policy Council meeting on 5 October 1950, top Army planners therefore decided to obtain Mr. Truman's approval in writing of the Army's recent and projected actions in support of South Korean forces. The Secretary of the Army, Frank Pace, Jr., requested this approval on 1 November, and three days later the President signed an endorsement.[19]

The U.S. Army Chief of Staff, General J. Lawton Collins, was also concerned in October about the need for working up a postwar troop basis and a system of supply for the Far East Command, and the ROK Army. With victory seemingly in the offing, he reminded the JCS on 3 October that decisions on these matters might soon have to be made. Two days later Collins

---

[18] (1) Ltr, Col Greenwood. (2) GO 149, Hq EUSAK, 18 Mar 51. (3) Ltr, Chief, KMAG, to CG EUSAK, 6 Apr 51, sub: Reorganization of Bulk Authorization Unit (KMAG), KMAG File 320.4.

[19] (1) G–4 Staff Study with Memo for Secy Def, 7 Oct 50, sub: Approval for Issue of Equipment to South Korean Army, KMAG File, FE&Pac Br, G–3, folder 1, index 6. (2) Memo for the President from Secy of the Army, 1 Nov 50, sub: Logistic Support to Republic of Korea Army, KMAG File, FE&Pac Br, G–3, folder 2, bk. 1, tab E.

CHART 2—KMAG TABLE OF DISTRIBUTION, MARCH 1951

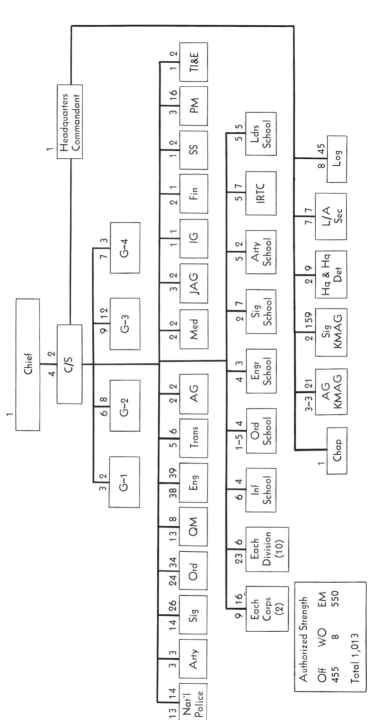

Source: EUSAK File AG 322.

directed his own staff to develop a definitive program of support for the ROK forces, including budgeting and funding aspects.[20]

At this same time, the Department of the Army asked the Far East Command to draw up a new Table of Organization and Equipment (T/O&E) for the ROK divisions. The original T/O&E had been hastily contrived and the Army now desired a permanent table. Using the U.S. Army's T/O&E 7N of 1948 as a model, KMAG tailored the tables in line with the ROK Army's capabilities. The result was a ROK divisional T/O&E of 13,554 (712 officers, 38 warrant officers, and 12,804 enlisted men) as compared with the U.S. division's strength of 18,855 (939 officers, 164 warrant officers, and 17,752 enlisted men). The new tables, designated T/O&E 7–ROK, were approved by the Department of the Army on 21 February 1951.[21]

Under T/O&E 7–ROK, the majority of heavy armament employed by U.S. divisions was omitted or greatly reduced. Each ROK division would have only one battalion of 105-mm. howitzers and one battalion of 155-mm. howitzers as artillery. Organic armor would consist of one medium tank company at the division level. There would no recoilless weapons. Additional artillery and tank support, if needed, would come from attached Eighth Army units. In addition, there would be one less engineer company in each engineer combat battalion, one less ordnance maintenance platoon in each division ordnance company, no bath and laundry section in the quartermaster company, and no filler personnel. An important feature in omitting or reducing the number of heavier and more complicated pieces of equipment in Korean divisions was the resultant reduction in support and maintenance units, always a great problem in the ROK Army.[22]

---

[20] (1) JCS 1776/124, 4 Oct 50. (2) G–4 Staff Study, 7 Oct 50, cited preceding note.

[21] (1) Msg, WAR 93553, CSGPO to CINCFE, 6 Oct 50. (2) Ltr, CG EUSAK to CINCFE, 28 Oct 50, sub: T/O&E for ROKA Div, EUSAK, AG 322. (3) G–3 Memo for Rcd, 3 Jan 51, sub: T/O&E for ROKA Div, KMAG, FE&Pac Br, G–3, folder 1, tab 16. (4) G–3 His of DA Activities Relating to the Korean Conflict, Unit and Equipment Sec, pp. 3–4.

[22] (1) G–3 Memo for Rcd, 3 Jan 51, T/O&E for ROK Army Div, cited preceding note. (2) MS, U.S. Military Advisory Group to the Republic of Korea, no date, KMAG File, FE&Pac Br, G–3, folder 19, tab M. (3) Advisor's Handbook, 1 Mar 51, p. 3.

The upsurge in interest in the future strength and organization of the ROK armed forces continued throughout October, then was eclipsed by the entry of the Chinese Communists into the war in November. As the UNC forces fell back toward the 38th Parallel and beyond, the question of survival again arose. Until it was certain that the U.N. Command could remain in Korea and continue the fight, planning for postwar ROK forces seemed to be academic. The situation in Korea at the end of 1950 appeared quite dismal. The enemy drove south of the Parallel and on 4 January Seoul fell for the second time. With the Chinese and North Korean troops pressing the attack south, the outlook for the U.N. and ROK forces was hardly reassuring.

Syngman Rhee, despite the setbacks, informed the United States that his country was determined to carry on the struggle. He requested that the United States arm large numbers of young Koreans, including the members of a national organization called the Korean Youth Corps, who had already received some military training. General of the Army George C. Marshall, who had become Secretary of Defense in September, asked the JCS to consider Rhee's request. In early January 1951, the JCS was able to notify MacArthur that rifles, carbines, automatic rifles, and submachine guns could be made available to arm an additional 100,000 Koreans.[23]

But MacArthur was dubious about the value of more ROK forces in the immediate future. In early January the fortunes of the U.N. Command were at a low point, and MacArthur was inclined to be pessimistic about the outcome of the war. He pointed out that the performance of ROK troops had not been outstanding in the past, that the battlefield would probably be limited in extent, and that the equipping of a Japanese National Police Reserve force should be accorded a high priority. The available Korean manpower, he went on, could be used to replace losses rather than to create new units.[24]

---

[23] (1) Memo, Chief, International Br, G–3 for Maj Gen [Cortlandt V. R] Schuyler, no date, sub: Proposed Arming of Korean Youth Corps, G–3 091 Korea, case 137. (2) Msg, JCS 80254, JCS to CINCUNC, 4 Jan 51. (3) G–3 Hist of DA Activities Relating to the Korean Conflict, Incl. A, pp. 12, 14. (4) Schnabel, Korean War, ch. IX, pp. 26–28.
[24] Msg, C 52879, CINCFE to DEPTAR, 6 Jan 51.

In view of the United Nations commander's reluctance to expand the ROK Army organization, the JCS told General Marshall that, from a military point of view, it appeared that the Korean Youth Corps and other available manpower could be best employed as replacements for casualties in the ROK units already in being.[25]

The gloom of January was replaced by the rising spirit of optimism in February 1951. The Eighth Army had an energetic new commander, Lt. Gen. Matthew B. Ridgway, and the forces under his command began to take on the semblance of a fighting army again.[26] After stabilizing the front, Ridgway pushed the enemy north of the 38th Parallel for the second time.

As the U.N. Command prospects brightened during the winter, the Department of the Army restudied its position on future commitments to Korean forces and on the size of the postwar ROK Army. Assuming first that the U.N. Command would be able to stabilize the ground action in Korea so that ROK forces could contain the enemy without the aid of major UNC forces, and second that Chinese Communist troops would be withdrawn eventually from the peninsula, the Army concluded that the size of the ROK forces should be ten infantry divisions, with necessary combat and support units, not to exceed a total strength of 300,000 men. Such an army would be capable of maintaining internal security, resisting attacks by other than a major power, and, if driven out of Korea, could materially assist the United States in executing certain war plans in the Pacific area. While conceding that the ROK Army's training doctrine and methods were satisfactory, the study concluded that ROK infantry division Tables of Organization and Equipment should be revised in the light of recent experience.[27]

---

[25] (1) Memo, JCS for Secy Defense, 17 Jan 51. (2) See also G–3 Hist of DA Activities Relating to the Korean Conflict, p. 14. It is interesting to note that when battlefield conditions improved, MacArthur took advantage of the Korean manpower and authorized an increase of 25 percent in ROK division strength. The increase was in riflemen only and totaled 33,885 men, for which he asked and received DA support in rifles and other equipment. See Memo, Duff for Bolté, 1 May 51, KMAG, FE&Pac Br, G–3, folder 2, tab H.

[26] General Walker was killed in an accident just before Christmas.

[27] Msg, DA 86891, Deputy CofS for Plans (sgd Bolté) to CINCFE, 7 Mar 51.

The Deputy Chief of Staff for Plans, Maj. Gen. Charles L. Bolté, informed General MacArthur of these conclusions on 7 March 1951 and requested that MacArthur's comments include recommended priorities for organizing and equipping units. MacArthur answered on 5 April 1951, stating that he considered his "previously indicated concept" of ten divisions and appropriate supporting units with a total strength of 250,000 was "still sound." Moreover, he recommended that no change be made in the ROK infantry division organization recently approved by the Department of the Army.[28] As for priority in organizing and equipping ROK units, the U.N. commander stated that it was not then practicable for him to make sound recommendations on the matter. It appeared reasonable, he said, to assume that ROK divisions would have been fully organized and largely equipped when Allied ground forces were withdrawn from Korea; thereafter priorities for equipping additional units would depend on the situation existing at that time. If the assumptions upon which the Army based its conclusions proved to be valid, MacArthur concluded, he still thought that the Japanese National Police Reserve should receive higher priority than similar projects for the Korean Army.[29]

The following day MacArthur told Ridgway that, as U.N. commander, he had no authority to establish strength levels for Korean forces. As a sovereign nation only the Republic of Korea could do that. His recommendations were made on the basis of availability of equipment rather than on personnel ceilings.[30]

Less than a week later General MacArthur was recalled by Mr. Truman. General Ridgway succeeded MacArthur as U.N. and Far East Commander and as Supreme Commander, Allied Powers, and Lt. Gen. James A. Van Fleet became Eighth Army Commander.

On 18 April General Collins approved, for planning purposes,

---

[28] See above.
[29] Msg, C 59376, CINCFE to DEPTAR, 5 Apr 51.
[30] Msg, CX 59480, CINCFE to CG, Army Eight, 6 Apr 51, cited in Schnabel, Korean War, ch. X, p. 18.

a postwar ROK Army of ten divisions plus supporting units, with a 250,000-man ceiling.[31]

ROK officials, however, were not content with a ten-division army. In April, Col. Ben C. Limb, the ROK representative to the United Nations, publicly appealed for U.S. arms for 375,000 South Koreans who, he said, were immediately available for military service. President Rhee followed on 23 April with a request to Ridgway that the United States arm and equip ten additional divisions. Mr. Rhee's request could hardly have arrived at a worse time, for on 22 April a ROK division had unnecessarily suffered a disastrous defeat at the hands of the North Koreans. The incident, involving the flight of the ROK 6th Division before inferior enemy forces, endangered the entire United Nations line and was serious enough to command General Ridgway's personal attention. Immediately he launched a study to determine what should be done to increase the effectiveness of the Republic of Korea Army.[32]

Following conferences with General Van Fleet, Ambassador Muccio, and President Rhee, General Ridgway concluded that the ROK Army's primary needs were leadership and training, not manpower and equipment. Until the ROK forces then in being could demonstrate an ability to perform suitably in battle, there seemed to be little point in arming and equipping additional units.[33] One possibility considered during the course of this study was that U.S. Army officers be used to command elements of the Korean Army. Such a possibility had been proposed to General of the Army Omar N. Bradley by Colonel Limb on 18 April 1951, and General Marshall had expressed interest in the idea. However, General Ridgway, Ambassador Muccio, and President Rhee rejected this course of action as impracticable in view of the large number of American officers that would be required, the ever-present language barrier, and the fact that successful command of Korean units by U.S. officers would

---

[31] G–3 Hist of DA Activities Relating to the Korean Conflict, Unit and Equipment Sec, p. 8.

[32] See CINCFE G–3 Presentation for Mr. Archibald S. Alexander, Under Secretary of the Army, no date, G–3 File 091 Korea (1951), case 187/7, tab C.

[33] (1) Msg, C 61433, CINCFE to DEPTAR, Personal for Collins, 1 May 51. (2) Msg, C 61856, CINCFE to DEPTAR for Lt Gen John E. Hull, 5 May 51.

require a prerequisite of complete authority to administer and discipline forces of a friendly sovereign nation.[34]

A practical solution was suggested by General Ridgway himself on 2 May when he directed General Van Fleet to investigate the feasibility of conducting a special training course for ROK officers to correct deficiencies in leadership. Col. Gilman C. Mudgett, EUSAK G–3, suggested in turn that some type of command, possibly like the replacement and school command established by the U.S. Army during World War II, be established within the Korean Army. A United States general officer could be assigned as advisor to the command and, so as to insure proper co-ordination with the ROK Army's combat requirements, be a member of the U.S. Military Advisory Group.[35]

Colonel Mudgett noted in passing that KMAG at its current strength was unable to furnish enough advisors to ROK Army schools and recommended that KMAG strength be increased. In February 1951 the Ground General School at Tongnae had been redesignated the Infantry School when separate training centers (schools) were established for the signal, engineer, ordnance, quartermaster, and artillery branches, along with military police and field finance schools. Operating independently, these branch schools (training centers) by May 1951 were conducting every basic course then offered in U.S. Army service schools, and advanced courses were scheduled to begin on 15 May 1951. The Infantry School had five advisors, the Engineer School had three, the Artillery School had two, and most of the others each had one advisor.[36]

General Farrell agreed with Mudgett's proposals but emphasized that a training command for the ROK Army should be

---

[34] (1) CINCFE G–3 Presentation for Mr. Alexander. (2) Summary Sheet, Joint War Plans, 25 Apr 51, sub: Steps To Be Taken To Arm and Equip an Additional Ten South Korean Divisions, (sgd Maj Gen Maxwell D. Taylor), G–3 091 Korea, case 174. (3) Memo, General Wade H. Haislip, Vice CofS for Bradley, 28 Apr 51, sub: Additional Korean Divs, G–3 091 Korea, case 174.

[35] (1) Comment Sheet (sgd Mudgett), 4 May 51, sub: Troop Leadership School for Senior Korean Officers, KMAG File AG 353. (2) See also Msg, C 61856, CINCFE to DEPTAR for Hull, 5 May 51.

[36] (1) Comment Sheet (sgd Mudgett). (2) Advisor's Handbook, 1 Mar 51, G–3 an., sec. III, pp. 2, 3. (3) Office of the Army Attaché Seoul, Rpt R–24–52, 19 Jan 52, G–2 Doc Lib, DA, ID 871088. (4) Excerpt from DATT 4456 (Teletype Conference), ref note 1, DATT 4449, 6 Mar 51, FE&Pac Br Files, G–3.

under his direction for co-ordination. Regarding an increase in KMAG's strength, Farrell pointed out that there were then only 33 officers and 34 enlisted men assigned to ROK training installations. In order for such a training command to be successful, KMAG training personnel would have to be augmented by at least 68 officers and 85 enlisted men. He based this increase on his concept of advisory functions at training installations, as follows:

1. General supervision of installations operations.
2. Personal instruction of the Korean instructor cadre in each phase of training.
3. Direct supervision of the development and preparation of programs of instruction and lesson plans.
4. Direct supervision of classroom presentation.
5. Critique of instruction.
6. Revisions in U.S. Army training literature before it was translated into Korean.

He recommended, however, that any action to change KMAG's Table of Distribution be delayed until the officer who was to take over training command had had an opportunity to determine his requirements.[37]

Generals Ridgway and Van Fleet selected Col. Arthur S. Champeny, Deputy Chief of Staff, General Headquarters, Far East Command, as the officer best qualified to head such a program. Involvement in Korean affairs was nothing new to Colonel Champeny, who had been the Director of National Defense under U.S. Army Military Government in Korea (USAMGIK) when the Korean Constabulary was formed in January 1946, and later Deputy Military Governor of Korea.[38] He had commanded a U.S. regiment early in the war, was wounded in September 1950, and, until May 1951, had been on duty in both Korea and Japan.[39]

---

[37] Comment (2) by Gen Farrell, Chief, KMAG, 13 May 51 (Troop Leadership School for Senior Korean Officers), KMAG File AG 353.
[38] See ch. I, above.
[39] (1) Ltr, Brig Gen Arthur S. Champeny (Ret), 17 Nov 53. (2) See also Memo for Secy Army from Gen Hull, Dep CofS for O&R, 17 Jul 51, sub: Development of ROK Officers and NCO Corps, KMAG File, FE&Pac Br, G–3, folder 2, tab J.

Lt. Gen. Doyle O. Hickey, FEC chief of staff, called Colonel Champeny to his office in the Dai Ichi Building in Tokyo on 7 May 1951 and informed him of his appointment as General Ridgway's personal representative. He was, said Hickey, to go to Korea the next day to look things over and decide what was needed for the United States to improve the ROK Army's training, return to Japan on the following day, and depart immediately for the

COLONEL CHAMPENY

States. Champeny was surprised at the limited time given him to make his analysis, and said so, but General Hickey replied simply that General Headquarters could not allow him more time than that.

After a conference with Maj. Gen. Henry I. Hodes, deputy commander of the Eighth Army, in Taegu the next day, Colonel Champeny reported to General Farrell at KMAG Headquarters. The chief of KMAG outlined for him the facilities and equipment that were available to the advisory group and suggested that he inspect the schools and training installations located at Tongnae. Champeny left immediately in a liaison-type plane furnished for his use by General Hodes, and on the following day he visited as many training installations as possible in the Pusan area. To have visited all ROK Army training areas in South Korea or, indeed, to have thoroughly inspected those installations around Pusan would have required at least two weeks. Colonel Champeny accomplished as much as he could in the time available to him and returned to Japan on 9 May. He left for the United States two days later.

After conferring in Washington with representatives of the Assistant Chief of Staff, G–3, Maj. Gen. Maxwell D. Taylor, Colonel Champeny went on to Headquarters, Army Field Forces, at Fort Monroe. There he worked out an itinerary of visits to various schools and training installations, where he hoped to obtain viewpoints and suggestions, training materials, and, most important, instructor personnel for assignment to KMAG. During the following weeks he visited the Infantry and Artillery Schools at Forts Benning and Sill; he observed basic training conducted by the 10th Mountain Division at Fort Riley, the 3d Armored Division at Fort Knox, and the 9th Infantry Division at Fort Dix; and he concluded his tour at Fort Monmouth, where he inspected the training of U.S. Army signal personnel. Later, on his way back to the Far East, he stopped off at Fort Bliss, to observe training at the Antiaircraft School, and at Camp Roberts and Fort Ord.

Colonel Champeny had learned at Fort Monroe that Korean officers attending courses at the Infantry and Artillery Schools were not benefiting greatly unless they had a good knowledge of the English language. At these schools, therefore, he proposed that Korean officers be assigned to groups of from 150 to 200 and that the school instructors deliver their instruction through interpreters; suitable interpreters, he thought, could be obtained from a large Korean group resident in Hawaii. Because he felt that the ROK Army's primary need was for infantry and artillery officers, Champeny recommended that such group instruction of Korean officer students be confined to the aforementioned schools.[40] In this connection, his conviction that the situation in Korea called for trained Korean fighters and leaders rather than technicians led Colonel Champeny to inspect leaders courses conducted by the 10th Mountain Division, 3d Armored Division, and 9th Division, and similar courses at Fort Ord and Camp Roberts. Although he planned to develop leaders courses for the Republic of Korea Army, Champeny felt that the courses as given in the United States placed too much emphasis on methods

---

[40] (1) Ltr, Gen Champeny, 17 Nov 53. (2) Also see Ltr, Gen Champeny to CG EUSAK, 24 Jul 51, sub: Agreements Relative to Groups of Korean Officers Going to the United States for Attendance at Service Schools, KMAG File AG 350.2; Ltr, Gen Champeny to CG EUSAK, 24 Jul 51, sub: Rpt of Trip to Zone of Interior on Leadership Schools, KMAG File AG 352.

of instruction and neglected the aspects of leadership needed in combat. For that reason, in his opinion, the U.S. courses were not appropriate for the Koreans.

Back in Washington he informed General Taylor of the plan for instructing groups of Korean officers through interpreters and cited the approval of Army Field Forces and the schools concerned. Although U.S. policy with respect to the use of funds for schooling would have to be modified for this purpose, General Taylor assured Colonel Champeny of G–3 support and suggested that he work out the details with the chief of KMAG upon his return to Korea. Champeny later discussed the matter of interpreters with the Korean consul in Hawaii, but that gentleman was not enthusiastic.

At each service school, Colonel Champeny also obtained the names of officers who were on orders to the Far East Command, along with the schools' recommendations as to their abilities as instructors. It was his thought that KMAG could request the assignment of outstanding officers to the advisory group upon their arrival in the Orient. He further screened personnel records in Washington but was not overly successful in securing instructors or training personnel. However, he did obtain the services of an officer who proved to be of great value to him in establishing the ROK Army training command, Col. William W. O'Hearn, whom he had recalled to extended active duty from civilian life. Like Champeny, O'Hearn had a background of service in Korea during the early years of the American occupation.

Not long after Colonel Champeny's return to Korea, in July, the Department of the Army asked General Ridgway for his estimate of what was needed to make the Republic of Korea forces completely effective. General Ridgway replied on 22 July that the ROK Army needed first of all officer and noncommissioned officer corps of adequate professional competence. These corps had to be thoroughly imbued with a will to fight, be capable of aggressive leadership, and be inspired with such essential qualities as love of country, honor, integrity, devotion to duty, and professional pride. Under the conditions of that time, it would require at least three years to develop an effective ROK Army; if the war in Korea ended, the job could be done in two years.[41]

Several courses of action were necessary, in Ridgway's opinion, if this objective were to be attained. Among these were:

1. The establishment of a replacement training and school command to supervise the ROK Army's schooling and training.
2. The establishment of a U.S. Army-type military reservation, and a centralization of ROK Army training installations for the combat arms.
3. An increase in the number of U.S. Army personnel at ROK Army training installations.
4. An intensive leadership program for the ROK Army.
5. More training of ROK officers in U.S. Army service schools.
6. Pressure on the Republic of Korea Government to insure disciplinary measures against incompetent, corrupt, or cowardly ROK officers and governmental officials.
7. A rehabilitation program for all ROK infantry divisions.
8. The development of service units for a ten-division ROK Army.
9. An increase in the number of automatic weapons, artillery, and tanks in the ROK Army, as units demonstrated an ability to absorb and use additional equipment.

The United Nations commander emphasized his opinion that the United States could not afford to enter an armament race with the Soviet Union through the medium of U.S.-equipped Republic of Korea divisions versus Russian-equipped North Korean or Chinese Communist divisions. The ROK Army's effectiveness should be based on its strength of ten divisions, rather than on the estimated requirements of a ROK Army capable of withstanding future Communist aggression.

As the Korean War entered a new phase in the summer of 1951, the task that confronted KMAG remained the same. The ROK Army still needed thorough training and instruction on all levels to build up its confidence and to develop its leadership. There was no easy or quick solution to this problem; in the past, the pressure of the battlefield had not allowed adequate time for the training that was required. But as the U.N. Command and

---

[41] (1) Msgs, DA 96162, DA to CINCFE, 12 Jul 51, and DA 96459, DA to CINCFE, 16 Jul 51, cited in Memo, Col Louis A. Walsh, Jr., Acting Chief, FE&Pac Br, G-3, for Brig Gen Ridgley Gaither, 24 Jul 51, sub: Status of Efforts in Improving the ROK Army, KMAG File, FE&Pac Br, G-3, folder 2, tab K. (2) Msg, CX 67484, CINCFE, to DEPTAR, 22 Jul 51.

the enemy negotiators met at Kaesong in July to discuss the possibility of concluding a truce, the pace at the front slackened. For the first time there seemed to be enough time to institute training programs and to work on the ROK Army's basic weaknesses.

CHAPTER IX

A Firm Foundation

During the last two years of the war, the action in Korea took place on a ten-mile-wide strip of land that straddled the 38th Parallel on the western end and reached toward the north along the east coast. Each side mounted limited objective attacks from time to time to apply military pressure upon the other and influence the course of the truce negotiations at Kaesong and later at Panmunjom. For the most part, however, the front was static, and the character of the war was defensive.

The slowdown in operations on the battlefield was of great help to the KMAG staff. The advisory group finally had enough time, personnel, and facilities to carry out its mission under relatively favorable conditions. Both the United States and the Republic of Korea were anxious to see a well-trained and well-equipped ROK Army in being, one that would be able to defend the country successfully against another aggression. With the sharp reduction in the scale of fighting at the front, the moment seemed propitious to improve the ROK Army.

Strengthening the School System

Most of the weaknesses that had appeared in the ROK forces could be traced to inadequate training, and it was in this field that KMAG concentrated its efforts during the first year of the truce negotiations. Operating under the direct command of the Eighth Army for all training functions, KMAG sought to expand and strengthen the ROKA school system and training establishment. To carry out an augmented program of assistance and guidance, KMAG in January 1952 requested and won approval of a new Table of Distribution that called for a total of 1,815 spaces—578 officers and 1,237 enlisted men. KMAG was also authorized a temporary overstrength of 39 officers and 99 en-

178

listed men. At full strength KMAG could thus attain a total of 1953 men.[1]

Since time was no longer so essential, the emphasis in the schools shifted to a more adequate preparation of ROK soldiers and units for combat. By devoting more time to training and more attention to the development of leadership qualities, KMAG hoped to produce a professionally competent officer and noncommissioned officer corps and to build up the morale and confidence of all ranks.

During late 1951 and early 1952 KMAG began to stimulate the growth of the existing educational facilities and to establish new ones. Schools that had been closed by the North Korean invasion were resited and reopened. By the first of October 1951 the ROKA schools were operating with a capacity of over 10,000 students at a time. Similar progress was made in the expansion of the training establishments. Under the Replacement Training and School Command (RTSC) set up by General Champeny, facilities were developed by October to handle over 23,000 men simultaneously.

In an effort to centralize school and training installations, the RTSC successfully urged that the Infantry, Artillery, and Signal Schools all be located at Kwangju in southeastern Korea. In early January the consolidated school, later called the Korean Army Training Center (KATC) opened at the new site and soon was able to accommodate up to 15,000 men at a time.

The KATC was a well-planned facility with pistol and rifle ranges within easy walking distance of the main post and artillery ranges for all calibers of guns. KATC also had adequate space for carrying out small unit tactical problems and sufficient classrooms to house all the students in the event of bad weather.

To provide additional training for future company grade officers, the courses at the officer candidate schools were lengthened from eighteen to twenty-four weeks during the winter of

---

[1] Unless otherwise specified, this section is based upon: (1) Walter G. Hermes, Truce Tent and Fighting Front, a forthcoming volume in the UNITED STATES ARMY IN THE KOREAN WAR series; (2) Kenneth W. Myers, The U.S. Military Advisory Group to the Republic of Korea, pt. IV, KMAG's Wartime Experiences, 11 July 1951–27 July 1953, MS in OCMH files. Hereafter cited as KMAG's Wartime Experiences.

KOREAN STUDENTS AT THE INFANTRY SCHOOL, FORT BENNING. *Maj. Gen. Withers A. Burr, commanding general of the school, with Brig. Gen. Lee Hyung Koon and Lt. Col. C. K. Chang.*

1951, and the Korean Military Academy was re-established in a new location at Chinhae. On 1 January 1952 a full four-year course patterned after West Point was initiated, and the first class of 200 cadets began their instructions. For field grade officers the Command and General Staff School was reopened on 11 December 1951 at Taegu to instruct the ROK senior officers in the intricacies of good staff and command procedures.

To supplement the ROK Army school system, the Department of the Army had approved a KMAG request for 250 ROK officers to attend U.S. service schools in late 1951. A hundred and fifty officers were enrolled at the Infantry School at Fort Benning, and the other hundred participated in the course given at the Artillery School at Fort Sill. In addition to the technical and professional benefits gained at the U.S. schools, many of the ROK officers were able to learn some English as well. Since the members of the group selected for training in U.S. schools were of high caliber, they attained good grades in their studies and were especially well qualified to serve as instructors upon their return to Korea. When the first group graduated in March 1952, a second contingent of 250 was sent to the United States to begin the next cycle.

In addition to raising officer standards KMAG also sought to bolster the morale and combat capabilities of the troops at the front. In late July 1951 General Van Fleet appointed Brig. Gen. Thomas J. Cross, deputy commander of the U.S. IX Corps, as Commanding General, Field Training Command (FTC). During the succeeding three months members of the KMAG staff helped supervise the establishment of four training camps, one in each corps area, to retrain the ROK Army. Since many individuals and units had been forced by the exigencies of battle to enter combat with very little training, the respite on the battlefield provided a chance for the ROK divisions to fill in some of the gaps in their military education. As each division came back from the front and went into corps reserve, it was sent to a FTC camp for nine weeks of basic training. Refresher instruction in weapons and tactics began with the individual and worked up to the squad, platoon, and company level. At the end of the course a battalion problem was presented and worked out. In the two months of intense training the ROK soldiers became more skilled members of the combat team, and the ROK divisions approached a common standard of battle effectiveness. As it happened, the demands of the front prevented some of the divisions from completing the full nine-week cycle, but by late 1952 all of the ten original ROK divisions had received at least five weeks of refresher training. Some had returned several times to the FTC camps and accumulated as much as eleven weeks of training.

The problems faced by the KMAG advisors during the rapid expansion of school and training facilities were not greatly different from those encountered before the war. There was still a dearth of qualified ROK instructors. The lack of textbooks in Korean and the difficulties in procuring training aids and equipment for classes and demonstrations also made the task of instruction a great deal harder. Moreover, the old obstacle of communication had not been overcome; the translation of military concepts and technical designations into Korean was still complicated and open to misinterpretation and misunderstanding.

The Build-up of ROKA Support

In addition to the education and training of ROKA manpower, KMAG attempted to increase the effectiveness of the combat forces by providing them with more support in the field. In the past the ROK infantryman often had to double as a porter. The rough terrain and the poor communications system in the sectors most frequently manned by ROK troops made the problem of resupply an onerous task. Food, ammunition, and equipment had to be brought in by human carrier, and this often meant the infantryman since he was the only one available. To lighten this logistical burden and to improve the efficiency of the front-line forces, General Ridgway gave Van Fleet permission in November 1951 to increase the Korean Service Corps (KSC) to 60,000 men. The KSC consisted of laborers and porters who could relieve the combat soldiers of their service-type responsibilities. Ridgway eventually hoped to increase the KSC to 75,000 so that the infantrymen could concentrate upon their prime purpose—fighting the enemy.[2]

KMAG was also instrumental in securing the support of Ridgway and Van Fleet in another field in which the ROK Army had a basic weakness. The lack of adequate integral artillery in the ROK division had been recognized early in the war, for the ROK Army only had one 105-mm. howitzer battalion assigned to a division while the American counterpart had three 105-mm. and one 155-mm. howitzer battalions as a normal complement. Moreover, the U.S. division also had a tank battalion and heavy mortar companies to call upon for additional fire support. As long as the war had been in a mobile phase, the Far East Command and the Eighth Army staffs had frowned upon increasing the ROK artillery. They had felt that the rugged terrain, the

[2] Msg, DA–IN 354, CINCFE to DEPTAR, 18 Nov 51.

KMAG Artillery Advisor *watches ROK soldiers load 105-mm. howitzer.*

lifficulty of ammunition resupply, the lack of trained ROK irtillerymen, and the shortage of artillery pieces all argued igainst expansion.[3]

Time and the stalemate at the front overcame these objections. In September 1951 Ridgway authorized four 155-mm. howitzer battalions to be activated before the end of the year. As each was activated it was attached to a U.S. corps and trained for eight weeks. Three headquarters batteries and six 105-mm. howitzer battalions were authorized in November 1951 and began their raining two months later. The continued lull on the battlefield ind the availability of more artillery pieces and of trained ROKA artillery officers as they returned from the U.S. Artillery School provided added incentive for further increases. Ridgway set up a program that eventually would produce sufficient 05-mm. and 155-mm. battalions to give each of the ten ROK

---

[3] Hermes, Truce Tent and Fighting Front, ch. X.

divisions a full complement of three 105-mm. and one 155-mm. howitzer artillery battalions. In May 1952 the Department of the Army granted the Far East commander interim authority to go ahead with this plan.[4]

During the remainder of 1952 the artillery program made great headway. By October sixteen battalions of 105-mm. howitzers were ready for duty and four others were scheduled to join the ROK Army before the close of the year. In the meantime the cadres of six ROK 155-mm. howitzer battalions had undergone training with U.S. divisional artillery and by November were ready to take their battalion firing tests.[5]

To strengthen the ROK fire power, KMAG began to train armored troops at the Infantry School in April 1951. The object was to provide one tank company for each ROK division, plus the maintenance personnel to keep the tanks operational. In October the first two companies were activated and trained on M36 gun motor carriages, which were equipped with 90-mm. guns. One company went on that month to join the ROK I Corps, but the lack of tanks prevented the second company from completing its training. It was not until the spring of 1952 that M24 light tanks arrived from the United States and that additional tank companies could be prepared for operations. By October a Marine and four ROK Army tank companies had been formed and had their tanks; three others awaited their equipment, en route from the United States, to make them operational.[6] With the provision of full artillery and some tank support, the combat capabilities of the ROK divisions would be bolstered considerably, and it was hoped that reliance upon U.S. divisions for combat support would be materially lessened.

In the field of supply and procurement, KMAG had to instruct and train the ROKA troops in the practice of sound military supply procedures. U.S. logistical support of the ROK Army was restricted to the items the Republic of Korea could

---

[4] Msg, DA 909826, G–3 to CINCFE, 27 May 52.
[5] Hq Eighth Army, Command Reports, Sec. I, Narrative, October and November, 1951.
[6] Myers, KMAG's Wartime Experiences, pp. 211 ff.

not produce domestically. Therefore KMAG attempted to stimulate, whenever possible, ROK efforts to attain self-sufficiency. It supervised ROKA procurement agencies, gathered information concerning the production potential of Korean industry, and made suggestions upon the modification of ROKA equipment and matériel so that the South Koreans could themselves manufacture some of these items.[7]

Besides this responsibility for developing ROK supply resources, KMAG also had to insure that logistical support furnished by the United States was properly utilized. KMAG advisors had to work closely with their ROK counterparts in the preparation of supply requisitions, which were then forwarded to the KMAG G–4 senior advisor for review, approval, consolidation, and submission to the Eighth Army. When the Eighth Army approved a requisition, the KMAG advisors had to insure that the ROK units employed or expended the supplies judiciously.[8]

By mid-1952 the pattern of KMAG operations for the remainder of the war had been established. The school and training program and facilities had been set up and were capable of handling large groups of students or trainees. In the Field Training Command camps, the ROK divisions received refresher instruction that helped create a standard of training for the ROK Army as a whole. Specialists were being turned out in increasing numbers to satisfy the mounting demands for their skills within the Army. And combat and service support forces were strengthening the offensive and defensive capabilities of the ROKA organizations.

Ahead lay the great period of expansion when the ROK Army would double the numbers of personnel and divisions under its jurisdiction with the resultant growing pains and dilution of quality that wholesale increases always produced. But the machinery had been created and the cadres formed—the ROK Army had a foundation upon which to build, one KMAG had largely helped to lay down.

---

[7] *Ibid.*, pp. 252 ff.
[8] *Ibid.*

KMAG in Retrospect

The accomplishments of KMAG can be properly appreciated only when they are viewed against the background of its limitations, and in the early phase of its history, these were many. In the Department of the Army directive of June 1949 that established KMAG, the prime limitation was set forth: KMAG would develop Korean security forces, which the Korean economy could eventually support. The emphasis thus was placed upon internal security forces that could preserve order and defend the border areas rather than upon the formation of an army capable of defense and offense. This restriction provided the framework within which KMAG had to operate. The United States reinforced this framework by supplying the ROK defense forces with light weapons and equipment that were more suitable for a constabulary than for an army. In the prewar period neither the United States nor General MacArthur seemed to regard the new republic as a vital link in the U.S. defense system; the military aid in dollars was comparatively small, and there was little effort to provide it swiftly.

The KMAG group itself was also fairly small, especially when measured against the spiraling growth of the ROK forces. Designed originally to train a modest army of 50,000 men, KMAG's strength in the year before the war remained static while the ROK Army constantly expanded. Thus KMAG advisors frequently had to divide their services between several units instead of concentrating on one, and the dilution of their over-all efforts could not fail to be reflected in the lower training status of the ROK Army.

Working in an atmosphere of domestic unrest with the government facing urban political opposition while fighting continuously against guerrillas and brigands scattered throughout the rural areas, KMAG had to operate on makeshift training schedules that were dependent upon the exigencies of the moment. The American group had to surmount the military inexperience of the Korean leaders and people and their different standards of efficiency and methods of operation. They had to face the problems of language and communication to give the ROKA forces a basic understanding of modern military con-

:epts. Since the United States did not judge it appropriate, and .he Republic of Korea could not afford, to support the ROK orces completely, the supplies, equipment, and pay of the troops were less than adequate. KMAG had to try to fashion a trained army out of soldiers who lacked, in many cases, everything but spirit.

Perhaps the most important limitation imposed upon KMAG was that of time itself. Given sufficient time to finish the training of the ROK units—to develop a core of professionally qualified leaders and build up the equipment and weapons of the ROK forces—KMAG might well have produced an army that could have withstood and turned back the North Korean attack.

In the year before the invasion KMAG made a beginning. It improved and strengthened the ROK Army's organization and disposition and established an integrated training program that brought most units up through company-level exercises. By setting up military schools, KMAG started to raise the quality and competence of ROKA leadership. And some progress had been made in the KMAG effort to tie in the ROKA logistical support with the country's economy. The individual KMAG effort during the prewar period on the whole was excellent despite the obstacles besetting the advisors. They labored long and hard with the materials at hand to lay a firm foundation, and it was to their credit that the ROK Army was even 50 percent combat effective when the war broke out.[9] Unfortunately, time ran out, and the first effort by KMAG was doomed to failure.

The attack by the better trained North Korean forces equipped with superior artillery and supported by tanks and aircraft smashed through the ROKA defenses and disrupted most of the ROK units in its path. The new-laid foundation cracked and crumbled under the impact, and KMAG was forced to do a hasty job of patching and improvising during the succeeding months of retreat and stabilization along the Pusan Perimeter.

In the pursuit of the North Korean forces to the Yalu, the ROK units moved swiftly and performed well, but the strain and stress caused by the Communist Chinese assaults again im-

---

[9] See KMAG, SA Rpt, 15 Jun 50, an. V.

posed too heavy a burden upon the insufficiently trained ROK troops. For a second time they broke and retreated.

Again the task of reconstitution began, but little definitive progress could be made so long as the press of combat remained. Only after the front became static along the 38th Parallel could KMAG secure the time, personnel, and facilities to build and train a sound army.

During the last two years of the war the ROK Army steadily improved and assumed an increasingly important role in the defense of its country. Despite several lapses, the over-all performance of the ROK Army was encouraging and showed the efforts KMAG had made to increase its efficiency and competence. Time, hard work, patience, and determination all contributed toward the fashioning of a better ROK Army, and KMAG could understandably be proud of its part in this development.

Bibliographical Note

Most historical works on recent events are based primarily upon written records—either official or unofficial—supplemented by interviews and correspondence with the participants concerned. But the records pertaining to the activities of the U.S. Military Advisory Group to the Republic of Korea are sparse and contain little information on the problems of the officers and men engaged in organizing and training the South Korean forces. Therefore, of necessity, great reliance has been placed in this study upon the memories of the former members of the KMAG team, especially when the narrative touches upon events below the level of the major headquarters. Efforts have been made to compensate for the well-known inaccuracy of the human memory by reaching as many participants as possible. All letters and interviews mentioned in the footnotes are in OCMH files unless otherwise specified.

Although there are a number of studies dealing with the activities of U.S. Army Forces in Korea (USAFIK), including the U.S. Army Military Government in Korea (USAMGIK), few of them contain details about the development of Korean security forces. For example, on the formation of Constabulary regiments in the spring of 1946, a three-part manuscript history of U.S. Military Government in Korea written by the USAMGIK Statistical Research Division has one brief reference to a "recruiting drive" by the "newly-formed Constabulary." An official monthly publication of General Headquarters, Far East Command, *Summation of Non-Military Activities in Korea,* Volumes 6–22, March 1946 to July 1947, contains brief references to the Korean Constabulary and Coast Guard, but the U.S. military advisors with those organizations are not mentioned. A USAMGIK publication, *South Korean Interim Government Activities,* Volumes 26–36, November 1947 to September–November 1948, which superseded the latter, makes no mention whatsoever of Korean security forces or their advisors.

The official USAFIK and USAMGIK files are not much better. These are confined largely to records dealing with routine administrative matters, and to occupation problems such as the development of Korean economy and the complicated political situation existing in Korea after World War II. Much of the information concerning the background and planning for Korean security forces is to be found in JCS documents. On the U.S. Coast Guard Detachment to Korea, the U.S. Coast Guard files in Washington contained a copy of Captain McCabe's little paper, and nothing more.

Lt. Gen. John R. Hodge wrote in March 1952 that, while commanding general of USAFIK, he had kept a "Commanding General's file of radiograms, teletype messages, etc. from all sources which affected everything we did." This file, he noted, remained in Korea when he returned to the United States in 1948, but was later removed, possibly to Japan. According to General Hodge, no historical account of the U.S. occupation of Korea should be written without reference to this file, which was not available to any other portion of the occupation forces, including the military government. Efforts to locate the file were unsuccessful, although it is possible that its contents have been incorporated with the regular USAFIK files.

The records of the Provisional Military Advisory Group were few and inadequate for definitive historical purposes.

KMAG records from July 1949 to June 1950 were more satisfactory, though they left much to be filled in from other sources. KMAG historical and semiannual reports were helpful, enabling the writer to build up a general outline of KMAG's activities and problems during the period. But here again interviews and correspondence with former KMAG personnel were necessary in order to round out the KMAG story.

Official Records

U.S. Army Forces in Korea (USAFIK)

Adjutant General's files, 1945 to 30 June 1949, are located in the Federal Records Center, General Services Administration, (GSA), Kansas City, Missouri. These records deal mainly with routine administrative matters and problems connected with the occupation of Korea. They are helpful in providing a background for the U.S. Military Government in Korea and are valuable because of details concerning the withdrawal of U.S. forces from Korea in 1948 and 1949.

U.S. Army Military Government in Korea (USAMGIK)

Adjutant General's files, August 1945 to December 1948, are in the custody of the National Archives and Records Service of the General Services Administration, Washington 25, D.C. These records concern the development of Korean economy and government after World War II and the political situation then existing in Korea. They furnish considerable information about the U.S. Military Government in Korea but are remarkable for the lack of information dealing with the U.S. Army officers and men in the Department of National Defense (later Internal Security) of USAMGIK, who organized and developed South Korean security forces.

Provisional Military Advisory Group (PMAG)

Adjutant General's files, 1948 and 1949, are located in the Federal Records Center, Kansas City. These records deal primarily with routine administrative matters and are of some help in reconstructing PMAG's organization and strength. There is little about advisory problems here.

U.S. Military Advisory Group to the Republic of Korea (KMAG)

Adjutant General's files, 1949 and 1950, are located in the Federal Records Center, Kansas City. Besides routine administrative records, this file contains correspondence with the Department of the Army, Far East Command, and American Mission in Korea, all of which provide depth to the KMAG story. General and special orders are here.

Department of the Army, ACofS, G-3

P&O (Plans and Operations) files are in the custody of the National Archives and Records Service, GSA, Washington 25, D.C. These files are an invaluable source of information concerning South Korean security forces, PMAG, and KMAG, and provide the background and planning so necessary to an understanding of those subjects. Besides official correspondence, radio messages, and the like, G–3 files contain such items as personal correspondence between Brig. Gen. William L. Roberts and Maj. Gen. Charles L. Bolté.

Joint Chiefs of Staff (JCS) Documents, 1945–50

The complete file is in the custody of G–3 Records Section, DA. These documents, consisting of JCS studies and decisions, cover many and varied subjects including the establishment and developing of South Korean security forces and U.S. military aid to Korea. Those JCS documents cited in this monograph are in this file.

Reports and Manuals

Historical Report, U.S. Military Advisory Group to the Republic of Korea (KMAG), 1 July 1949 to 31 December 1949, contains a summary of events during the years 1945–49, inclusive, and reports from each advisory section of KMAG (PMAG) from 1 April 1949 to 31 December 1949. The summary should be used with caution, for other research has shown that some of the statements therein are in error. The section reports appear to be accurate and contain much useful information. Unless otherwise specified, all of the items mentioned in this section will be found in the custody of the National Archives and Records Service, GSA, Washington 25, D.C.

Semiannual Reports, U.S. Military Advisory Group to the Republic of Korea (KMAG), 1 July 1949 to 31 December 1949 and 1 January 1950 to 30 June 1950, are extremely useful and give a comprehensive picture of KMAG and its activities during the period covered. The 1950 report actually covers the period 1 January to 15 June.

Weekly Intelligence Reports, DA, ACofS, G–2, Nos. 1–75, 25 February 1949 to 28 July 1950, in G–2 Documentary Library, DA, contain information pertaining to guerrilla activity in Korea, actions along the 38th Parallel, ROK combat police battalions, and the ROK Army's counterguerrilla measures.

Annual Historical Reports for 1949 and 1950, General Headquarters, Far East Command, are useful in obtaining background information regarding KMAG, with particular reference to its relationship with the Far East Command. Many of the reports, Office of the Army Attaché, Seoul, Korea, 1949 and 1950, in the G–2 Documentary Library, DA, contain information regarding KMAG, the ROK Army, and collateral subjects.

Advisor's Handbook, U.S. Military Advisory Group to the Republic of Korea (KMAG), dated 17 October 1949, outlines in considerable detail KMAG's organization, mission, and standing operating procedures. A copy is included as Annex 3 to the KMAG Semiannual Report, 1 July–31 December 1949.

Manual of Military Government Organization and Functions, Headquarters, U.S. Army Military Government in Korea (USAMGIK), Office of Administration, 1946, outlines the USAMGIK organization and discusses its mission.

Manuscript Histories

Headquarters, U.S. Army Forces in Korea, History of the Occupation of Korea: Part I of this history describes the movement of the XXIV Corps to Korea, the Japanese surrender, the release of Allied prisoners of war, the occupation of the provinces, the evacuation and demilitarization of Japanese forces, the establishment of U.S. Army Military Government in Korea, and the administration of U.S. Army Forces in Korea. Part II covers Korean politics and people (1946–47) and American-Soviet relations (1945–47). Unless otherwise specified, all of the manuscripts mentioned in this section will be found in OCMH files.

History of the United States Military Government in Korea, prepared by the Statistical Research Division, U.S. Army Military Government in Korea, Parts I, II, and III, covering the period from September 1945 to 30 June 1946: Part I, Volume 1, describes the structure of U.S. Military Government in Korea at national and provincial levels, the procurement and assignment of military government personnel, economic problems, political parties and leaders, the establishment of a Korean government, and relations with the Soviets. Part II, Volume 1, describes the organization, functions, and activities of the various military government sections, including the Directorate of National Defense and the Korean National Police. Part II, volumes 1 and 2, describe conditions in the various provinces of South Korea upon liberation, the measures taken by military government agencies to solve problems, and local events for the period.

History of Department of Internal Security to 1 July 1948, prepared under the direction of Capt. James H. Hausman, Headquarters, Provisional Military Advisory Group (PMAG), contains a great deal of useful information about U.S. military advisors in Korea, the Korean Constabulary, and the Korean Coast Guard. It is not well organized, however, and should be used cautiously.

History of the U.S. Coast Guard Detachment in Korea, 2 September 1946 to 25 February 1947, by Capt. George E. McCabe, USCG, is a brief description of the Korean Coast Guard during this period and its progress under the supervision of U.S. Coast Guard advisors. As far as is known, this is the only such history in existence.

Military History of Korea, prepared by the Republic of Korea, translated from the Korean by the 500th Military Intelligence Service Group, Headquarters U.S. Army Forces, Far East (USAFFE), is a detailed account of the development of ROK armed forces from 1945 to the end of 1949. While valuable in many respects, this history should be used with great caution. Noteworthy among its defects is a complete disregard of the U.S. military advisors, who were instrumental in organizing and training Korean forces. Still, the history contains details not available elsewhere.

Hq, U.S. Army, Japan, the U.S. Military Advisory Group to the Republic of Korea, pt. IV, KMAG's Wartime Experiences, 11 July 1951–27 July 1953, prepared by Kenneth W. Myers, is a detailed account of the KMAG organization and efforts during the last two years of the war.

Hq, Far East Command/United Nations Command, History of the Korean War, 25 June 1950–30 April 1951, prepared by Maj. James F. Schnabel, contains a great deal of valuable information on the status of forces and the conditions in Korea during the first months of the war.

Policy and Direction: The First Year, June 1950–July 1951, prepared by James F. Schnabel, is an amplification of the previous monograph and covers the Washington events as well. It will be published in the UNITED STATES ARMY IN THE KOREAN WAR series.

Truce Tent and Fighting Front, prepared by Walter G. Hermes, is a detailed account of the last two years of the war and contains several sections on KMAG activities during the period. It will also be published in the UNITED STATES ARMY IN THE KOREAN WAR series.

Published Works

Appleman, Roy E. *South to the Naktong, North to the Yalu.* UNITED STATES ARMY IN THE KOREAN WAR. Washington, 1961.

Department of State. *The Conflict in Korea.* Washington, 1951.

Department of State. *Korea 1945 to 1948.* Washington, 1948.

Department of State. *Korea's Independence.* Washington, 1947.

Department of State. *Mutual Defense Assistance Program.* A Fact Sheet. Publication 3826. General Foreign Policy Series 25. April 1950. Washington, 1950.

Department of State. *North Korea: A Case Study of a Soviet Satellite.* Report 5600. Washington, 20 May 1951.

General Headquarters, Commander in Chief, Far East, U.S. Army Forces Pacific. *Summation of Non-Military Activities in Korea.* Vol. 6, March 1946, through vol. 22, July 1947.

Grajdanzev, Andrew J. *Modern Korea.* New York: The John Day Company, 1944.

KMAG Public Information Office. *The United States Military Advisory Group to the Republic of Korea, 1945–1955.* Tokyo: Daito Art Printing Co., Ltd, no date.

McCune, George M. *Korea Today.* Cambridge: Harvard University Press, 1950.

Meade, E. Grant. *American Military Government in Korea.* New York: King's Crown Press, Columbia University, 1951.

National Economic Board (USAMGIK). *South Korean Interim Government Activities.* No. 23, August 1947, through No. 36, September–November 1948.

Nelson, M. Frederick. *Korea and the Old Orders in Eastern Asia.* Baton Rouge: Louisiana State University Press, 1946.

Oliver, Robert T. *Korea—Forgotten Nation.* Washington, Public Affairs Press, 1944.

Supreme Commander for the Allied Powers. *Summation of Non-Military Activities in Japan and Korea.* Nos. 1–5, September–October 1945, through February 1946.

U.S. House of Representatives, 81st Congress, 2d Session. *First Semiannual Report on the Mutual Defense Assistance Program.* House Document 613. 1950.

U.S. House of Representatives, 81st Congress, 2d Session, Committee on Foreign Affairs. *Background Information on Korea.* House Report 2495. 1950.

U.S. Senate, 82d Congress, 1st Session, *Hearings Before the Committee on Armed Services and the Committee on Foreign Relations on the Military Situation in the Far East.* 5 vols. Washington, 1951.

U.S. Senate, 83d Congress, 1st Session. *The United States and the Korean Problem, Documents 1943–1953.* Senate Document 74. Washington, 1953.

Periodical

Skroch, Major Ernest J. "Quartermaster Advisors in Korea." *The Quartermaster Review,* September–October 1951.

Miscellaneous

Orientation Folder, compiled by Brig. Gen. William L. Roberts in the spring of 1950 for his successor as chief of KMAG, contains descriptions of each KMAG staff and advisory section including its organization and functions and covers such subjects as MDAP, the ROK Army training program, and the ROK Army school system. In addition, it supplies many details about living conditions in Korea, with related subjects. The folder is extremely helpful; photostatic copy in OCMH files.

The Road to Ruin, an address delivered on 20 February 1950 at the ROK Army Staff School by Lt. Col. Lewis D. Vieman, reviews ROK Army logistical status and recommends measures to improve the situation. Transcript in OCMH files.

The Truth About the Yosu Incident, author unknown, was loaned to OCMH by Maj. John P. Reed, former PMAG–KMAG G–2 Advisor, who stated the paper was written by a U.S. field-grade officer then on duty in the Far East as a Japanese language and area student. Copy on OCMH files.

Summary of Operations, Korean Army, undated, by Capt. Harold S. Fischgrund, former KMAG G–3 Advisor covers guerrilla activity and actions along the 38th Parallel in 1948 and 1949. Loaned to OCMH by Captain Fischgrund.

Glossary

ADCOM	Advance Command
ACofS	Assistant Chief of Staff
AMIK	American Mission in Korea
ASCOM	Army Service Command
CINCAFPAC	Commander in Chief, Army Forces, Pacific
CINCFE	Commander in Chief, Far East
CINCUNC	Commander in Chief, United Nations Command
CofS	Chief of Staff
Comdr	Commander
COMNAVFE	U.S. Commander of Naval Forces, Far East
DA	Department of the Army
DEPTAR	Department of the Army
Dir	Director
D.I.S.	Department of Internal Security
ECA	Economic Cooperation Administration
EST	Eastern Standard Time
EUSAK	Eighth United States Army in Korea
FE	Far East
FEC	Far East Command
FTC	Field Training Command
G–1	Personnel section of division or higher staff
G–2	Intelligence section of division or higher staff
G–3	Operations and training section of division or higher staff
G–4	Supply section of division or higher staff
GHQ	General Headquarters
GO	General Orders
GSA	General Services Administration

Hist _____ Historical; history
HR–KMAG _____ Historical Report–Korea Military Advisory Group

JAS _____ Joint Administration Services
JCS _____ Joint Chiefs of Staff
JUSMAGPHIL _____ Joint U.S. Military Advisory Group to the Republic of the Philippines

KATC _____ Korean Army Training Center
KATUSA _____ Korean Augmentation to the U.S. Army
KMA _____ Korea Military Academy
KMAG _____ United States Military Advisory Group to the Republic of Korea
KSC _____ Korea Service Corps

LST _____ Landing Ship, Tank

MDAP _____ Mutual Defense Assistance Program
MHK _____ Military History of Korea
MOS _____ Military occupational specialty
MTP _____ U.S. Army Mobilization Training Program

NCO _____ Noncommissioned officer
N.K. _____ North Korean
NSC _____ National Security Council

O&T _____ Operations and Training
OACofS _____ Office of the Assistant Chief of Staff
OCS _____ Officer Candidate School
Opns _____ Operations
ORO _____ Operations Research Office
OTS _____ Officer Training School

P&CO _____ Plans and Combat Operations
P&O _____ Plans and Operations
PC _____ Patrol Vessel, Submarine Chaser
PMAG _____ Provisional Military Advisory Group

Rcd _____ Record
ROK _____ Republic of Korea

ROKA _____ Republic of Korea Army
RTSC _____ Replacement and Training School
                   Command
RTC _____ Replacement training center

SCAP _____ Supreme Commander for the Allied
                   Powers
SO _____ Special Orders
SWNCC _____ State-War-Navy Coordinating Com-
                   mittee

TAG _____ The Adjutant General
T/D _____ Table of Distribution
T/O&E _____ Table of Organization and Equipment

U.N. _____ United Nations
UNC _____ United Nations Command
USAFFE _____ United States Army Forces in the Far
                   East
USAFIK _____ U.S. Army Forces in Korea
USAFPAC _____ United States Army Forces, Pacific
USAMGIK _____ United States Army Military Govern-
                   ment in Korea
USCG _____ U.S. Coast Guard

WIR _____ Weekly Intelligence Report

⊠ (XX) _____ Infantry Division

⊠ (X) _____ Infantry Brigade

Armored Regiment

Mtrcl _____ Motorcycle Regiment

Index

Acheson, Dean G., 102
ADCOM. *See* General Headquarters
    Advance Command and Liaison
    Group.
Adjutant General's Section, KMAG,
    54–55
Advisor's Handbook, 57
Aid to Korea. *See entries under* South
    Korea; Republic of Korea.
Aircraft
    North Korean, 94, 104, 105
    ROK, 94–95, 106
    USSR, 94, 104
    U.S., 94, 102
Air evacuation service, 53
American Mission in Korea (AMIK),
    45, 46, 47, 48, 51, 55, 98, 121, 123,
    131
    and evacuation plan CRULLER, 110–
    11
    on Yosu revolt, 39
American schools in Korea, 51–52
AMIK. *See* American Mission in
    Korea.
Ammunition
    ROK need of, 120
    MacArthur sends to ROK, 123
Anjung-ni, 120
Argo, Col. Reamer W., 8, 8n
Armed Forces Organization Act, ROK,
    41
Armies, U.S., *See* Eighth U.S. Army in
    Korea (EUSAK).
Armistice negotiations. *See* Truce ne-
    gotiations.
Armor, ROKA
    armored cars (M8), 106
    half-tracks (M2) (M3A2), 106
    medium tank company, 166
Army Administrative Area, Foreign As-
    signment Activity, 46, 155
Army Policy Council, 164
Artillery
    North Korean Army, 105–06
    ROKA, 67, 70–71, 76, 100
        37-mm. guns, 38, 106
        57-mm. guns, 67, 106, 117, 141
        90-mm. guns, 184

Artillery—Continued
    ROKA—Continued
        105-mm. cannon, 38
        105-mm. howitzers, 67, 102, 106,
        120, 141, 153, 166, 182–84
        155-mm. howitzers, 100, 141,
        166, 182–84
        3-inch guns, 102
    U.S.
        105-mm. howitzers, 182
        155-mm. howitzers, 182
Arnold, Maj. Gen. Archibald V., 8, 20
ASCOM (Army Service Command)
    City, 43n, 57, 84, 111, 159
    processing center set up, 121
    ROKA technical services installations
    at, 51
Assistant Chief of Staff, G–3, U.S. Army,
    162, 173
AT–6 trainer planes, 94
AT–10 trainer planes, 106
Automatic weapons. *See* Weapons,
    automatic.

Back, Brig. Gen. George I., 131, 132
BAMBOO plan, 13–14
Barros, Lt. Col. Russell D.
    and Constabulary build-up, 23
    Director of National Defense, 20n
Bartosik, Lt. Col. Matthew J., 43, 44
Battalions
    ROK National Police, 77, 78
    ROKA, 76, 78, 150
        antitank, 76
        artillery, 67, 76, 84, 166, 183–84
        engineer, 76, 83, 128, 166
        ordnance, 67
        quartermaster, 67
        signal, 67
    U.S. Army
        artillery, 38, 182
        tank, 182
Bernard, Lt. Col. Lyle W., 20n
Bolté, Maj. Gen. Charles L., 169
Bradley, General of the Army Omar N.,
    170
Branch immaterial training, 84n, 85
Branch material training, 84n, 85

Parallel, 38th. *See* 38th Parallel.
PC (Patrol Vessel, Submarine Chaser), 92n
Peiping, 155
Pentagon, 47, 164
Philippines. *See* Republic of the Philippines.
Pioneer Dale, USS, 131
PMAG. *See* Provisional Military Advisory Group.
P'ohang-dong, 18, 144
Polgyo-ri, 40
Posong, 40
Potsdam Conference of 1945, 6
Price, Col. Terrill E., 20n, 22, 31, 47
Provisional Korean Military Advisory Group Headquarters, Pusan, 132
Provisional Military Advisory Group (PMAG), 35–45
Provisional Military Advisory Group Board, 43–44
Public Law 329, 97
Pukhan River, 109
Pup'yong-ni, 109
Pusan, 16, 18, 23, 30, 52, 77, 111, 112, 118, 120, 122, 129, 130, 131, 132, 135, 136, 137, 142, 149, 151, 173
Pusan Perimeter, 137, 138, 140
Putnam, Capt. Gerald D., 131, 132
P'yongch'ang, 118
P'yongyang, 113

Quartermaster battalions. *See* Battalions, quartermaster.
Quartermaster Clothing Factory, ROKA, 99

Radio Station WVTP, 111, 122
Recoilless rifles, 153
Recruitment, ROKA, 144, 147
Reed, Capt. John P., 40, 56
Regimental Combat Team, U.S., 5th, 37, 38, 42, 45
Regiments
  North Korean, 105
  ROKA, 70, 77, 84, 114
    5th, 120
    10th, 117
    12th, 115
    14th, 39–40
    17th, 110, 114, 115
    18th, 110
    21st, 117
    22d, 128–29, 136
    23d, 131
    26th, 144, 147
    Cavalry, 66, 67, 71, 110

Regiments—Continued
  U.S. Army
    5th, 70
    32d, 37
Reiner, Thomas, 131
Reinholt, Norwegian ship, 121, 122
Replacements, ROKA, 148–50, 153–54
Replacement Training Centers, ROKA, 148–49, 150
Replacement Training and School Command, 179
Republic of China, 102, 104, 123n
Republic of Korea, 34, 36, 45, 52, 107–09, 113, 149–50. *See also* South Korea.
  aircraft secured by, 94
  anti-Communist purges, 75
  appointment of General Chung as ROKA Chief of Staff, 143
  armed forces strength, 1950, 106
  Armed Forces Organization Act, 41
  arsenal program, 99–100
  conditions in, 36, 51–52
  defense area, 107–10
  disturbances in, 39
  elections, 1950, 113
  establishment of Air Force, 93
  establishment of National Defense Army, 41
  and evacuation plan CRULLER, 111
  and expansion of armed forces, 35, 41–42, 58
  fall of Seoul, 118–28
  Government formed, 33
  guerrillas in, 54, 97
  and increased U.S. arms, 170
  internal security problems, 73–74, 97
  invasion of by North Korea, 114–18
  and KMAG terms of reference, 57
  lack of heavy artillery, tanks, and aircraft, 106
  and legal status of KMAG, 48
  military assistance to, 96–104, 164
  and military appointments, 65
  MDAP survey teams visit, 101
  postwar relationship between United States and, 160
  recognition by United States, 37
  reorganization of defense administration, 41
  Rhee first president of, 33
  road and rail net of, 107–09
  United Nations asks for assistance to, 128
  U.S. policy excludes defense of, 102

Republic of Korea Air Force
  aircraft, 94, 106
  established, 93
  KMAG and, 94–95
  strength of, 94, 106
Republic of Korea Army, 53, 58, 60–61,
    65, 66, 72, 93, 98–99, 124, 133,
    134, 152, 168, 169. *See also*
    Armor; Artillery; Battalions; Com-
    panies; Corps; Divisions; Mortars,
    ROKA; Regiments; Schools,
    ROKA; Tanks.
  activation of two divisions, 58
  additional advisors for, 42–43
  air liaison detachment, 67
  ammunition expended by, 69, 98
  anti-Communist purges in, 75
  artillery and armor, 1950, 106
  artillery expansion, 183–84
  assignment of faculty to academy, 81–
    82
  battalion command post exercises in,
    75
  casualties in June 1950, 134
  Central Procurement Agency set up,
    98
  Chief of Staff, 41, 58
  Church asks automatic supply for, 142
  and Command and General Staff Col-
    lege, 88
  defense plans for, 109–10
  deficiencies in, 62–66, 69, 79, 106,
    152, 170, 176
  deployment of, 67, 110
  deserters from, 73–74
  and destruction of Han River bridge,
    125–26
  discipline, 61
  equipment, 38, 98
  establishment of, 41
  expansion of, 58, 75, 146
  graduates of U.S. service schools in,
    88
  guerrilla activity delays training in,
    66, 74–75, 77–78
  headquarters set up at Taegu, 138
  infantry division T/O&E, 166
  and KMAG advisor system, 58–59
  KMAG commands during retreat, 140
  and KMAG mission, June 1950, 121
  and Korean Military Academy, 89–90
  and lack of military language, 62–65
  and lack of recoilless rifles, 70
  and lack of tanks and heavy artillery,
    106

Republic of Korea Army—Continued
  Lee, Brig. Gen. Hyung Koon, Chief
    of Staff of, 41
  logistical problems of, 142–43
  loss of weapons and equipment in
    initial invasion, 141
  MacArthur on support of, 144–45,
    162
  and manufacture of clothing and
    equipment, 99–100
  military dictionary compiled, 64
  mission of, 106
  morale of, 126
  and national pride, 69
  and need for flexible training pro-
    gram, 69
  and need for more U.S. advisors, 159
  officers sent to Japan, 89
  ordnance supply and maintenance in-
    stallations, 159
  organization, 1949, 67
  performance in battle, 170
  and political appointments, 65
  reconstitution of, 1950, 140
  and recruitment of ROK 2d Division,
    147
  relationship with KMAG Chief of
    Staff, 60
  reluctance to assign personnel to
    schools, 79–80
  reorganization of July 1950, 141–44
  replacements and training, 148–50,
    153–54
  and revolt in 1948, 39–41
  Ridgway on, 175–76
  rifle instruction for, 72, 148, 149, 153,
    154
  shoe repair for, 99
  shortages, 38, 72
  status of aid for, 1950, 103–04
  strength of, 41, 106, 141
  supply discipline, 98
  supply system, 141, 182
  support forces, 182–85
  technical services, 67, 69, 71, 76, 78,
    98
  ten-division program approved for,
    164
  training of, 67–90
  and truce negotiations, 178
  U.S. plans for postwar, 169–70
  and use of U.S. service schools, 88,
    174–75
  weakness in leadership, 79
  weapons, 1948, 38
  withdrawal to southeast Korea, 137

United States National Security Council on arms for ROK forces—Continued
on military aid to ROK, 37–38, 97
and review of U.S. policy on Korea, 37–38
and withdrawal of U.S. forces, 37
USAFFE. *See* United States Army Forces, Far East.
USSR. *See* Union of Soviet Socialist Republics.

Van Fleet, Lt. Gen. James A., 169, 170, 171, 172, 181
Vice Minister of Defense, ROK, 126n
Vieman, Lt. Col. Lewis D., 80–81, 85, 87, 126

Wake Island conference, 161–62
Walker, Lt. Gen. Walton H., 149, 155, 156n, 164
and disagreement with MacArthur on ROKA, 145–46
and establishment of EUSAK, 137
on expansion of ROKA, 145–46
and KMAG expansion, 160–61
takes command in Korea, 137
War Department, 18
Weapons, 167
automatic, 105, 148
carbines, 120, 141
M1 rifles, 39, 72, 72n, 76, 78, 141, 148
machine guns, 102, 117, 141, 148
Model 99 rifles, 93, 99

White, Lt. Col. Ralph B., 85
Willoughby, Maj. Gen. Charles A., 132
Wonju, 54, 118, 132
Wonsan, 108, 109
World War II, 3, 6, 171
Wright, Col. W. H. Sterling, 60, 119, 124, 127n, 134, 136, 141
and efforts to cross Han River, 126–27
and evacuation of Seoul, 122–28
KMAG Chief of Staff, 57
KMAG members recalled by, 125
ordered to take command of KMAG, 119
and relationship with ROKA Chief of Staff, 60
return to Korea, 122
return to U.S., 138
and ROKA stragglers, 134
WVTP, Radio Station, 111, 122

YAK–3 fighter planes, 94, 105
Yalu River, 140, 154, 155
Yesong River, 107
Yim, 2d Lt. Soon Ha, 22
Yokohama, 89, 123
Yongam, 26
Yongdungp'o, 51
Yonghae, 136
Yongju, 120
Yosu, 39, 91
Yosu revolt, 39–41, 73
Yu, Col. Sung Yul, 128

U.S. GOVERNMENT PRINTING OFFICE : 1966 O—216-985